Why the Bank of Japan Has Failed to Conquer Deflation in Japan

Shigeyuki Hattori

Why the Bank of Japan Has Failed to Conquer Deflation in Japan

Springer

Shigeyuki Hattori
Faculty of Commerce
Doshisha University
Kyoto, Japan

ISBN 978-981-97-9407-2 ISBN 978-981-97-9408-9 (eBook)
https://doi.org/10.1007/978-981-97-9408-9

This Springer imprint is published by the registered company Springer Nature Singapore Pte Ltd.
The registered company address is: 152 Beach Road, #21-01/04 Gateway East, Singapore 189721, Singapore

Preface: What Is Wrong with the Reflationist Theory?

> *To begin with, reflationists are those who believe that past deflationary recessions were caused by monetary policy failures and that the real interest rate should be lowered to get out of deflationary recessions by setting an inflation target of around 2% and by making a bold change in monetary easing policy. (Harada, 2021, p. 54)*
>
> *When the QQE [quantitative and qualitative monetary easing] started in April 2013, I honestly thought that 2% in two years would be difficult, but I did not think that we are not able to accomplish still today. Of course, there were the effects of the 2014 and 2019 consumption tax hikes, unexpected overseas economic slowdowns, frequent natural disasters, and so on, but still. (Harada, 2021, p. 401)*

In 2013, the Bank of Japan (BOJ), under the leadership of Governor Kuroda, began its quantitative and qualitative monetary easing (QQE) policy to overcome deflation. This book is the first book in English to seriously discuss why this historical experiment by the BOJ failed (there are not a few books discussing it in Japanese).

We do not believe that people who cannot read Japanese fully understand what the BOJ under Kuroda and the reflationists who theoretically supported Kuroda were thinking and doing. For example, Kikuo Iwata, a representative of the reflationists who served as the deputy governor from March 2013 to March 2018, argued that the BOJ can end deflation by working on inflation expectations. His tools of achieving this are an inflation target, for which the BOJ was committed by setting an achievement deadline, and a massive supply of the monetary base. However, we are unaware of anyone in the English language literature that discusses this peculiar monetary policy of reflationists in Japan. Furthermore, as discussed in this book, these policies advocated by reflationists ended after only three years. Since then, the BOJ, while claiming to strengthen easing, proceeded to taper it. Not a few economists in Japan have also discussed these realities, but we are not aware of any literature written in English. Most of them probably do not even know that the controversy over the money supply occurred in Japan in the early 1990s, which we discuss in Chap. 5.

Since the 1990s, the BOJ has been the focus of intense attention from economists worldwide interested in monetary policy. After 1999, the BOJ introduced unconventional monetary policies such as the zero interest rate policy, the Quantitative Easing (QE) policy, and forward guidance. After the global financial crisis of 2008, central banks in the United States (U.S.) and Europe adopted some of these new policies and even took a page from the BOJ's policies, including its failures. The fiasco of the BOJ under Kuroda's historical experiment must also have much to learn for central bankers and economists worldwide.

Since the bursting of the bubble economy in the early 1990s, the Japanese economy fell into secular stagnation. During that period, reflationists led by Iwata argued that only the BOJ's monetary policy would help to overcome the country's chronic deflation and secular stagnation. The opening quotation at the beginning of "Preface" is by Yutaka Harada, a reflationist who was a member of the BOJ Policy Board from March 2015 to March 2020. Harada defines a reflationist as someone who believes that deflation is the result of the BOJ's failed monetary policy and that setting an inflation target along with aggressive monetary easing can help overcome deflation.

Reflationists insisted that the inflation target must set a deadline for achievement and clarify the commitment of the BOJ. On this basis, a massive supply of the monetary base would pull Japan out of deflation and revive its economy. According to Harada (2021, pp. 18–21), the growth rate of the monetary base is linked to the nominal GDP growth rate with a lag.

In March 2013, the late Prime Minister Shinzo Abe nominated Haruhiko Kuroda as the governor of the BOJ and Iwata as the deputy governor. From April 2013 onward, a large supply of the monetary base was implemented based on the reflationist theory. The inflation target had already been set in January 2013 based on the arguments of reflationists. Thus, the historical monetary policy experiment based on the reflationist theory began. However, as we (Hattori, 2014) anticipated at the beginning, ten years later, Kuroda stepped down without achieving the 2% inflation target.

Kuroda's historic experiment ended in a fiasco. The second quote at the beginning of "Preface" is from the greeting given by Harada when he retired in March 2020. He admits that the BOJ under Kuroda did not achieve its target of overcoming deflation. However, he emphasizes achievements such as higher stock prices and improved employment.

In this book, we emphasize that import prices and costs drive consumer price (CPI) and not the monetary base or inflation expectations. That is why the 2% inflation target, which the BOJ could not achieve under Kuroda even after ten years, was easily achieved by imported inflation from 2022 onward. At the same time, we also reveal that when CPI rises due to imported inflation, consumption declines in real terms. This proves that there is no basis for reflationists to claim that the Japanese economy can be revived if deflation is overcome.

We also emphasize that the monetary policy based on reflationist theory was conducted for less than the first three years. By 2016, it was expected that the BOJ would be unable to purchase a large amount of long-term Japanese government bonds. Therefore, in February 2016, the BOJ introduced a negative interest rate policy. Furthermore, in September of the same year, it changed its negative interest rate policy to yield curve control (YCC). After this, the BOJ rapidly reduced the supply of the monetary base. Although Japan entered a period of recession after October 2018, it reduced the monetary base. Thus, one of the policy tools of reflationists was abandoned.

Reflationists argued that the inflation target should be set by a deadline to clarify the BOJ's commitment. However, in April 2018, the BOJ under Kuroda stopped announcing the outlook when the inflation target would be achieved. In the context of the reflationist theory, this indicates that the BOJ has abandoned its main goal of overcoming deflation.

After the introduction of YCC, the BOJ did the opposite of what reflationists advocated. Logically speaking, the BOJ has succumbed to those who opposed reflationists. However, this would damage the positions and reputations of both the BOJ under Kuroda and the reflationists. Therefore, the BOJ and reflationists were actually implementing theories and policies that opposed reflationists; however, they attempted to make it seem as if reflationists' monetary policies were continuing and the attempts to overcome deflation were progressing smoothly. Thus, the wrong monetary policy turned into a deceptive monetary policy.

In *Defure to Tatakau* (*Fighting Deflation*), Harada (2021, p. 415) also wrote, "Unfortunately, I feel that the Japanese elite have a weak feeling that they cannot succeed by lying." He takes Japan's invasion war against China since the 1930s as a prime example. We completely agree with this, but it is the same with the BOJ under Kuroda and reflationists who continued to pursue their monetary policies that could not succeed through falsehoods. However, as Japanese, we would like to deny that this is something unique to Japan. In September 2008, policymakers in the U.S. allowed the Lehman Brothers to collapse, triggering the global financial crisis. Worldwide, people doubted why the U.S. policymakers would allow Lehman to fail, but this failure occurred because policymakers did not believe that Lehman's bankruptcy would triggere one of the most severe financial crises in history. However, they falsely claimed that the failure was due to a lack of legal authority to bail out Lehman (this point is discussed in Sect. 3.4.1).

James K. Galbraith (2016, p. 100) stated that, in the world of economic policy, policymakers can explain unanticipated failures so that they do not have to admit policy failure. First, they argue that the initial conditions were poor; second, that the policy was not fully fledged; and third, that there was not enough time to implement the policy effectively. If monetary easing cannot conquer deflation, then by definition monetary easing is always insufficient. Therefore, reflationists can criticize the BOJ for not pursuing sufficient monetary easing; indeed, they had done so until the time Shirakawa was the governor of the BOJ. In this book, we clarify that under Kuroda, the BOJ did not implement the policies advocated by reflationists. However, criticizing the BOJ under Kuroda for not fully implementing its policies would damage the positions and reputations of the BOJ and reflationists. Therefore, there was not much criticism that monetary policies of reflationists were not fully implemented (not entirely absent). Except for this, both the BOJ and reflationists have reacted, as Galbraith pointed out.

Galbraith (2016, p. 100) also said, "Economists are not ranked by the results of their recommendations. They are ranked by what one might call the a priori analytical correctness of their point of view, by intellectual power according to the judgment of others in their profession. It's a bit like a priesthood, perhaps not accidentally." The BOJ under Kuroda could not achieve its inflation target even after ten years. If judged by the results of their proposals, the hierarchy of reflationists would be at the bottom. However, the structural hierarchy of reflationists is maintained by intellectual power and the judgment of their peers that their policies were successful.

The BOJ's monetary policy under Kuroda has already become history. The essence of human history is also a history of failures. The global financial crisis of 2008 is another history of failed economics and economic policy. Why and how the BOJ failed under Kuroda will be a question for economists and historians to answer. If there is something to contribute to this issue, we would be happy to do so.

Kyoto, Japan Shigeyuki Hattori
August 15, 2024
Anniversary of the End of the
Asia-Pacific War in Japan

References

In Japanese

Harada, Y. (2021). *Defure to Tatakau: Nichigin Shingi Iin Kutō to Shikō Sakugo no Go Nenkan (Fighting deflation: Five years of struggle and trial and error for the members of the policy board of the Bank of Japan).* Chuokoron-Shinsha.

Hattori, S. (2014). *Abenomikusu no Shūen (The End of Abenomics).* Iwanami Shoten.

In English

Galbraith, J. K. (2016). *Welcome to the poisoned chalice: The destruction of Greece and the future of Europe.* Yale University Press.

Acknowledgments

We have written two books on the BOJ under Kuroda and Abenomics in Japanese, *Abenomikusu no Shūen* (*The End of Abenomics*) (Tokyo: Iwanami Shoten, 2014) and *Itsuwari no Keizai Seisaku: Kakusa to Teitai no Abenomikusu* (*Deceptive Economic Policies: Abenomics of Inequality and Stagnation*) (Tokyo: Iwanami Shoten, 2017). This is our third book.

In writing this book, we had discussions with the following people, and their comments were helpful: Prof. Emeritus Yoshinori Shiozawa (Osaka City University), Prof. Tosihiro Oka (Kyoto University), Prof. Makoto Nishibe (Senshu University), Prof. Hiroshi Nish (Hannan University), Prof. Emeritus Tetsuji Kawamura (Hosei University), Prof. Akira Matsumoto (Ritsumeikan University), Prof. Yoshihiro Yamazaki (Fukuoka University), Prof. Emeritus Satoshi Niimura (Okayama University), Former Prof. Tatsuhiko Aoki (Shinshu University), Prof. Taichi Tabuchi (Doshisha University), Senior Specially Appointed Prof. Kimihito Sakurai (Rikkyo University), Prof. Kenshiro Ninomiya (Rikkyo University), Prof. Taiji Hagiwara (Okayama Shoka University), and Prof. Shigehiro Naruse (Kanagawa University). We express our gratitude to them all. However, we are responsible for all possible errors.

In writing this book, we were personally provided 10-year breakeven inflation rates by Japan Bond Trading Co., Ltd. For this, we express our gratitude to Japan Bond Trading Co., Ltd. We are grateful to the Japan Society for the Promotion of Science (JSPS) for funding this research with Grant-in-Aid for Scientific Research (c) 21K01417, "Contemporary Significance of Ricardian Trade Theory." We would like to thank Editage (www.editage.jp) for the English language editing. We are also grateful to Prof. Emeritus Yuji Aruka (Chuo University), and Mr. Yutaka Hirachi and Ms. Mano Priya S. of Springer Nature Japan for their help in publishing this book.

It has only been 24 years since the beginning of the twenty-first century, but we have witnessed two historic economic policy failures: the global financial crisis of 2008 and the BOJ's monetary policy under Kuroda. I believe that I have clarified why these two major failures occurred. However, it is attributable to the contributions of Prof. Emeritus Mitsuharu Ito (Kyoto University and Fukui Prefectural University), who was my supervisor at Kyoto University and Graduate School, and Prof. Michał

Kalecki and Prof. Hyman P. Minsky, whom I have never met, rather than my own effort. Once again, I express my deep gratitude and indebtedness to them.

Contents

About the Author

Shigeyuki Hattori has been a Professor at Doshisha University since 2016. He was Professor at Fukui Prefectural University from 2007 to 2016. He is currently a member of the Japan Association for Evolutionary Economics, The Japanese Society for the History of Economic Thought, and the Japanese Economic Association. He has written two books which clarified the failure of Abenomics and the Bank of Japan under Governor Haruhiko Kuroda—End of Abenomics (in Japanese) (2014) and Economic Policy of Deception: Inequality and Stagnation under Abenomics (in Japanese) (2017). He also wrote several books, including Crisis, Instability, and Capitalism: Economics of Hyman P. Minsky (in Japanese) (2013); Consequences of Neoliberalism: Why is the World Economy Stagnant? (in Japanese) (2014); and Crisis of the Global Financial Capitalism: The World in Turmoil and Economics (in Japanese) (2023). His research interests are monetary policy, financial crisis, income distribution and growth, and the evolution of the capitalist economic system.

Chapter 1
Introduction: Historical Fiasco of the Monetary Policy

Abstract Kikuo Iwata, who was the Deputy Governor of the Bank of Japan (BOJ), and other reflationists argue that deflation in Japan could be solved by the monetary policy of the BOJ, which works on inflation expectations. Their tools are a Japanese-style inflation target with a deadline and clearing responsibilities of the BOJ and a massive supply of monetary base. Based on this theory, the BOJ under Kuroda started implementing quantitative and qualitative monetary easing in March 2013, but eventually, Kuroda stepped down without achieving the target. We show that this failure was theoretically inevitable. Instead, what drives consumer prices in Japan are costs, especially import prices. Reflationists, however, argue that the policies they advocate are standard in mainstream American economics. Conversely, Bernanke and Gertler now realize that the BOJ cannot solve deflation. We also show that both the massive supply of monetary base and the Japanese-style inflation target advocated by the reflationists have been abandoned after only about three years. Logically, this would mean a complete defeat for the BOJ and the reflationists, but in order to save their positions and reputations, the BOJ under Kuroda continued to pretend the policies advocated by reflationists were in place and succeeding.

Keywords Abenomics · The Bank of Japan under Kuroda · Deflation in Japan · Quantitative and qualitative monetary easing · Japanese-style inflation target · Inflation expectations · Reflationists · Kikuo Iwata · Monetary policy

> In general, even at the effective lower bound, monetary policy can boost aggregate demand, employment, and inflation in one of two complementary ways—by easing financial conditions (for example, by lowering longer-term interest rates, depreciating the currency, or lifting the stock market)—which stimulates aggregate demand directly; or by raising the public's expectations of inflation, thereby lowering real interest rates as well as increasing expectations of future growth …
>
> In any case, in Japan both channels of monetary policy transmission seem to be approaching their limits. First, today, not only are short-term interest rates in Japan at or near their effective lower bound but so are very long-term interest rates—a sort of "super liquidity trap," if you will. (Bernanke, 2017, p. 30)

S. Hattori, *Why the Bank of Japan Has Failed to Conquer Deflation in Japan*,
https://doi.org/10.1007/978-981-97-9408-9_1

> Inflation expectations in Japan did rise after the initial announcement of QQE [the quantitative and qualitative monetary easing], but overall they have been less responsive than hoped (Bank of Japan, 2016), particularly when headline inflation was depressed by declining oil prices and other factors. It's sometimes said that Japanese inflation expectations are adaptive, or that institutions like national wage bargaining lead to backward-looking behavior. These are less explanations than different ways of restating the basic puzzle, that inflation expectations in Japan have seemed overly sensitive to current developments and relatively unresponsive to central bank talk, even when that talk has been accompanied by vigorous measures such as large-scale asset purchases. (Bernanke, 2017, p. 31)

1.1 Inevitable Failure

The Japanese economy plunged into secular stagnation when the bubble burst in the early 1990s. As interest rates have a zero lower bound, there was much debate about what else monetary policy could achieve. During such periods, reflationists, led by Kikuo Iwata, argued that monetary policy would be effective by working on inflation expectations. When prices rise, the value of money decreases. As a result, even if nominal interest rates are zero, real interest rates can be lowered to negative. Iwata (e.g., 2012, 2013) and others adopted the Japanese-style inflation target and massive supply of the monetary base as a concrete tool to achieve this. Iwata stated that the inflation target must be set with a deadline for achievement and that the Bank of Japan's (BOJ's) responsibility must be clearly defined. That is why we added the Japanese style.

Shinzo Abe, who called for bold monetary easing, became prime minister in December 2012. In March 2013, Haruhiko Kuroda was nominated as the governor of the BOJ, and Iwata was the deputy governor. The quantitative and qualitative monetary easing (QQE) policy was implemented in April, and a large monetary base was supplied based on the reflationist theory. In January 2013, the BOJ set the inflation target based on the arguments of reflationists. However, Governor Shirakawa at the time was against reflationists, and in line with his views, not only was there no deadline set for achieving the target, but the responsibility for achieving it was also a joint responsibility with the government.

Thus began the historical experiment of monetary policy based on the reflationist theory. Ten years later, Kuroda stepped down from the helm of the BOJ without achieving the 2% inflation target. Iwata himself had retired five years earlier when his term of office expired. The failure was exactly what we had predicted at the beginning (see Hattori, 2014), and we were not surprised; however, it is difficult to understand why neither Iwata nor Kuroda, nor Masazumi Wakatabe, who had succeeded Iwata as the deputy governor, nor Abe, who had appointed them, intended to take the blame for their failure. Since 2022, the consumer price (CPI) inflation rate in Japan exceeded 2% and peaked at over 4%. However, this is because, as the BOJ under Kuroda itself admitted, import prices soared with the surge in global food and energy prices following Russia's invasion of Ukraine and the rapid depreciation of the yen.

The fact that the BOJ under Kuroda could not achieve its 2% inflation target even after ten years of hard work—which could have easily been reached due to soaring import prices—shows that the BOJ under Kuroda and reflationists was doubly wrong. The fundamental error of the reflationist theory is that it did not recognize that costs are crucial to price fluctuations in Japan, not monetary policy or inflation expectations. It is theoretically inevitable that the BOJ under Kuroda, which is based on the wrong price theory, will fail to overcome deflation.

Reflationists have argued that overcoming deflation is the key to reviving the Japanese economy. However, after 2022, when prices rose due to imported inflation, the Japanese people complained that rising prices had eroded their real incomes and that their lives had become difficult. The "bad weak yen" was also among the top ten buzzwords of 2022. The government also took measures to limit the impact of rising prices, such as subsidizing soaring electricity charges. A key assumption of the BOJ's policies under Kuroda and reflationists was that when prices rose, wages also rose, creating a virtuous economic cycle. However, it was revealed that this assumption was merely an assumption.

The solution to this problem, as Prime Minister Fumio Kishida says, is wage increases exceeding price rises. The BOJ continued with monetary easing, claiming that even if the increasing rate of CPI significantly exceeded 2%, it would not be accompanied by wage increases. Therefore, if we consider whether monetary easing will be enough to raise wages, it will probably be impossible. Thus, it became clear that reflationists are not only wrong in their theory of prices but also in all their strategies based on the wrong theory.

However, the BOJ under Kuroda, reflationists, and politicians who support Abenomics have argued that Abenomics revived the Japanese economy, citing seemingly fruitful data such as rising stock prices, a sharp improvement in corporate profits, and an increase in the number of employed persons. However, in standard macroeconomics, economic growth refers to the high rate of increase in real gross domestic product (GDP). Achieving a 2% increase in real GDP was one of the targets when Abenomics began at the end of 2012. From the fourth quarter of 2012, when the Abe administration took office, to the second quarter of 2019, real GDP increased at an annual rate of only 1.2%. Since then, real GDP has fallen sharply due to the consumption tax hike and the spread of COVID-19. This is not only short of the 2% target but also lower than before Abenomics.

Japan is now considered a declining country, and it could lose its developed country status in the near future. Neighboring East and South East Asian countries are the fastest-growing regions in the world (except North Korea, Myanmar, and other countries). As a result, Japan's decline is conspicuous. Of course, China is much larger in terms of the scale of its economy, and the gap is widening year by year. However, as China's population is ten times that of Japan, it is natural for China's overall economy to be overwhelmingly larger than Japan's. In contrast, it is not well known that GDP per capita, measured by purchasing power parity, was surpassed by Taiwan in 2009 and South Korea in 2018.

Since the Meiji Restoration, "datsua" (leaving Asia) has been an option for Japan. Previously, leaving Asia meant "leaving barbaric Asia and joining the ranks of

Western civilizations." Now, a new leaving Asia has occurred, that is, "dropping out of Asia, the center of global economic growth." It is simple, fake news that Abenomics and the BOJ under Kuroda have revived the Japanese economy.

1.2 Monetary Policy Based on the Reflationist Theory Has Also Been Abandoned

The target inflation rate was reached only until after 2022 when imported inflation occurred. The economic growth rate was also at a level that can be called stagnant. According to the teachings of reflationists, the monetary base should be increased even more rapidly to raise inflation expectations. Kuroda, Iwata, and Wakatabe should accept the responsibility for not achieving their inflation target. Since 2016, however, the pace of increase in the monetary base began to slow down. In 2018, the BOJ under Kuroda stopped publishing its outlook for achieving its inflation target, primarily to avoid being blamed for its failures. The BOJ under Kuroda effectively abandoned monetary policy based on the reflationist theory.

Instead, the BOJ adopted yield curve control (YCC) (specifically, keeping not only short-term interest rates but also long-term interest rates close to zero) in September 2016. Fixing interest rates in both the short and long terms implies not lowering nominal interest rates further. Iwata (2018, p. 419) posits that YCC does not have the power to raise inflation expectations. This means that real interest rates cannot be lowered either. Reflationists have argued that monetary easing is possible by raising the expected inflation rate even if the nominal interest rate reaches the lower bound. Admitting that the expected inflation rate cannot be raised is, in effect, a declaration of defeat for the reflationist theory. Under YCC, real interest rates automatically rise as deflation progresses. This is a pro-deflationary monetary policy, which is contrary to the reflationist philosophy of monetary policy. Besides, according to the mainstream theory, long-term interest rates cannot be controlled because they rise when inflation occurs due to monetary easing. Conversely, the fact that long-term interest rates are close to zero shows that the market believed that the BOJ under Kuroda would not be able to overcome deflation.

Reflationists have articulated that the policies they advocate are the common sense of mainstream economists in the United States (U.S.). However, not only was the global financial crisis that occurred in the U.S. in 2008 a crisis that was theoretically impossible in mainstream economics, but the U.S. economic recovery was not satisfactory despite the aggressive monetary easing that followed. In response, mainstream economics in the U.S. have changed. In addition, the failure of the BOJ under Kuroda further changed their thinking. There is no basis for the claim that policies recommended by reflationists are the global standard.

For example, Bernanke, who served as chair of the U.S. Federal Reserve Board during the global financial crisis in 2008 and won the 2022 Sveriges Riksbank Prize in Economic Sciences in Memory of Alfred Nobel, gave a lecture at the Institute of

Monetary and Economic Studies, the BOJ in 2017. The quote at the beginning of this chapter is from this lecture. He argued that even as short-term interest rates fall into the zero bound, theoretically, there are policies to change the financial environment, such as lowering long-term interest rates and raising inflation expectations. He stated that, in practice, Japan's long-term interest rates were close to zero, leaving no further room for a cut, and inflation expectations had not been successfully raised. He stated that there was almost nothing more the BOJ could achieve under Kuroda.

Gertler (2017, p. 40), who spoke next, began with the following words.

> Recent events in the global economy have forced a reevaluation of much of what we know in macroeconomics. Chief among the challenges is accounting for the sustained low inflation and economic weakness in Japan. It is no longer possible to blame the stagnation in Japan on mismanagement of monetary policy. Since the spring of 2013, through the introduction of Quantitative and Qualitative Monetary Easing (QQE), the Bank of Japan has implemented what many view as a state-of-the-art policy program.

Finally, he (Gertler, 2017, p. 55) stated that the central bank's skill alone to create inflation is not enough; "it is also going to involve luck." In the preface to the Japanese edition of *21st Century Monetary Policy*, Bernanke (2023, p. 12) also stated that under Kuroda, the BOJ's failure to end deflation was not due to lack of effort.

Since the 1990s, the BOJ until Shirakawa had argued that monetary policy can not solve deflation in Japan. For example, in February 2011, Governor Shirakawa (2011, p. 5) stated, "It is sometimes said that deflation will only be solved if the central bank provides liquidity more aggressively. Provision of ample liquidity is important, of course, but this alone does not solve the problem of deflation." Both Bernanke and Gertler now agree with Shirakawa's assertions.

The BOJ under Kuroda failed to achieve its 2% CPI inflation target even after ten years. The monetary policy advocated by reflationists was abandoned long ago. Now, mainstream economists in the U.S. conjecture that Kuroda's policies are at a standstill. However, the government, the BOJ, and reflationist economists blame everything but the monetary policy for their policy failures. One example is the persistent deflationary mindset. This story is that deflation has persisted for so long that the deflationary mindset has set in, and we cannot get out of deflation in Japan. However, Iwata and other reflationists argued that inflation expectations will rise if the BOJ eases the monetary policy. Therefore, a persistent deflationary mindset refutes the reflationist theory.

In addition, in 2022, the CPI inflation rate exceeded 4% due to soaring import prices. If a deflationary mindset really exists, CPI will not rise by as much as 4%. The true story is that the soaring import prices raise CPI, but the BOJ under Kuroda simply does not have the ability to raise CPI. Ironically, the quote at the beginning of this chapter shows that Bernanke was one of the critics of such blame-shifting by the BOJ and the reflationists.

1.3 Outline of This Book

Chapter 2 clarifies that import prices drive CPI in Japan. This indicates that costs are critical for gauging fluctuations in CPI. Next, it shows that consumption is declining in real terms due to a decrease in households' disposable income when prices are rising. These results imply that both the reflationist price theory and its strategies are wrong. However, it will be consistent with the feelings of those who suffered in Japan from imported inflation after 2022.

Chapter 3 criticizes monetary policy working on inflation expectations. Iwata argued that a sharp increase in the monetary base would raise inflation expectations. The biggest problem with his claim is that there is no theoretical basis for it. Reflationists argued that monetary policy that worked on inflation expectations was the standard policy of mainstream economics in the U.S. We make it clear that this claim is also unfounded. However, Iwata argues that his assertion has been proven correct by showing a positive correlation between the monetary base and inflation expectations. This chapter also makes it clear that this alleged evidence is also false. Inevitably, a theory that had no theoretical basis or evidence would fail.

Chapter 4 points out that monetary policy works on inflation expectations, as advocated by reflationists such as Iwata, has already ended in the first three years or so. However, as mentioned earlier, Iwata and the BOJ under Kuroda blame everything for the failure to overcome deflation but do not admit their lapses. This chapter shows that some of these blame-shifting theories are correct, but all of them, including the correct ones, are self-denial of reflationist theory. The theories and policies of reflationists have now collapsed. As this would have been detrimental to their positions, they pretended that the monetary policy advocated by reflationists was continuing and that the Japanese economy was finally overcoming the deflation.

In the early 1990s, the controversy on the money supply between Iwata and Kunio Okina arose. It was about whether the BOJ could increase its money stock. In this controversy, Iwata argued that the money stock will increase even if lending does not increase. The BOJ under Kuroda demonstrated the error of Iwata's assertion. This is because the monetary base surged, but the money stock did not increase correspondingly. Thus, the controversy on the money supply also ended, delivering a crushing defeat to Iwata. Chapter 5 examines why an increase in the monetary base did not lead to an increase in money stock based on the BOJ's results under Kuroda. Conversely, we also find that fiscal deficit policy has a substantial impact on increasing the money stock.

Chapter 6 is the conclusion.

When the 2008 global financial crisis broke out, mainstream macroeconomics and monetary policy theory were criticized. What determines prices and why money stock does not increase even if the monetary base is rapidly increased are fundamental macroeconomic issues. Therefore, similar to the failures that led to the global financial crisis, the failure of the reflationist theory and the BOJ under Kuroda are theoretical failures of macroeconomics and monetary policy theory. We believe that we have theoretically answered these questions, but it is up to the reader to judge the veracity of our analyses.

References

In Japanese

Bernanke, B. S. (2023). Nihon Go Ban e no Jobun (Preface to the Japanese edition). *21 Seiki no Kin'yū Seisaku: Dai Infure kara Korona Kiki made no Kyōkun (Japanese edition of 21st century monetary policy: The Federal Reserve from the great inflation to COVID-19)* (pp. 7–12). Nikkei Business Publications and Nikkei Publishing.

Hattori, S. (2014) *Abenomikusu no Shūen (The end of Abenomics).* Iwanami Shoten.

Iwata, K. (2012). *Nippon Ginkō: Defure no Ban'nin (The Bank of Japan: Keeper of deflation).* Nikkei Publishing.

Iwata, K. (2013). *Rifure wa Tadashii: Abenomikusu de Fukkatsu Suru Nihon Keizai (Reflation is correct: The Japanese economy revived by Abenomics).* PHP Institute.

Iwata, K. (2018). *Nichigin Nikki: Go Nenkan no Defure to no Tatakai (Diary in the Bank of Japan: Fighting deflation for five years).* Chikuma Shobo.

In English

Bernanke, B. S. (2017). The Mayekawa lecture: Some reflections on Japanese monetary policy. *Monetary and Economic Studies, 35*, 23–37.

Gertler, M. (2017). Rethinking the power of forward guidance: Lessons from Japan. *Monetary and Economic Studies, 35*, 39–57.

Shirakawa, M. (2011). Toward a revitalization of Japan's economy. Speech at the Foreign Correspondents, Club of Japan, February 7.

The Bank of Japan. (2016). Comprehensive assessment: Developments in economic activity and prices as well as policy effects since the introduction of quantitative and qualitative monetary easing (QQE): The background. September 21.

Chapter 2
Consumer Prices in Japan Are Determined by Costs

Abstract Reflationists have argued that if the Bank of Japan (BOJ) sets a Japanese-style inflation target and supplies a large monetary base, inflation expectations will rise, thereby allowing deflation to end. We show that these reflationist claims are false and that, using Kalecki's cost-determined price theory, what drives consumer prices (CPI) in Japan are costs, especially import prices. Hence, the 2% CPI inflation rate, which the BOJ under Kuroda could not achieve even after ten years, was easily achieved when imported inflation occurred after 2022. However, imported price inflation has caused consumption to stagnate through declines in real wages and real disposable income of the households. There is no basis for reflationists' claim that overcoming deflation will revive the Japanese economy. The BOJ under Kuroda and reflationists have claimed that Abenomics and the monetary policy by the BOJ have revived the Japanese economy, citing rising stock prices, surging corporate profits, and an increase in the number of employed persons. We show that this is also a mistake and that the stagnation of the Japanese economy has advanced further.

Keywords Abenomics · The Bank of Japan under Kuroda · Deflation in Japan · Price theory · Michał Kalecki · Imported inflation · Stagnation in Japan · Inflation expectations

> After the new Bank of Japan law came into effect in 1998, it can be said that the Japanese economy has continued to experience its macroeconomic performance that is close to the worst of any country in the world, as explained in the next chapter.
>
> The main reason is that the Bank of Japan's monetary policy has been austere for a little more than 15 years in the past, leading to deflation and a very strong yen. (Hamada, 2013, pp. 25–26)
>
> What is causing great suffering in the lives of the Japanese people today is deflation and the appreciation of the yen. Deflation is caused by the relative price of the yen against goods, while the appreciation of the yen is caused by the relative price of the yen against foreign currencies: in other words, it is a monetary problem.
>
> Therefore, deflation can be resolved only through monetary policy, and it is the Bank of Japan's commitment to deal with deflation through monetary policy. (Hamada, 2013, pp. 26–27)

S. Hattori, *Why the Bank of Japan Has Failed to Conquer Deflation in Japan*,
https://doi.org/10.1007/978-981-97-9408-9_2

2.1 Introduction

The quote at the beginning of this chapter is from Koichi Hamada, who served as Special Advisor to the Cabinet under the Abe administration. Whether he belongs to reflationists is delicate. At least, as far as we know, he does not claim that monetary policy works on raising inflation expectations. However, he also argued that only the Bank of Japan (BOJ) could solve the deflation problem in Japan. Moreover, he was deeply critical of the governor of the BOJ at the time (in the year 2012), Masaaki Shirakawa, who was his former student, declaring that he had not eased monetary policy and left deflation and a strong yen unchecked.

Based on the arguments of Hamada and reflationists, the BOJ under Kuroda implemented monetary policy but did not achieve the target of a 2% increase in consumer prices (CPI). This showed that the perception that the power of money could raise CPI in Japan was just a delusion of Hamada and the reflationists. However, since 2022, soaring import prices have raised Japan's CPI through rising costs. This chapter reaffirms that prices fluctuated in Japan, not due to monetary policy, the monetary base, or inflation expectations, but due to costs, especially import prices.

Reflationists state that although they have failed to overcome deflation, the real economy has improved, with employment growth and corporate profits soaring. Conversely, this chapter shows that the real GDP growth rate is sluggish. Specifically, the sluggish consumption is remarkable. Imported inflation caused stagnation in consumption by reducing real wages and incomes. This is also contrary to reflationists' claim that the Japanese economy will revive once deflation is resolved. Conversely, this is consistent with our assertion that Japan's CPI fluctuates due to import prices. At least there is no contradiction. The reflationist price theory not only failed to explain price fluctuations in Japan, but policies based on the wrong price theory were also flawed.

Section 2.2 explains the monetary policy that works on inflation expectations as conceived by the reflationists. Section 2.3 clarifies that what drives CPI in Japan is not inflation expectations or the monetary base, as the reflationists believe, but costs, especially import prices. In addition, we show that when prices rise, real wages and household disposable income decline, and consumption also declines in real terms. Section 2.4 explains the cost-determined price theory and shows that Japan's output deflator fluctuates in tandem with the import deflator. Section 2.5 clarifies the economic stagnation during the Abenomics period. Section 2.6 concludes. In the Appendix, we develop a mathematical model of cost-determined price theory and use Granger causality and vector error correction models (VECMs) to show that what drives CPI and expected inflation in Japan is not the monetary base but wages and especially import prices.

2.2 Monetary Policy Based on the Reflationist Theory

2.2.1 How the Monetary Policy Works

In discussing the reflationist monetary policy, we briefly explain the mechanism of monetary policy. Some banks and other financial institutions may be short of funds, while others may have excess funds. Therefore, financial institutions lend and borrow short-term funds in the interbank market. The interest rate in Japan's interbank market is called the call rate. When the BOJ supplies funds, there are excess funds in the interbank market, and the call rate falls. Conversely, when the BOJ collects funds, the call rate rises. The BOJ conducts monetary policy by manipulating the call rate. Currently, the call rate is considered representative of short-term interest rates in Japan.

However, the BOJ does not provide printed money for free. In the first place, the BOJ transacts only with financial institutions such as banks. There are two channels through which the BOJ supplies money to financial institutions. One route is to purchase financial assets such as Japanese government bonds (JGBs). The other route is to lend to banks. In these ways, the BOJ transfers money to the current accounts held by banks at the BOJ. However, when depositors withdraw deposits, banks cash out the current account at the BOJ and pay them. Therefore, the monetary base is the sum of the current accounts held by banks at the BOJ and cash.

A current account held at the BOJ operates through three functions. One is the settlement of money between banks. When one bank changes the name of its current account at the BOJ to another bank, it pays money to the other bank without transporting the current account at the BOJ. The next would be to guarantee that depositors will cash out their deposits when they attempt to withdraw them. Banks earn profits by using deposits for lending and purchasing securities. However, if too many deposits are used for lending, depositors may not be able to withdraw their deposits even if they want to. To prevent this, the BOJ has established rules on the minimum amount of current accounts held at the BOJ, which should be accumulated according to deposits. These are called legal reserves.

The last is the monetary policy tool. The BOJ has set its legal reserves at a level that exceeds the reserves required by banks. The BOJ conducts monetary policy by manipulating call rates. As call rates are determined by the supply and demand of funds in the interbank market, to manipulate call rates, the BOJ must match the supply of funds with the demand for reserves at the given call rate. However, it is difficult to know the demand for reserves in real-time. Legal reserves are supposed to be accumulated as a statutory amount within a one-month period. Therefore, when call rates are lower than the BOJ's target rate, banks try to borrow funds at lower call rates and accumulate more reserves. Conversely, when call rates are higher, banks reduce the amounts of reserves they accumulate. Thus, interest rates can be easily controlled by making the demand for reserves sensitive to high and low interest rates. According to Bernanke (2022, p. 248), this method of interest rate manipulation is the scarce reserve regime.

In Japan, however, short-term interest rates fell to almost zero in 1999. After the global financial crisis of 2008, short-term interest rates were reduced to almost zero in the United States (U.S.) and Europe. The quantitative easing (QE) policy was introduced in Japan, the U.S., and Europe to further ease the monetary policy. A large amount of the monetary base supplied became excess reserves over legal reserves. This method of normalizing excess reserves is the ample reserve regime (Bernanke, 2022, pp. 248–252). While exiting QE, the Federal Reserve decided to raise short-term interest rates by raising the interest rate on excess reserves. If interest rates on loans and other assets fall below this rate, financial institutions will not use them for lending and other purposes, and the interest rate on excess reserves will theoretically become the minimum level for short-term interest rates. Furthermore, in January 2019, the Federal Reserve decided to have excess reserves in place permanently and control short-term interest rates by manipulating the rate of interest on excess reserves.

Under the scarce reserve regime, the central bank must monitor reserve demand in real-time to control the short-term interest rate. In contrast, under the ample reserve regime, even if the supply of reserves is wrong, excess reserves act as a buffer, and miscalculations do not affect the interest rate. Therefore, the Federal Reserve believed it would be easier to manipulate interest rates. This indicates that the Federal Reserve considers that excess reserves have no policy implications.

In economics, what is treated as money is not the monetary base but money stock comprising cash and bank deposits (excluding those held by the central government and financial institutions). The reason for omitting the holdings of financial institutions is that they serve as intermediaries between borrowers and lenders of funds, and the money they hold is considered to have no impact on the real economy. However, according to the money multiplier approach, when the BOJ supplies the monetary base to banks, the receiving banks increase their money stock by lending to firms and purchasing securities. In Chap. 5, we will show that this mechanism does not work, at least in Japan today.

2.2.2 *Monetary Policy to Work on Inflation Expectations*

Short-term interest rates have been close to zero in Japan since the mid-1990s. As interest rates have a zero lower bound, an important question arose as to what more monetary policy can do. Strictly speaking, zero is not the lower bound, as short-term interest rates in Japan sometimes become negative. However, as short-term interest rates will not be lowered to, say, − 1%, it is almost certainly at the lower bound.

However, when prices rise, the value of money decreases. Therefore, in the current mainstream monetary policy theory, interest rates must be judged by the real rate of interest that considers fluctuations in the value of money. Furthermore, mainstream monetary policy theory is based on the Wicksellian theoretical framework. Wicksellian's believe that there is a neutral real interest rate that will sustain the current inflation rate. If real interest rates are higher than that, the inflation rate will decline further. If nominal interest rates do not change even if the inflation rate declines, real interest rates will rise, and the inflation rate will decline further. Therefore, in a situation where nominal interest rates reach the zero lower bound and cannot be lowered further, as in Japan, deflation will proceed cumulatively. In theory, however, if the neutral rate is negative, it can exacerbate inflation cumulatively. However, if that were the case, deflation in Japan would have ended long ago. Therefore, a policy that fixes nominal interest rates at almost zero is pro-deflationary and catastrophic. Strangely, this is important, but it is not indicated.

Nonetheless, reflationists such as Iwata (e.g., 2012, 2013) argued that monetary policy would become effective by raising inflation expectations. What they used as a means were the Japanese-style inflation target and a large supply of the monetary base. In *Nippon Ginkō* (*The Bank of Japan*), Iwata (2012, pp. 217–220) argues that overcoming deflation does not require any increase in lending or money stock. In *Nippon Ginkō*, Iwata (2012, p. 39) noted that the BOJ Act should be amended to mandate the BOJ to achieve an inflation rate of 2–3% so that the inflation target is effective. In addition, Iwata argued that the BOJ must clarify its commitment by setting a deadline for achieving the inflation target. The reason for labeling the inflation target, which is now a policy adopted by many countries, as a uniquely Japanese style is that reflationists insisted that it was essential to clarify the BOJ's commitment by setting a deadline.

In February 2012, when Shirakawa was the governor, the BOJ set the "medo" (goal) of aiming for an inflation rate of 0–2%, or 1% in the interim. However, Iwata (2012, pp. 169–185) criticized this "medo" because the 1% target is too low. The other reason is that there is no deadline to achieve; therefore, even if the goal is not achieved or maintained, there would be no denunciation. He (Iwata, 2012, p. 179) criticized that "the BOJ 'only needs to pose as if it is making efforts until it can outlook to achieve it.'" It is true that unless there is no deadline, even if the BOJ cannot achieve the "medo," it can postpone and avoid taking the blame. In *Rifure wa Tadashii* (*Reflation is Right*) (Iwata, 2013, pp. 32–37), the monetary base in the U.S. and Europe surged after the global financial crisis. However, only the BOJ did not surge the monetary base; therefore, only Japan was in a state of deflation.

Hamada (2013, p. 26) also criticized the target 1% inflation rate as halfway. He (Hamada, 2013, p. 26) pointed out that the BOJ had translated the "medo" into English as the goal. He argues that, effectively, the "medo" is an inflation goal and that it is the BOJ's sophistry logic to say that the "medo" is different from the inflation target. However, what the BOJ, until Shirakawa, disliked most was to be held responsible for the failure to achieve their unattainable inflation targets. Therefore, there is a big difference between the "medo" and target. Conversely, if the "medo" and the target were the same, then "medo" would not matter. In January 2012, the Federal Reserve adopted a long-run goal for inflation. This is generally understood to be an inflation target. However, Bernanke (Federal Open Market Committee, 2012, p. 23) stated at the press conference that if the inflation target puts price stability first and other goals second, it is not an inflation target. The Federal Reserve aims for price stability and maximum employment with equal weight. There is no single absolute definition of inflation targeting, even among supporters of inflation targets.

Besides, Hamada (2013, p. 36) argues that the BOJ's declaration of the "medo" (goal) might imply a change of mind by the BOJ; in reality, he criticized it, saying, "So to speak, it turned out to be nothing more than a policy of deflection of criticism, in which the BOJ makes promises and does not implement them or alternatively postpones them altogether, under the guise of monetary easing."

Furthermore, Iwata (2013, pp. 81–86) criticized Former Governor Shirakawa's thinking, calling it the BOJ's theory on the QE. This theory is that "when there is no liquidity shortage in the private sector, prices will not rise even if the Bank of Japan increases liquidity" (Iwata, 2013, p. 81). The BOJ increases the monetary base only when there is a liquidity problem, such as the Great East Japan Earthquake, but recovers it when the liquidity problem is resolved. He criticized that this is why deflation cannot be overcome. Iwata (2012, pp. 125–126) also criticizes the BOJ's policy-based finance on the ground that the BOJ does not have the ability to discern a growing industry.

In December 2012, Shinzo Abe was formally elected as the prime minister of Japan. Immediately, he began to implement the monetary policy based on the reflationist theory. In January 2013, he imposed the inflation target on the BOJ. However, Shirakawa, governor of the BOJ at the time, resisted the reflationists. For this reason, there was no specific deadline to achieve the inflation target, and Shirakawa himself explains that the responsibility for achieving the inflation target lies with both the BOJ and the government (Shirakawa, 2021, pp. 349–351). The joint statement with the government was actually written, as Shirakawa claims. We can say that Shirakawa retained his position as a central banker.

In March 2013, Haruhiko Kuroda was nominated as the governor of the BOJ, and Iwata became the deputy governor. At their inaugural press conference, they (The Bank of Japan, 2013) boasted of achieving a 2% inflation target within two years. Furthermore, Iwata (The Bank of Japan, 2013, p. 18) boasted,

> If, two years later, we are still unable to achieve 2%, or if, close to 2%, but we are still unable to achieved it, I think the first thing we should fulfill is accountability. However, if I am unable to fulfill that accountability, or if it is just my misjudgment, I think the best way to take the blame is to resign. First of all, I think the fundamental thing is whether we can fulfill our accountability.

Five years later, at the end of his term as the deputy governor, there was no prospect of achieving the inflation target. Iwata did not resign but retired at the end of his term. Even after ten years, the BOJ under Kuroda failed to achieve its target, excluding imported inflation. However, neither Kuroda nor Wakatabe, who succeeded Iwata as the deputy governor, were blamed or resigned.

In April 2013, the quantitative and qualitative monetary easing (QQE) policy was introduced. Under Kuroda, the BOJ decided to expand the monetary base at an annual pace of about ¥60–¥70 trillion per year. This corresponds to the quantitative part of the QQE. The BOJ also decided to increase long-term JGBs at an annual pace of ¥50 trillion. The average remaining maturity of long-term JGBs was set at about seven years. In addition, the purchase of exchange-traded funds and Japan real estate investment trusts also increased. These measures correspond to the qualitative part of the QQE. Attributable to its enormous scale, it was also called "monetary easing of different dimensions" or "Kuroda bazooka."

Thus, monetary policy designed based on reflationist theory was initiated.

2.3 Overcoming Deflation Is Forever Only Halfway

2.3.1 Import Prices that Drive Consumer Prices

Ten years after his inauguration, Governor Kuroda stepped down after failing to achieve the inflation target. Iwata and Kuroda demonstrated for themselves that the BOJ has no power to overcome deflation. However, why did they fail?

Figure 2.1 shows CPI inflation, import price inflation, and inflation expectations. The BOJ's inflation target is based on the index less fresh food; therefore, we used this index in the figure. Commonly used indicators of inflation expectations are the breakeven inflation rate (BEI) and ESP forecasts conducted by the Japan Center for Economic Research, which are illustrated in the figure.

BEI is the difference between the interest rate on 10-year JGBs and the interest rate on 10-year inflation-linked bonds. Inflation-linked bonds are JGBs in which the principal is indexed to inflation or deflation. Investors will likely prefer the more advantageous of the common JGBs and inflation-linked bonds. Through these investor actions, theoretically, the two rates of return will eventually coincide. However, as prices ten years from now are not known precisely at the present time, the rate of price increase is merely an expectation. Moreover, as expectations could deviate, a liquidity premium is added. As a result, in theory,

$$\begin{aligned}&\text{Interest Rate on Inflation-Linked Bonds}\\&\quad = \text{Interest Rate on JGBs} + \text{Expected Inflation Rate}\\&\qquad + \text{Liquidity Premium}\end{aligned}$$

$$\begin{aligned}&\text{Breakeven Inflation Rate}\\&\quad = \text{Interest Rate on JGBs} - \text{Interest Rate on Inflation-Linked Bonds}\\&\quad = \text{Expected Inflation Rate} + \text{Liquidity Premium}.\end{aligned}$$

If the liquidity premium is zero, BEI is equal to expected inflation. If it does not change at a constant value, even if it is not zero, and the difference is constant, there would be no practical problem.

The ESP forecasts are the average forecast of the rate of increase in CPI less fresh food for the same quarter of the following year by experts who specialize in economic

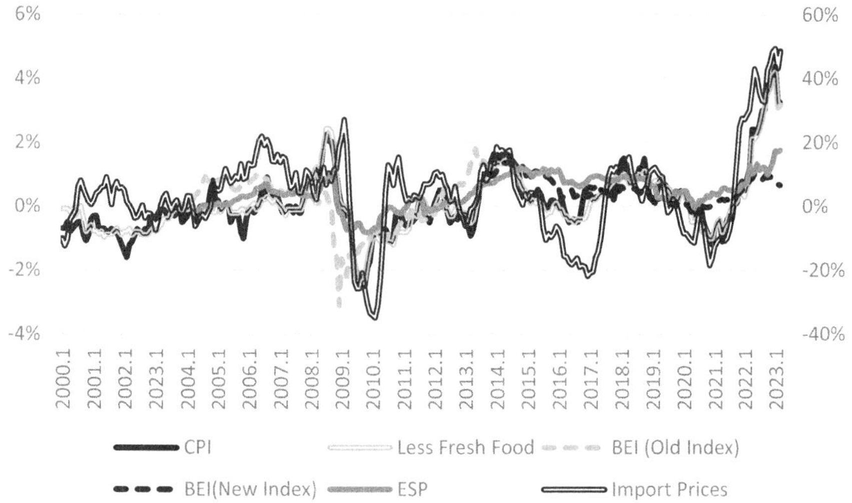

Fig. 2.1 Consumer price inflation rate, import price inflation rate, and inflation expectations (January 2000–March 2023). *Source* Statistics Bureau, Ministry of Internal Affairs and Communications, Japan (2023a), the Bank of Japan (2023b), Japan Bond Trading Co., Ltd. (2023), and Japan Center for Economic Research (2023). *Note 1* "Import prices" are indicated on the right-hand side axis, while others are indicated on the left-hand side. *Note 2* Inflation rates are year-on-year growth rates. *Note 3* "Less fresh food" is CPI less fresh food, which is subject to the BOJ's inflation target. The "BEI" is a 10-year BEI. Data from March 2004. A new index from October 2013. The old index has no principal guarantee for inflation-linked bonds, and the new index has a principal guarantee. BEI data are for the 10th of each month in the figure. However, if data were not available for the 10th, the next available day of data was used. "ESP" is the average estimate of CPI inflation rates less food for the same quarter of the following year by ESP forecast experts in Japan since May 2004. *Note 4* "CPI" and inflation expectations by the ESP forecast exclude the impact of the consumption tax hikes and other factors. Import prices were six months ago. *Note 5* Japan Bond Trading Co., Ltd. personally provided us with the data on the BEI. We would like to express our gratitude to Japan Bond Trading Co., Ltd.

forecasting. The figure shows the expected rate of increase during the same quarter of the following year for the month when the survey was conducted.

However, monetary policy that works on inflation expectations is intended to raise CPI by increasing inflation expectations. So, the inflation expectations of financial markets or experts are not necessarily an appropriate indicator to determine whether monetary policy that works on inflation expectations is having an effect. In the Appendix and Fig. 3.2, we focus on consumers' inflation expectations.

In the nine years since Kuroda became the governor in 2013, the 2% inflation target could not be achieved. However, in April 2022, it exceeded the target of 2%. Furthermore, the CPI inflation rate rose and reached 4% in December 2022. Examining the figure, the rate of increase in import prices began to rise in early 2021, reaching 40% by the end of the year. This surge in import prices led to a rise in the CPI with a lag of about six months.

If you examine the figure closely, it can be observed that when import prices decline sharply, the CPI also reduces, but to a smaller extent than when import prices rise. Very often, a downward rigidity in prices has been noted. Corresponding with this, according to Watanabe (2022, pp. 266–268), if the CPI inflation rate remains the same, Japanese firms are more likely to keep prices unchanged than their counterparts in the U.S. and Europe. In addition, Japanese firms show that the proportion of firms that keep prices unchanged in negative inflation zones is considerably higher than the proportion of firms that keep prices unchanged in positive zones. This means that price rigidity has suppressed deflation in Japan. However, Watanabe (2022, 268–271) himself uses this fact as evidence to prove that prices will not rise because most consumers do not tolerate price increases; however, this is contradictory.

While researching for *Abenomikusu no Shūen* (*The End of Abenomics*) (Hattori, 2014, pp. 29–32), we noticed that the CPI reacts to import prices with a lag of about six months in Japan. Based on this, we wrote that the rise in CPI at that time would also end when the surge in import prices concluded. When the imported inflation rate declined sharply from the beginning of 2014, the CPI inflation rate also declined, accompanied by a lag of about six months, as we expected. Yukio Noguchi (2022, p. 52) has also pointed out that Japan's CPI is linked to import prices with a lag of about six months.

Kichikawa et al. (2020) used the complex Hilbert principal component analysis to demonstrate that price fluctuations in Japan move in one direction, and that the clusters of price changes move from upstream to downstream because upstream price changes alter downstream prices by modifying downstream costs. Even though we had taken this for granted, after reading Kichikawa et al., we realized that even economists who discuss prices do not always understand this obvious phenomenon.

The BOJ under Kuroda was unable to raise the CPI inflation rate to 2% despite making efforts for ten years; however, when import prices rose, the CPI inflation rate could easily rise to 4% in about six months. This shows that import prices and costs drive the CPI in Japan, and not monetary policy, monetary base, or inflation expectations, as emphasized by reflationists. Historically, it was inevitable that policies based on the reflationist theory, which could not understand what drives CPI fluctuations in Japan, should fail.

2.3.2 Declining Expected Inflation Rates

Expected inflation rates declined sharply after the global financial crisis. Thereafter, expected Inflation rates rose in parallel with the end of the financial crisis. Iwata (e.g., 2012, pp. 109–117) argued that the rise in expected inflation rates after the global financial crisis was the result of the BOJ's monetary base expansion. He also claimed that this proved his own claim.

Since the inauguration of the Abe administration, expected Inflation rates have risen further. Subsequently, the expected inflation rates began to decline in both indicators. BEI peaked in May 2013, shortly after Kuroda took office. While it fell sharply in October 2013, it was due to a switch in index. Under the new index, it rose for a while but peaked in June 2014, after which it declined again. From the beginning of 2016, inflation expectations by ESP forecasts also started to decline. However, in 2020, both started to rise. If Iwata's claim were accurate, expected inflation rates would continue to rise even more sharply as the BOJ under Kuroda expanded the monetary base at an unprecedented pace. However, under Kuroda, the expected inflation rate rose only for a short period of time initially and began to decline thereafter.

Why did this happen? The figure shows that inflation expectations rose and declined repeatedly in irregular cycles. Let us assume that these seemingly irregular cycles do not correspond to the increases or decreases in the monetary base. Nevertheless, an increase in the monetary base could coincide with a period of rising inflation expectations. Therefore, even if an increase in the monetary base coincides with a rise in inflation expectations, it does not prove Iwata's argument. Conversely, if both were just coincidentally rising simultaneously, the expected inflation rate could *coincidently* decline as the monetary base continues to increase. In fact, even after the arrival of the BOJ under Kuroda, the expected inflation rate declined. Thus, Iwata's claims were completely shattered by the BOJ under Kuroda and Iwata.

After the global financial crisis, import prices plummeted due to the sharp decline in crude oil and energy prices worldwide and the rapid appreciation of the yen. Therefore, contrary to 2022 and beyond, the CPI inflation rate was significantly negative. Naturally, the CPI inflation rate will rise once the sharp decline in import prices subsides. Accordingly, inflation expectations will improve. In addition, BEI is also affected by liquidity premiums. Shortly before the global financial crisis, credit uncertainty spread worldwide. As a result, interest rates on JGBs, which are safe-haven assets, declined. Conversely, interest rates on inflation-linked bonds, which have a small market, rose. Thus, a rise in liquidity premiums also lowered BEI. By contrast, if the financial crisis subsided and liquidity premiums declined, BEI rose accordingly.

As Fig. 2.1 illustrates, the rise in CPI with the start of Abenomics resulted from soaring import prices due to a depreciating yen (see also Fig. 4.2). The rise in inflation expectations was also the result of imported inflation. If this is the case, inflation expectations are expected to decline once imported inflation subsides, and this is indeed happening as expected. Therefore, an increase in inflation expectations after the global financial crisis subsides or after the Abe administration takes office does not prove Iwata's assertion correct. If Iwata's claim were precise, the BOJ under Kuroda's massive supply of the monetary base would have further raised both inflation expectations and actual inflation rates. However, shortly after the BOJ under Kuroda took over, inflation expectations began to decline. This is conclusive as a counter-proof.

Thus, Kuroda and Iwata proved that there is no monetary policy working on inflation expectations, as advocated by reflationists.

Fig. 2.2 Consumer prices inflation rate and rate of growth in real wages (January 2000–March 2023). *Source* Statistics Bureau, Ministry of Internal Affairs and Communications, Japan (2023a) and Ministry of Health, Labor and Welfare, Japan (2023). *Note 1* Year-on-year growth rates. *Note 2* "CPI" is a tax-adjusted index less imputed rent. "Real wage" is calculated by dividing the scheduled cash earnings of regular workers by the consumption tax-adjusted CPI less imputed rent

2.3.3 Imported Inflation and Stagnation of Consumption

Since 2022, BOJ's inflation target has been achieved through soaring import prices. However, most people in Japan consider the current imported inflation to be a weighing factor on household budgets. Thus, reflationists' strategy of reviving the Japanese economy by overcoming deflation had no basis. Hauseman et al. (2021) point out that monetary policy during Abenomics lowered nominal interest rates, weakened the yen, and boosted stock prices, but consumption remained stagnant. They further point out that consumption fluctuations do not vary much across households with different ratios of debt or financial assets to income, as well as income and age. Based on this, they conclude that the effects of monetary policy were limited.

Figure 2.2 illustrates the relationship between the rate of increase in the CPI and the rate of increase in regular workers' real wages. The wages of regular workers are based on scheduled cash earnings.[1] In addition, the CPI is an index less imputed rent, which is the rent amount payable when you lease the house you own. As imputed rent is not actually paid, this is omitted from the calculation of real wages. The figure omits inflation due to the hike in consumption tax, among others.

[1] Scheduled cash earnings are earnings paid according to method and conditions previously determined by labor contracts, collective agreements, or wage regulations of establishments, excluding overtime pay.

Reflationists believe that overcoming deflation would lead to economic recovery and higher wages. However, the figure shows that although the rate of increase in real wages fluctuates widely month-by-month, it generally fluctuates in the opposite direction to the CPI inflation rate. In fact, real wages were declining during periods of inflation, which is the exact opposite of what reflationists expect; however, if the rise in Japan's CPI is caused by imported inflation, it is rather natural (see Hattori, 2023b, pp. 44–45).

Figure 2.3 uses GDP data to illustrate the growth rate (year-on-year) of real disposal income of households, real consumption and consumption deflator in Japan. This figure shows that the rate of increase in the consumption deflator and real disposable income or real consumption generally fluctuate in opposite directions.

Using the same data, we estimated the consumption function (which shows what determines consumption). Table 2.1 shows the results. The estimated period is from the first quarter of 2001 to the third quarter of 2019. The reason for closing in the third quarter of 2019 is attributable to the fact that the estimated results are distant because of the consumption tax hike during the fourth quarter and the outbreak of COVID-19 from 2020 onward. "Real Net Financial Assets" denote households in the previous quarter. The Durbin–Watson statistics are also presented, and although these values are low, this is a natural result because we are using quarterly data and creating a model compared to the same period of the previous year. For periods related to the 2008 global financial crisis, the 2011 Great East Japan Earthquake, and

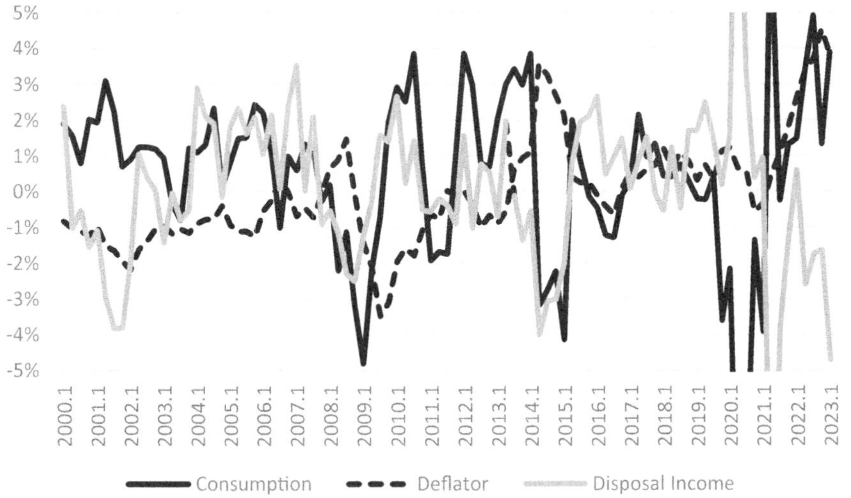

Fig. 2.3 Rate of growth in real disposable income, real consumption, and household consumption deflator (2000.Q1–2023.Q1). *Source* Economic and Social Research Institute, Cabinet Office, Japan (2023c). *Note 1* Year-on-year growth rates. *Note 2* "Consumption" is household consumption (less imputed rent). "Deflator" is that of household consumption (less imputed rent). "Disposable income" is the real disposable income of households

the 2014 consumption tax hike, dummy variables are included because consumption fluctuated greatly due to these shocks.

The first estimate used real disposable income and real net financial assets as independent variables. This result stands to reason because when real disposable income and real net financial assets increase, consumption also increases in real terms. The second estimate changes disposable income to nominal and adds consumption deflators to the independent variables. The coefficient of the deflator is -0.31, and the t-value is also high. In contrast, the coefficient of disposable income was no longer significant. The third estimate shows the relationship between real consumption and the consumption deflator. The coefficient and t-value of the consumption deflator are almost the same as that of the second estimation. Finally, the relationship between real disposable income and the deflator was also estimated. The results showed that a 1% increase in the deflator would reduce real disposable income by over 0.5%. Importantly, these results support our argument that imported inflation reduces consumption by reducing real disposable income and real net financial assets.

2.3.4 *Overcoming Deflation that Did Not Exist from the Beginning*

In 2012, the CPI inflation rate was negative for several months. However, after Kuroda became the governor of the BOJ, the inflation rate became positive and continued to rise. Inflation expectations also rose. However, inflation expectations were on a recovery trend after the sharp decline following the global financial crisis. In response, the BOJ under Kuroda, the government, and reflationist economists boasted that they had proven the accuracy of the reflationist theory. This is still the case (e.g., Iwata, 2018; The Bank of Japan, 2016a, 2016b; Wakatabe, 2022, pp. 16–17).

However, as noted earlier, the rise in CPI at that time resulted from the surge in import prices, and we (Hattori, 2014, pp. 29–32) predicted that once the surge in import prices ended, the rise in CPI would also end. This happened after 2014, precisely as we had expected. We are not the only ones who noticed that the general increase in prices at that time was due to imported inflation. The same is true of Yukio Noguchi (2022, p. 52), mentioned earlier. Director General for Economic Research, Cabinet Office, Japan (2014, pp. 54–55) also pointed out that the rise in import prices had raised the CPI at different rates for different items. It also projected that this price pass-through would end in nine months.

Director General for Economic Research (2014, pp. 148–152) stated that the weaker yen had raised export prices in the manufacturing industry and improved value-added deflation. However, this applies only to the processing industry among manufacturing industries, which is a leading export industry in Japan, while the value-added deflation was exacerbated in the materials industry, which relies on imports for most raw materials (Director General for Economic Research, 2014, pp. 152–155). Furthermore, value-added deflation had worsened in the nonmanufacturing

Table 2.1 Estimation of consumption function (2001.Q1–2019.Q3)

Dependent variable: real consumption

	Coefficient	*t*-value		Coefficient	*t*-value
Constant	0.000	– 0.09	Constant	0.000	– 0.12
Real disposal income	0.193**	2.35	Nominal disposal income	0.144	1.66
Real net financial assets	0.150***	5.74	Real net financial assets	0.145***	5.59
D1	– 0.025***	– 3.60	Deflator	– 0.310***	– 2.86
D2	– 0.017**	– 2.48	D1	– 0.026***	– 3.77
D3	– 0.021***	– 3.17	D2	– 0.018**	– 2.62
D4	– 0.029***	– 4.22	D3	– 0.023***	– 3.40
D5	– 0.025***	– 3.65	D4	– 0.030***	– 4.41
D6	– 0.014**	– 2.01	D5	– 0.025***	– 3.71
D7	0.019***	2.83	D6	– 0.013**	– 1.94
D8	0.035***	5.11	D7	0.018***	2.72
D9	– 0.020***	– 2.84	D8	0.034***	5.12
R^2	0.779		D9	– 0.018**	– 2.64
$\bar{R}^2$	0.738		R^2	0.789	
DW	1.40		$\bar{R}^2$	0.746	
			DW	1.40	

	Coefficient	*t*-value
Constant	0.004***	2.73
Deflator	– 0.372***	– 3.08
D1	– 0.038***	– 4.39
D2	– 0.024***	– 2.85
D3	– 0.026***	– 3.01
D4	– 0.030***	– 3.51
D5	– 0.024***	– 2.79
D6	– 0.011	– 1.26
D7	0.023***	2.62
D8	0.038***	4.42
D9	– 0.020***	– 2.28
R^2	0.637	
$\bar{R}^2$	0.577	
DW	1.03	

Dependent variable: real disposable income

	Coefficient	*t*-value
Constant	0.003	1.58

(continued)

Table 2.1 (continued)

Dependent variable: real disposable income		
	Coefficient	t-value
Deflator	– 0.545***	– 4.04
D1	– 0.018*	– 1.81
R^2	0.229	
$\overline{R}^2$	0.206	
DW	1.09	

*** 1% significant, ** 5% significant, * 10% significant

Source Economic and Social Research Institute, Cabinet Office, Japan (2023c)

Note 1 Year-on-year growth rates, expect dummy variables

Note 2 "Consumption" and "disposable income" denote those of households (less imputed rent). "Deflator" corresponds to household consumption (less imputed rent). "Real net financial assets" denote households in the previous quarter

Note 3 D1 is a dummy variable with 1 for the first quarter of 2009 and – 1 for the first quarter of 2010. D2 is a dummy variable with 1 for the second quarter of 2009 and – 1 for the second quarter of 2010. D3 is a dummy variable with 1 for the third quarter of 2009 and – 1 for the third quarter of 2010. D4 is a dummy variable with 1 for the first quarter of 2011 and – 1 for the first quarter of 2012. D5 is a dummy variable with the second quarter of 2011 as 1 and the second quarter of 2012 as – 1. D6 is a dummy variable with the third quarter of 2011 as 1 and the third quarter of 2012 as – 1. D7 is a dummy variable with the fourth quarter of 2013 as 1 and the fourth quarter of 2014 as – 1. D8 is a dummy variable with the first quarter of 2014 as 1 and the first quarter of 2015 as – 1. D9 is a dummy variable with the second quarter of 2014 as 1 and the second quarter of 2015 as – 1

sector (Director General for Economic Research, 2014, pp. 158–164). The sharp depreciation of the yen raised export prices and improved value-added deflation in export industries; however, domestic-type industries could not pass on the increase in import prices completely to output prices, exacerbating value-added deflation.

Newspapers reported that soaring import prices triggered the price rise at that time and that it was a bad price rise. For example, Asahi Shimbun (2013) reported in August 2013 that the price increase from a negative increase was due to the weaker yen. It also informed that the government's notion of a good price increase, in which a weaker yen improves corporate profits, raises salaries, increases consumption, and improves corporate profits, had not occurred.

Table 2.2 shows the rate of increase in real GDP from the third quarter of 2012 to the second quarter of 2014. The year 2012 was marked by a recession, with negative growth continuing from the second quarter. However, after the Abe administration was inaugurated in December 2012, a high annual growth of nearly 6% was achieved in the first quarter of 2013. However, macroeconomic policies take more than six months to become effective. Moreover, no one would expect to sustain high growth beyond the bubble period of the 1980s, which was 6% per annum. Therefore, this high growth is nothing short of good luck. If the BOJ under Kuroda had succeeded in reviving Japan's economy, a relatively high growth level could have been maintained in the second half of 2013. However, the growth rate was negative in the fourth quarter of 2013.

Table 2.2 Growth in real GDP, contribution of each item to real GDP and consumer confidence index (2012.Q3–2014.Q2)

	GDP (%)	Consumption (%)	Durable goods (%)	Private housing (%)	Public demand (%)	CCI
2012.Q3	– 1.52	– 0.33	– 0.10	0.28	– 0.15	40.5
2012.Q4	– 0.21	0.81	– 1.35	0.33	0.11	39.3
2013.Q1	5.55	3.34	1.60	0.16	– 0.02	44.2
2013.Q2	3.67	1.58	0.32	0.13	2.00	44.8
2013.Q3	3.92	1.04	0.47	0.57	0.97	43.9
2013.Q4	– 0.43	– 0.44	0.31	0.52	0.70	40.6
2014.Q1	3.16	4.79	1.96	0.22	– 0.25	38.1
2014.Q2	– 6.97	– 10.65	– 2.74	– 1.34	– 0.95	38.8
2014.Q3	0.39	2.28	– 0.46	– 0.80	1.15	40.4
2014.Q4	1.88	0.37	0.47	0.03	0.18	37.3

Source Economic and Social Research Institute, Cabinet Office, Japan (2023d)
Note 1 "GDP" is the annualized growth rate from the previous quarter. Others (excluding CCI) are the annualized contribution to real GDP from the previous quarter
Note 2 "Consumption" is household consumption (less imputed rent). "Durable goods" include purchases in Japan by non-residents and do not include purchases made abroad by residents
Note 3 "CCI" was converted to quarterly data by averaging monthly data. Since April 2013, the survey has changed from a home-visit detention survey to a mail-in survey; therefore, the figures are not necessarily consistent with the previous surveys

In the second half of 2012, consumption of durable goods had plummeted due to a reactionary decline owing to the end of the home appliance eco-point system, a program that promotes the purchase of home appliances that consume less electricity and stimulate demand without increasing energy use. Conversely, in the first half of 2013, consumption of durable goods increased in reaction to the reactionary decline. Furthermore, in the second half, consumption of durable goods and housing investment swelled due to the last-minute surge in demand prior to the consumption tax hike. The table also shows that the contribution of public demand was high in 2013. Nevertheless, the contribution of consumption (other than durable goods) declined after the second quarter of 2013, thereby pushing the rate of real GDP growth lower.

The table also shows that the consumer confidence index (CCI) was low in 2012, the year of the recession, and it rose sharply in the first quarter of 2013 after the recession ended. The second quarter also showed a slight increase (note that the survey methodology was changed in April 2013, so it did not continue with the previous figures. However, there was no significant difference between March and April, so it is unlikely that there would be much difference following the change in survey methodology). However, it declined sharply from the third quarter onward. In the fourth quarter, it fell to the same level as in late 2012. In the first quarter of 2014, the rate of increase in consumption was extremely high due to the last-minute increase in demand prior to the consumption tax hike. However, the CCI fell below the second half of 2012. In fact, consumers also felt that their lives had deteriorated due to the imported inflation since the second half of 2013.

Asahi Noguchi (2021, pp. 167–168), a member of the Policy Board at the BOJ since April 2021, argues the exact opposite. He states that there was a remarkable economic recovery in 2013 when Abenomics began. Furthermore, according to the statistics at the time, the real GDP growth rate in the second quarter of 2013 reached 3.7% (GDP statistics, especially seasonally adjusted figures, change depending on the revision; besides, the GDP standard itself was revised in 2016). He even concluded that the remarkable economic growth generated by Abenomics led to the wrong decision to proceed with the consumption tax hike in 2014 as scheduled, thereby preventing the end of deflation.

As mentioned earlier, the high growth in the first half of 2013 cannot be attributed to Abenomics or the BOJ under Kuroda. Primarily, if the economy had recovered through Abenomics and the BOJ under Kuroda, the economic growth rate would have risen during 2013. In fact, the opposite is true: despite the large last-minute surge in demand prior to the consumption tax hike, the growth rate in the fourth quarter of 2013 was negative. Even consumption showed negative growth. In the first quarter of 2014, growth exceeded 3%. However, as the combined contribution of consumption and housing investment exceeds 5%, it can be considered as negative growth if the large last-minute demand surge is omitted.

The BOJ under Kuroda argued that imported inflation since 2022 was temporary and a bad one without wage increases, and it was different from the inflation it was aiming for. The price increase from 2013 onward was also temporary due to the imported inflation, and it was a bad price increase without corresponding wage hikes. In this sense, the progress of overcoming deflation has not yet begun.

2.4 Theory of Price Determined by Costs

2.4.1 History of Theory of Prices Determined by Costs

Kalecki (1954) developed the macroeconomics of cost-determined prices and production adjustment. He argued that prices of primary commodities, whose production is difficult to adjust, fluctuate with supply and demand, while the prices of manufactured goods, whose production is easy to adjust, are determined by costs. He developed macroeconomics based on cost-determined prices because primary commodities were unimportant in developed countries in the second half of the twentieth century. However, he does not deny that demand fluctuations determine the prices of primary commodities, which in turn changes manufacturing prices through fluctuations in the cost of raw materials.

Morishima (1984) also argues that in developed countries like Japan, where the production of primary commodities is negligible, the realistic macroeconomic model is prices determined by costs and production adjustment. However, countries like Japan also import primary raw materials from developing countries. Therefore, fluctuations in import prices from developing countries move prices in Japan.

The economy is not made up of one or two sectors. Therefore, price theory, which is determined by costs, also needs to be developed in multiple sectors, as developed by Sraffa (1960). Furthermore, Shiozawa's (2014, 2017) new theory of international values developed a price theory determined by a combination of costs as a multi-sectoral model, including foreign trade.

When supply is elastic, it is rather commonplace in economics that fluctuations in demand do not affect prices. Housing, especially housing in urban areas, has a low elasticity of supply. As a result, there was a housing bubble in the U.S. in the first half of the 2000s. However, Mian and Sufi (2011, Fig. 2, p. 2140) show that even in the U.S. during the housing bubble, prices did not rise much in the metropolitan areas where the housing supply was elastic. In empirical research, it has been repeatedly admitted, since the Oxford Survey (Hall & Hitch, 1939) in the 1930s, that cost determines the prices of manufactured products. A recent study by Blinder et al. (1998) focused on price rigidity, noting that prices do not vary sufficiently to match supply and demand. However, they (Blinder et al., 1998, p. 307) also found that firms set prices based on costs and raise them when industry-wide costs increase. However, firms do not raise prices when cost increases are expected to be temporary, and even when cost increases are expected in the future, they do not raise prices until the costs increase.

Using Kalecki's price theory, Yoshikawa (2013, Chaps. 5 and 6, pp. 149–193; 2022, pp. 149–167) attempted to elucidate deflation in Japan. He concluded that the lack of wage growth was the cause of deflation in Japan. Yoshikawa (2022, pp. 160–163) criticizes the reflationist theory that CPI fluctuates in response to money and inflation expectations, based on the empirical results of Kichikawa et al. (2020) that price changes spread in clusters from imported goods to CPI.

Deflation is said to begin in Japan after the economic bubble burst in the early 1990s. However, CPI began to decline continuously after the financial crisis of 1997–1998 in Japan. We believe that this is not a coincidence because cutting labor costs was a common phenomenon after the financial crisis. The U.S. could avoid deflation even after the global financial crisis, and we believe that this was possible because the nominal wage growth in the U.S. remained reasonably high even when the unemployment rate was high. Hoshi and Kashayap (2021) note that in Japan, wage fluctuations used to move prices, but this relationship was no longer observed after around 1998. We believe that the reason for this is that since then, wage fluctuations have become smaller, and their effect on the CPI has become smaller. The VECMs in the Appendix, shown below, also does not contradict this hypothesis.

The price theory, which is determined by costs, provides a generalized answer to the phenomenon that soaring import prices and consumption tax hikes raise the CPI, and these price rises were caused by rising costs. If the answer is given in this general form, it can be predicted that as wages are part of costs, any rise in wage costs will also raise prices. This is one of the important benefits of theory. Firstly, there is hardly anyone who would not admit that the consumption tax hike and the current surge in import prices have raised CPI through higher costs. While acknowledging these, it is a theoretical contradiction to think that wage stagnation does not create deflation.

In the first half of the 1970s, inflation was a worldwide phenomenon. Kaldor (1978 [1976]) argued that this global inflation was due to a cost-push from high oil prices. In addition, he states that workers demanded and achieved higher wages in the face of inflation, which further accelerated inflation due to higher wage costs. Blinder and Rudd (2013) attribute the notable spike in U.S. inflation during 1973–1975 and again during 1978–1980 to supply shocks. They point out that food prices rose alongside oil prices. Consistent with Kaldor, they also add that wage increases. As for the 1973–1975 inflation, the lifting of wage and price controls during the Nixon era impacted inflation, which was not a supply shock (as for the 1973–1975 inflation, see also Blinder, 1979). CPI rose in Japan after 2022 as import prices soared. However, unlike the 1970s, at least in Japan, a sharp increase in wages has not yet occurred, and this may explain the reason for the modest degree of inflation compared to the 1970s.

Of course, explaining all price fluctuations by a single factor, not just costs, is impossible. Instead, what we argue is that demand factors indicate a much smaller meaning than costs in response to changes in the CPI in Japan. In addition, there are almost no effects, such as an increase or decrease in the monetary base and inflation expectations, as emphasized by reflationists. Moreover, as monetary policy and wage growth are different dimensions, they are not necessarily theoretically exclusive. The original Phillips curve shows the relationship between a decline in unemployment and an increase in nominal wages (Phillips, 1958). If we add that when wages rise, prices also rise, we can create the commonly disseminated price version of the Phillips curve. It is logically possible that monetary policy, whether directly or indirectly, will raise the CPI by increasing wages and import prices. However, as it failed to do so, the BOJ under Kuroda, despite ten years of hard work, could not achieve its inflation target.

2.4.2 Analysis by Output Deflator

Costs include the cost of domestic intermediate goods, the cost of imported intermediate goods, and wage costs (for an analysis of this section, see also Hattori, 2024, pp. 41–43). The price is these costs multiplied by 1 + markup, plus indirect taxes minus subsidies. Now, if we take the price of Good 1 produced in Japan, p_{d}^{1},

$$p_{\mathrm{d}}^{1} = (1 + \text{Markup})(\text{Cost of Domestic Intermediate Goods} \\ + \text{Cost of Imported Intermediate Goods} + \text{Wage Cost}) \\ + \text{Indirect Taxes} - \text{Subsidies}.$$

Using the *Annual Report on National Accounts*, the rate of increase in the output deflator can be divided into the contributions of intermediate goods costs, wage costs, markups, and indirect tax subsidies, respectively.

However, as domestic intermediate goods are domestically produced, their prices change with changes in wages, other costs, and other factors. Therefore, the contribution of the cost of domestic intermediate goods due to price changes must be reduced to other factors (Appendix presents a mathematical model of price theory determined by cost and calculates pricing decisions). This reduction is not possible because *National Accounts* does not divide the costs of intermediate goods into those of domestic intermediate goods and those of imported intermediate goods. Therefore, the contribution of intermediate goods costs is divided into those due to changes in price and those due to changes in inputs. Logically, intermediate goods from Japan would also be used to produce imported goods. This is an exceedingly small amount, so we simply ignore it.

Figure 2.4 illustrates the contribution of intermediate goods costs and other factors to the rate of increase in the output deflator.[2] The increasing rate of import deflator is also shown in the figure. The figure shows that since 1995, fluctuations in the output deflator have been largely determined by the contribution of price fluctuations of intermediate goods. As mentioned earlier, when the prices of output goods change, the prices of intermediate goods also change, so it is natural that the correlation is high. However, they do not fully interlock because there is an intermediate input of imported goods, and the composition of the contents of domestic intermediate goods and all goods produced in Japan are different.

On the one hand, the correlation between the rate of increase in the value-added deflator and the rate of increase in the output deflator is close to zero, and the correlation between the rate of increase in the value-added deflator and the contribution of price changes in intermediate goods is negative. On the other hand, the correlation between the rate of increase in the import deflator and the rate of increase in the output deflator or the contribution of price fluctuations of intermediate goods is extremely high. This is also consistent with our assertion that price changes in imported goods drive the CPI in Japan. There will be a lag between the rate of increase in import

[2] The contribution of each is as follows:

Costs of intermediate goods (Inputs) or wage costs $= \lambda_{-1}(1 + k_{-1})g$,
Costs of intermediate goods (prices) $= \lambda(1 + k_{-1})g$,
Markups $= \frac{\theta}{p_{-1}}(k - k_{-1})$,

Indirect Taxes − Subsidies $= \lambda_{-1}g$,

where λ is the percentage of each cost in the price, k is the markup, g is the growth rate of each cost, θ is the gross profit including consumption of fixed capital per output, p is price, and the subscript -1 indicates data one year ago.

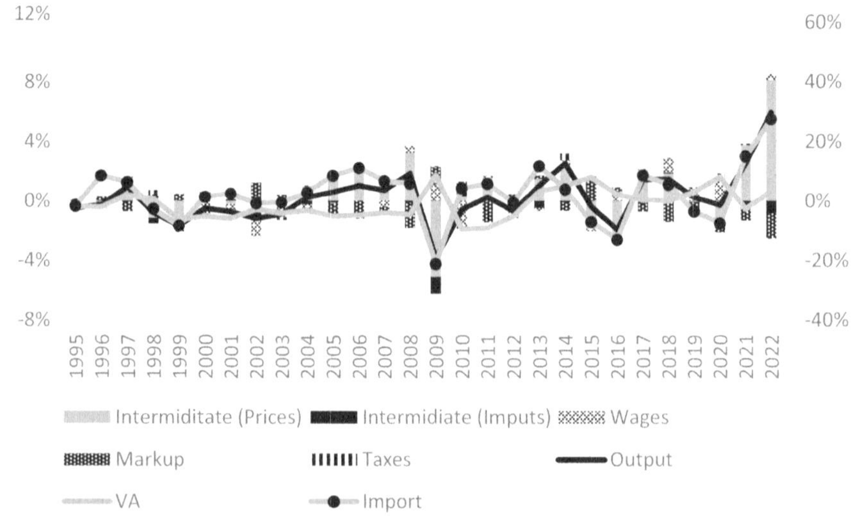

Fig. 2.4 Rate of increase in output deflator, value-added deflator and import deflator, and contribution of each item to the output deflator (1995–2022). *Source* Economic and Social Research Institute, Cabinet Office, Japan (2023c). *Note 1* "Import" is indicated on the right-hand side axis, while others are indicated on the left-hand side. *Note 2* "Output" and "import" are the rate of increase of each deflator. "VA" is the rate of increase in the deflator of value added without indirect taxes minus subsidies per output. "Intermediate (prices)," "intermediate (inputs)," and "wages" are the contributions of changes in the prices of intermediate goods, inputs of intermediate goods, and wage costs to the changes of output deflator, based on the assumption of no change of markup. "Markup" denotes the contributions of changes in markups. "Taxes" represents a contribution to the rate of increase of indirect taxes minus subsidies

deflator and the rate of increase in the contribution of price changes in intermediate goods. Therefore, there are limitations to the analysis using annual data.

In 2022, the output deflator increased at a high rate of 6%. However, the contribution of the price change of the intermediate goods, at 8%, exceeded the increase in the output deflator. The rate of increase in import deflator rose to 27%. In contrast, the increase in unit value-added deflator (excluding indirect taxes and subsidies) was not particularly high at 0.6%. Due to the soaring import deflators, import inflation in 2022 appeared extreme, but it can be deemed a continuation of past trends.

If we include the indirect effects of changes in wage costs on the cost of intermediate goods, then wage costs account for the majority of costs. However, the figure shows that the change in wage costs in Japan since 1995 had been negligible. In particular, since the financial crisis of 1997–1998, wage costs had been showing a declining trend. Based on these facts, we argue that the cause of deflation in Japan is that wage costs had not been rising but had been declining, albeit gradually. Furthermore, although insufficient, the Abe administration has called for wage increases and has achieved them. The figure shows that wage costs have been rising as a trend since 2014. We also argue that this has helped to alleviate deflation in Japan.

However, the complete increase in the cost of imported raw materials may not be passed on to prices entirely. Therefore, to the extent that they may not be passed on to prices, markups will decline. In the figure, the correlation between the rate of increase in the import deflator or the contribution of intermediate goods and the change in markups is negative. In Japan, firms try to avoid laying off regular employees even during recessions. As a result, firms' wage costs rise during recessions. However, firms will not pass on the temporary increase in wage costs, which increase for special reasons, to product prices. In fact, wage costs rose sharply during the severe recessions in 2008–2009 and 2020 (although overall costs, including intermediate goods costs, did not necessarily rise). In other words, in the short run, costs of imported raw materials, wage costs, and markups may not be completely independent factors.

The output deflator also includes export goods. Even though export prices of goods to foreign countries do not change in terms of the country's currency unit, they rise when converted into yen when the yen depreciates. The export deflator rose sharply in 2013 and 2022. Due to data limitations, however, it is not possible to calculate an output deflator for goods for domestic markets alone. For these reasons, the analysis is incomplete. Nevertheless, the conclusion that cost fluctuations, particularly those due to fluctuations in import prices, have been crucial to the fluctuation in the CPI in Japan since the 2000s may be supported.

In the Appendix, the Granger causality test and VECMs revealed that import prices and wages drive CPI in Japan and not the monetary base or money stock. As for inflation expectations, we show that import prices and wages have Granger causality, not the monetary base or money stock.

2.4.3 The Fallacy of the Dichotomy Between Relative Prices and Absolute Price

The BOJ under Kuroda admitted that the price rise since 2022 is cost-push inflation resulting from soaring import prices. However, it was Iwata (2012, pp. 81–84) who argued that soaring import prices cannot theoretically raise prices. We mentioned earlier that when Abenomics began, the media claimed that the rise in prices was due to the rise in import prices, which was a bad price rise (Asahi Shimbun, 2013). However, even then, Iwata (2014, pp. 10–11, Charts 16, 17) argued that a weaker yen could not raise the CPI in Japan. Iwata's rebuttal itself is evidence of the widespread recognition that the price rise at that time was caused by imported inflation.

The point of Iwata's rebuttal is the distinction between relative prices and absolute price. Iwata acknowledges that when the price of imported goods rises, the prices of goods that use them as raw materials and other inputs also increase. However, he believes that absolute price cannot rise. Moreover, distinguishing between relative prices and absolute price is fundamental to economics. This is a typical concept of the quantity theory. When you buy goods, you have to pay money for the price × the amount you purchase. When the price of some goods rises, so does the amount of money to buy them. Then, the amount of money that can be used to buy other goods decreases. As a result, the price of other goods decreases. Thus, the price of imported goods raises the price of some goods but does not raise absolute price.

By the same logic, Watanabe (2022, pp. 14–23) argues that soaring oil prices did not cause skyrocketing prices in 1974 in Japan, but the BOJ's excess money supply was responsible for this condition. He also confirmed that the reduction in mobile phone charges in 2019 would not lower absolute price. He declares that the theory that the sum of individual prices determines prices is a wrong accounting theory (as Stephen Cecchetti calls it). He added that individual price fluctuations are only transient.

The consumption tax in Japan was raised by 3% in 2014. However, as there are tax-exempt goods, the BOJ calculates that the impact of the consumption tax on rising prices is about 2%. The consumption tax hike in 2019 was 2%. As the consumption tax on food (excluding meals outside the home) was not raised, the impact of raising prices was about 1%, according to the BOJ's calculations, which are based on the accounting theory. If Iwata and Watanabe were correct, the consumption tax hike would not raise the CPI by lowering the price of tax-exempt goods. In 2019, food prices (excluding meals outside the home) should also decrease. However, nobody agrees with the claim that the consumption tax hike will not raise the CPI.

Iwata (2012, pp. 88–89) argued that stagnant wages cannot be the cause of deflation. This is also a natural conclusion, given the theory that fluctuations in costs do not affect absolute price.

What is the error in Iwata and Watanabe's claims? The most crucial mistake is assuming that production is constant. When the CPI rises due to higher consumption taxes or higher import prices, households will reduce their consumption. Therefore, even if prices rise, spending may remain the same in terms of amount. In short, they simply led to results that were different from reality by using assumptions that were likewise inconsistent with reality. Blinder and Rudd (2013, pp. 152–153) claim that the dichotomy between relative prices and absolute price, represented by Friedman, is a pre-Keynesian concept. In the presence of price rigidity, any change in relative prices will alter absolute price. Earlier in the discussion, we noted that the U.S. inflation of the 1970s was explained based on supply shocks. When a wage-price spiral develops, tightening monetary and fiscal policy to contain inflation will reduce demand and raise unemployment.

The economy does not consist of one sector, so it is necessary to consider from the perspective of multiple sectors. For example, Japanese financial institutions were healthy when the financial crisis broke out in the U.S. and Europe in 2008. Some Japanese financial institutions took over some of the failed U.S. financial institutions. However, triggered by a sharp decline in exports, Japan's economy was hit hard, and it experienced negative economic growth, which declined steeply more than the U.S., which was the epicenter of the crisis. Exporting firms reduced investment as production plummeted. When the incomes of workers in exporting firms declined, they cut back on consumption. Thus, a sharp drop in exports triggered a steep decline in domestic demand. This is the spillover process Keynes–Kalecki envisioned. However, if you assume, as Iwata does, that overall output is constant, then an expansion of domestic demand will offset a sharp decline in exports. The unrealistic nature of Iwata's assumption becomes even clearer when considered in the multisector model.

Broadly, the way in which the economic system is adjusted varies by country and era. For example, during the global financial crisis and the COVID-19 crisis, the Japanese economy suffered a massive setback, much worse than the U.S.; however, the decline in Japan's employment was much lower because when there is negative economic growth, American companies lay off workers, while Japanese companies try to protect full-time employment at least to the end.

Therefore, we do not believe that a simple model can be applied to the economies of all countries during all eras. In the future, some countries may have an economy where companies maintain prices at the expense of profits and wages to maintain production when import prices or consumption taxes rise. Presently, that is not the case in Japan.

2.5 Stagnant Economy

2.5.1 Further Stagnation in the Japanese Economy

The Japanese economy is stagnant. Some say that Japan will drop out of the developed world in the near future (e.g., Noguchi, 2022). There is no absolute boundary between the developed and developing countries. There are also relatively rich and relatively poor countries among developed countries. Therefore, what constitutes a developed country depends on where the line is drawn, and not all developed countries are equally rich. Nonetheless, Japan has certainly fallen to the bottom of the developed countries.

However, reflationists and politicians who support Abenomics claim that Abenomics has revived the economy. The reasons cited include rising stock prices, a sharp increase in corporate profits, and improved employment (e.g., Hamada, 2017, p. 125; Iwata, 2018, p. 85). However, it is common wisdom in macroeconomics that economic growth indicates an increase in real GDP. When Abenomics was implemented, the targets were set not only to increase the CPI inflation rate but also to increase GDP by 2% per year in real terms and 3% per year in nominal terms. However, economic affluence does not necessarily translate into happy people. Besides, even in terms of economic affluence, real GDP may not necessarily be an appropriate measure. We acknowledge the limitations of real GDP, but because of the lack of a more appropriate indicator, we use real GDP to reveal the stagnation of the Japanese economy under Abenomics.

As mentioned earlier, from the fourth quarter of 2012 to the second quarter of 2019, the real GDP growth rate was only 1.2% per year. In particular, the annual rate of increase in consumption is a miserable 0.3%. One argument for the cause of stagnation in consumption is the hike in consumption tax in April 2014. The last-minute increase in demand, prior to the consumption tax hike, was large, and it is only natural that the larger the last-minute increase in demand, the larger the reactionary decline will be. Besides, even starting from the second quarter of 2014, when consumption bottomed out due to the reactionary decline, the rate of increase in consumption was only 0.5% per year. Therefore, the consumption tax hike alone does not explain the slump in consumption.

After the 1997–1998 financial crisis, there were five business cycles in Japan. Therefore, let us clarify the stagnation of the Abenomics period by comparing it with other periods. However, the population started to decline in 2009. Considering this, a per capita rate of increase was adopted. If per capita is not adopted, the stagnation witnessed during the Abenomics period will be even more pronounced.

Figure 2.5 illustrates the changes in real GDP in these five business cycles. During periods of economic recovery, the growth rate may temporarily be high. Therefore, in the figure, real GDP is indexed to be 100 in the four quarters after the economic trough. The fourth quarter of 2012, when Abe became prime minister, was also an economic trough. The figure shows the Abenomics period up to the second quarter of 2020, which is the next economic trough. In the four business cycles, excluding the Abenomics period, real GDP per capita increased at an annual rate of about 1.5–2% during the boom periods, excluding the first four quarters of the recovery period. In contrast, the annual growth rate was only 0.9% during the Abenomics period. Real GDP indeed fell during the second quarter of 2014 due to the consumption tax hike; however, even if calculated from the second quarter of 2014, when consumption plummeted, it was only 1.2%.

Figure 2.5 also compares the rate of increase in demand during the Izanami boom period and the Abenomics period. As can be seen from the figure, exports surged during the Izanami boom period. Earnings from exports increased private demand, especially capital investment. Conversely, during the Abenomics period, although the yen depreciated substantially, the rate of increase in exports was not very high. Private demand also stagnated. This was because, despite the sharp depreciation of the yen, Japan did not earn much from exports, and the depreciation of the yen reduced households' disposable income and caused domestic consumption to stagnate. In addition, there was a consumption tax hike. Conversely, public demand declined during the Izanami boom period as Prime Minister Junichiro Koizumi cut public works as part of his structural reforms. Conversely, during the Abenomics period, public demand expanded steadily. In fact, the expansion was even more with the outbreak of the COVID-19 crisis.

The 30-year secular stagnation since the 1990s has not been equally stagnant. During the financial crisis of 1997–1998, the global financial crisis from 2008 onward, and the COVID-19 pandemic from 2020 onward, the economy fell sharply. Except during these crises, the economic growth rate of the Abenomics period was at its lowest level. Without the support of government spending, the economy would have stagnated further. We do not believe that bad outcomes and bad policies correspond one-to-one. Regardless of the cause, however, the Abenomics period was the most stagnant period outside other exceptional crises.

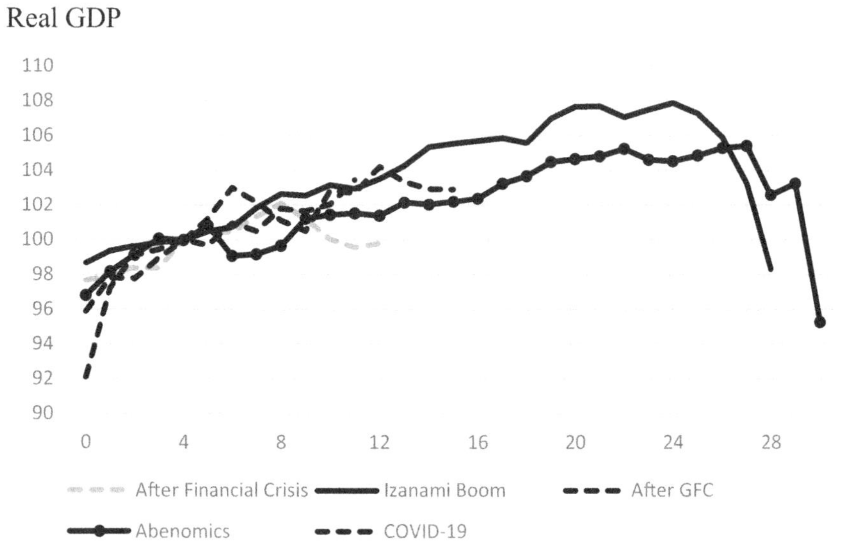

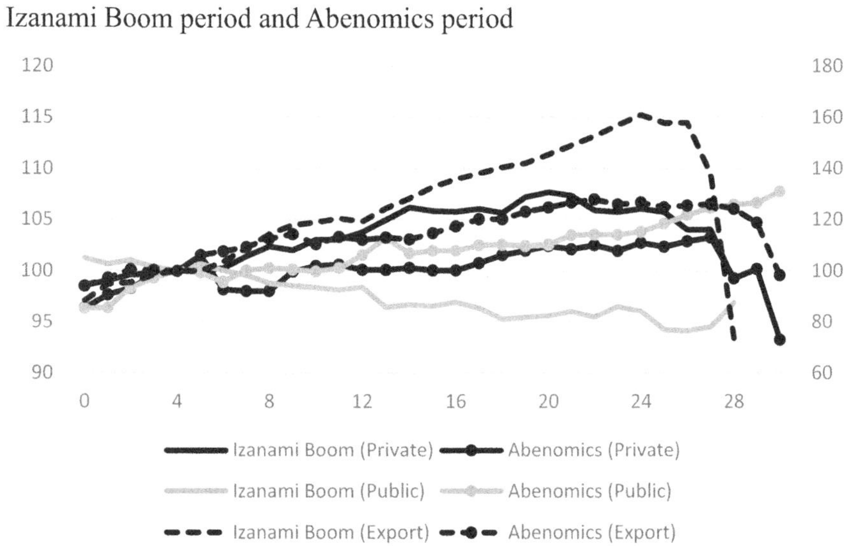

Fig. 2.5 Comparison of quarterly changes in real GDP and each item per capita by business cycle. *Source* Economic and Social Research Institute, Cabinet Office, Japan (2023d) and Statistics Bureau, Ministry of Internal Affairs and Communications, Japan (2023c). *Note 1* "Exports" are indicated on the right-hand side axis, while others are indicated on the left-hand side. *Note 2* Seasonally adjusted. Note 3 "After financial crisis" is defined from the first quarter of 1999 to the first quarter of 2002. "Izanami boom" is from the first quarter of 2002 to the first quarter of 2009. "After GFC (global financial crisis)" is from the first quarter of 2009 to the fourth quarter of 2012. "Abenomics" is from the fourth quarter of 2012 to the second quarter of 2020. "COVID-19" is from the second quarter of 2020 to the first quarter of 2023. "Private" is private demand, and "Public" is public demand. *Note 4* The trough of each business cycle is designated as period 0, and the trough up to the next trough is shown during the quarterly period. As the growth rate can be high during the first phase of economic recovery, the fourth period is set as an index of 100

2.5.2 *There Is No Virtuous Economic Cycle*

The story of a virtuous economic cycle has been repeated since the start of Abenomics. This is about creating a weaker yen through monetary easing and enabling companies to make profits through exports, which in turn leads to wage increases. If the increased wages are used for spending, companies will increase sales and realize further wage increases. Since Abenomics started, the yen depreciated rapidly, and corporate profits soared. Focusing just on these factors indicates that a virtuous economic cycle has begun.

This is also related to the measurement problem of estimating whether a company is making money. A company's profits are only a part of its sales. It is relatively easy to increase profits by cutting wages and other costs. Therefore, we must measure it not by profit but by sales or added value. Furthermore, it is natural that sales and added value will increase as prices rise. Hence, the effect of price increases must also be omitted. Similarly, to claim that the yen's depreciation has enabled companies to earn from exports, it is necessary to investigate whether exports are actually increasing. Strangely, such basic data analysis is not done (at least, it seems to us).

Figure 2.6 shows various indicators of "Financial Statements Statistics of Corporations by Industry" (Policy Research Institute, Ministry of Finance, Japan, 2023). The indicators are indexed with fiscal year 2012 as 100.[3] As income before income taxes fluctuates significantly, this is the only scale on the right. Evidently, there are two mountains in each indicator. The first mountain is the period of the Izanami boom period. Since around 2002, there have been housing bubbles in the U.S. and some European countries. It was also a time when the world economy was growing, and East and South East Asian countries were increasing their growth rates by expanding exports. Japan, like its neighbors, boosted its growth rate by expanding exports. However, the global financial crisis broke out in 2008 after the housing bubble burst. Although Japan and other East and South East Asian countries were not immune to the financial crisis, their economies declined sharply following a massive decrease in exports.

The next mountain is the Abenomics period. However, the Japanese economy peaked at the end of 2018 and entered into a recession. The reason seemed to be the U.S.-China trade war (we are not sure, but we cannot think of any other reason). If this was the case, neither the U.S. nor China, the directly concerned countries, were depressed to cause a recession; only Japan experienced a recession. Reflecting on this, most indicators peaked in fiscal year 2018. The decline did not begin with the consumption tax hike in 2019 or the spread of COVID-19 from 2020 onward. However, with the spread of the COVID-19 pandemic, various corporate indicators declined sharply in fiscal year 2020.

Net income before taxes soared from 18 in 2001 to 123 in 2006. Amid the global economic crisis, it fell sharply to 56 in fiscal year 2008 but recovered to 100 in fiscal year 2012. It rose further during the Abenomics period, peaking at 206 during fiscal year 2018. In fiscal years 2019 and 2020, it declined due to COVID-19 but recovered

[3] In Japan, the fiscal year begins in April and ends in March of the following year.

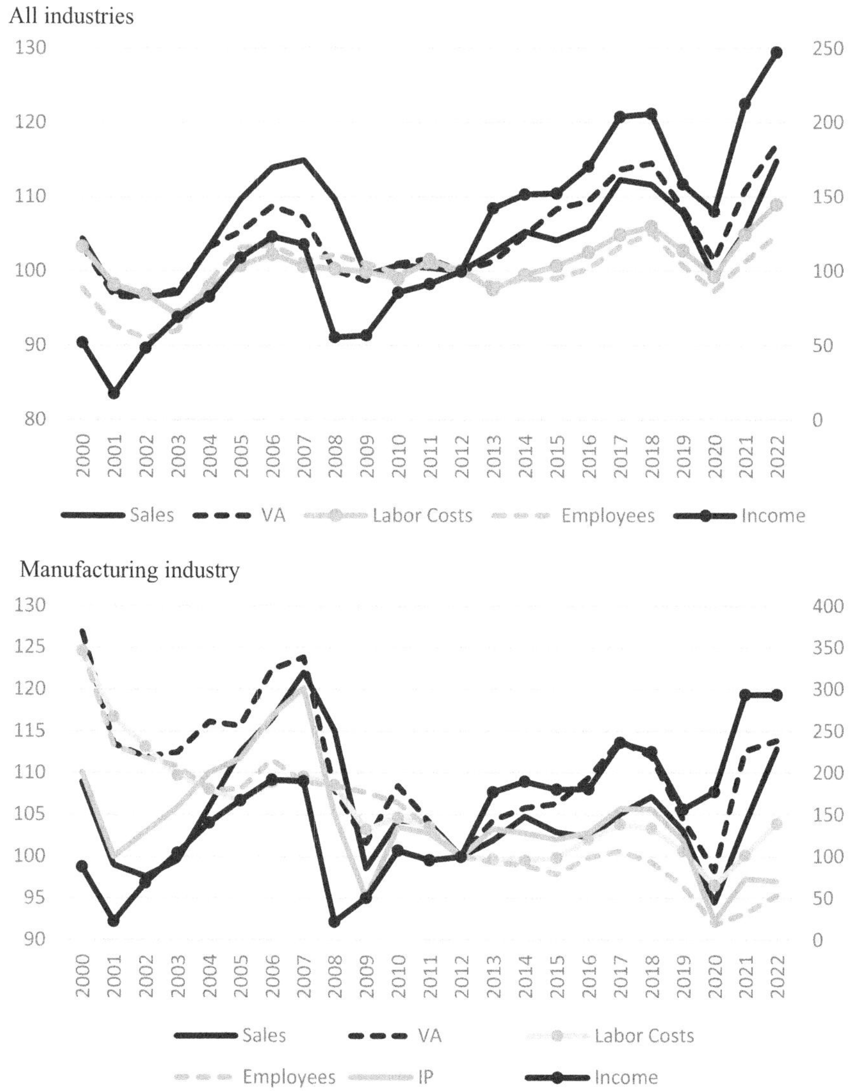

Fig. 2.6 Various indicators of corporate enterprises (FY2000–FY2022). *Source* Policy Research Institute, Ministry of Finance, Japan (2023) and Ministry of Economy, Trade and Industry, Japan (2023). *Note 1* "Income" is indicated on the right-hand side axis, while others are indicated on the left-hand side. *Note 2* "VA" is gross value added, including depreciation and amortization. Labor costs include those to executives. "Employees" are employees and executives. "Income" is the net income before taxes of corporations. "IP" is industrial production. *Note 3* Index with fiscal year 2012 as 100

starting in fiscal year 2021, reaching 247 in fiscal year 2022. In terms of net income before tax, corporate profits surged during the Abenomics period. However, this was also the case during the Izanami boom period.

Sales had also increased since the start of the Abenomics period, but they were not as significant as the Izanami boom period. Moreover, even at its peak during fiscal year 2017, it failed to surpass the peak of the Izanami boom period. The pace of increase in gross value added was relatively fast, and the peak value in fiscal year 2018 was higher than the peak of the Izanami boom period. However, this value was nominal. If the impact of inflation is subtracted, the increase in gross value added is not significant.

Compared with the Izanami boom period, the pace of increase in labor costs (including those to executives) and the number of employees and executives was not particularly remarkable. Labor costs remained mostly unchanged in real terms because of the rise in CPI. However, as prices did not rise in the same way during the Abenomics period, labor costs increased in real terms when the rate of price increases slowed. In fiscal year 2022, labor costs rose sharply, but not as much in real terms, because of the surge in CPI. The slow increase in the number of employees and executives seemed to contradict the claim that the increase in the number of employed persons is one of the greatest achievements of Abenomics. However, we (Hattori, 2017, Chap. 2, pp. 69–94) clarified in *Itsuwari no Keizai Seisaku* (*Deceptive Economic Policies*) that the number of employed persons working shorter hours increased sharply, and the number of employed persons who worked longer hours decreased, resulting in a flat or only slightly increased aggregate hours of work (see also Table 2.3).

In "Financial Statements Statistics of Corporations," when calculating the number of employees, temporary employees are calculated by dividing their aggregate hours of work by the average number of hours worked per month by regular employees. If the number of temporary employees working short hours increases rapidly, this would explain the slow growth in the number of employees in the "Financial Statements Statistics of Corporations."

The figure also shows various indicators for the manufacturing industry. Net income before income taxes in the manufacturing sector peaked in fiscal year 2017. It decreased from fiscal year 2018 onward but reversed in fiscal year 2020 to reach a record high in fiscal year 2021. In the manufacturing sector, profits soared during the Abenomics period. However, sales were flat. Gross value added increased only

Table 2.3 Annual growth rates in real GDP, employed persons, labor productivity and aggregate hours of work during the Izanami boom period and Abenomics period

	Real GDP (%)	Employed person (%)	Labor productivity (%)	Aggregate hours of work (%)
2002–2007	1.68	0.30	1.95	− 0.27
2012–2019	0.93	1.04	0.89	0.04

Source Economic and Social Research Institute, Cabinet Office, Japan (2023c) and Statistics Bureau, Ministry of Internal Affairs and Communications, Japan (2023b)
Note Labor productivity is real GDP divided by aggregate hours of work

slightly. This contrasts with the rapid increase in exports during the Izanami boom period, which led to an increase in both sales and gross added value. However, labor costs and the number of employees and executives remained flat during the Izanami boom period.

The figure also shows the industrial production index. During the Izanami boom period, industrial production surged while exports soared. Conversely, during the Abenomics period, production increases were not very large. The yen depreciated significantly, but the increase in exports was not significant. This suppressed the increase in industrial production. It was the Izanami boom period, not the Abenomics period, which earned from exports.

A company's profits account for only a small portion of sales and gross added value. Therefore, even if companies cannot make money from exports, it is not so difficult to sharpen profits by cutting costs. The scenario envisioned by Abenomics was that a weaker yen and an end to deflation would improve corporate performance, which in turn would lead to higher wages. This scenario failed to work from the beginning (see also Hattori, 2023b, pp. 45–47).

Conversely, the disadvantages of the yen's depreciation encompass a decrease in real disposable income due to imported inflation and declining consumption triggered by a sharp decrease in real disposable income. As mentioned earlier, these disadvantages are not only theoretical possibilities but were really observed. The depreciation of the yen, which did not lead to an increase in exports during the Abenomics period, caused the Japanese economy to stagnate further by slumping consumption. "Bad weak yen" entered the top ten buzzwords of 2022. This shows that many people believe that the rapid depreciation of the yen weighed on their lives. Our analysis shows that this "bad weak yen" claim is correct. However, after 2022, this was only an extreme form, and it can be concluded that Abenomics was a period of stagnant domestic demand, for the most part, attributable to a bad weak yen, bad price rises, and stagnant wages.

2.5.3 "Re-rethinking Japan"

When Hamada, Iwata, and other reflationists criticized the BOJ by claiming that only Japan was in deflation, it implied that the economies of the U.S. and Europe were growing steadily, and only Japan was stagnating. Rather, it is more important to note that Japan is the only country that has experienced economic stagnation. However, after the global financial crisis, the mainstream economists in the U.S., whose reflationists model, changed their minds and did not necessarily recognize that only Japan stagnated. For example, in 2015, Krugman (2015) stated in "Rethinking Japan" that if one considers the working-age population, Japan's growth rate since the 2000s has been higher than that of the U.S. However, Shirakawa (2012, p. 7, Chart 13) has already shown that Japan's growth rate in the 2000s was almost the same as that of the U. S. and the European countries in terms of real GDP per capita, and that Japan was even higher in terms of real GDP growth per working-age population.

We (Hattori, 2012a, 2012b) have also indicated that the growth rate per capita from 2002 to 2007 was the same for both Japan and the U.S. We further stated that stagnation in the U.S. began during the housing bubble period, as the U.S. growth rate was about the same as Japan's, notwithstanding its housing bubble. However, real GDP data are subject to revision. In the data used in Hattori (2012a, 2012b), the real growth rate per capita was slightly higher in Japan, but the latest data show a higher rate in the U.S. In 2013, Yoshikawa (2013, pp. 206–209) stated that since the 2000s, the real GDP growth rates per capita in Japan had been inferior to that of the 27 EU countries (including the United Kingdom and excluding Croatia at that time), but comparable to that of the U.S. Considering this, he also states that only the 1990s decade was lost. The high growth rate in the EU is due to the growth rates reported in Central and Eastern Europe, which are relatively less developed regions.

Now, however, it is necessary to focus on "re-rethinking Japan." Figure 2.7 illustrates the real GDP growth rates in Japan and the U.S. To eliminate short-term fluctuations, they are cumulative growth rates of two years. The figure shows that the real GDP growth rates are lower in Japan, but this is not the case for the growth rates per working-age population, as Krugman pointed out.

In the second half of 1990s, the U.S. achieved high growth amid the dot-com bubble. Conversely, in Japan, the financial crisis that began in 1997 caused the economy to stagnate. Thus, it can be stated that only Japan's economy crumbled during this period. However, when the U.S. dot-com bubble burst in 2000, the real GDP growth rate in the U.S. declined. Later, the housing bubble made the U.S.

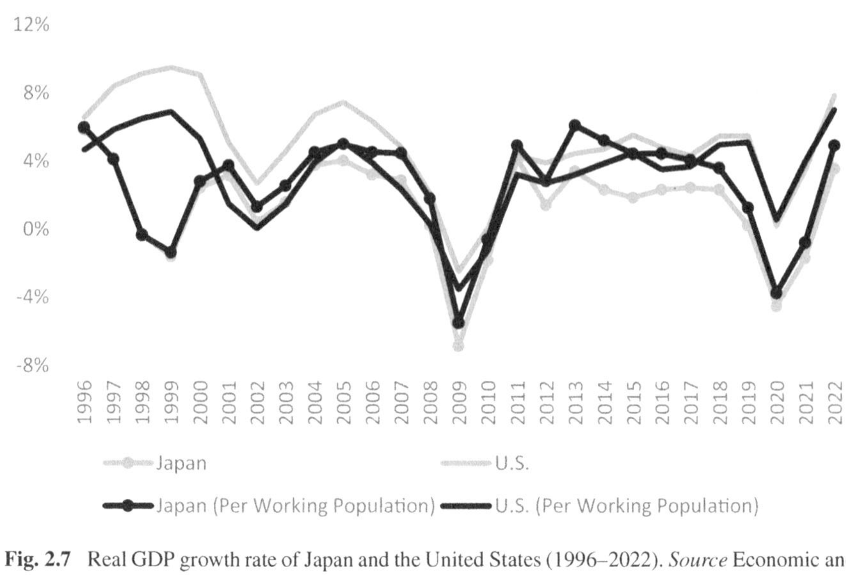

Fig. 2.7 Real GDP growth rate of Japan and the United States (1996–2022). *Source* Economic and Social Research Institute, Cabinet Office (2023c), Statistics Bureau, Ministry of Internal Affairs and Communications, Japan (2023b), Bureau of Economic Analysis, the U.S. (2023), and Federal Reserve Bank of St. Louis (2023). *Note 1* Growth rate is cumulative over two years. *Note 2* "Per working population" indicates the real GDP growth rate per population aged 15–64

economy seem to recover relatively quickly. However, American companies were burdened with excessive equipment and debt during the dot-com bubble. Therefore, even during the housing bubble, fixed investments by companies did not increase much. Therefore, despite the housing bubble, the real GDP growth rates in the U.S. were not very high. At least, compared to the dot-com bubble period, it ended at a much lower level. Amid the global bubble economy, Japan's exports surged, and the real GDP growth rates increased. As a result, during the housing bubble period, Japan's real GDP growth rates per working-age population overtook those of the U.S. After the financial crisis, the Japanese economy fell sharply, but the recovery was also better. As Krugman says, per working-age population, Japan grew more.

However, this was until the start of Abenomics. At the beginning of Abenomics, Japan's real GDP growth rates began to decline. Conversely, the U.S. recovered from the pain of the financial crisis, and its growth rate increased. As a result, the gap in the real GDP growth rates per working population narrowed. In addition, Japan has been in recession since 2018, and its growth rate dropped significantly. Thus, the growth rates of Japan and the U.S. reversed (Hattori, 2023a, pp. 116–119, 2023b, pp. 47–49 shows the economic stagnation during Abenomics based on a comparison of real GDP growth per capita, including developed countries other than the U.S.).

Furthermore, in 2020, the COVID-19 spread. The U.S. reported the highest number of COVID-19 deaths in the world (although some countries had higher death rates per population). In addition, drug deaths also increased sharply. For all these social blows, the U.S. economic downturn was comparatively small. However, in East and Southeast Asia, including Japan, the damage from the pandemic was insignificant compared to the U.S. and Europe. Thus, East and Southeast Asian countries experienced a minor economic downturn. An important exception is Japan, where the economic downturn was much greater than in the U.S., and the recovery was considerably slower than in the U.S.

Contrary to the claims of reflationists, the "Japanese-only" economic stagnation only began after Abenomics was launched.

2.5.4 Why Did the Number of Employed Persons Increase?

The increase in the number of employed persons has often been cited as an Abenomics achievement. However, the fact that the number of employed persons increased despite the low economic growth rate is itself a question. It would be strange not to consider it as a peculiar scenario. Figure 2.8 shows the increase in real GDP, employed persons, labor productivity, and aggregate work hours. Table 2.3 compares the rate of their increase between the Izanami boom period and the Abenomics period. However, the economy declined sharply in 2020 due to the COVID-19. Consequently, the Abenomics period ended in 2019.

Fig. 2.8 Growth in real GDP, employed persons, labor productivity and aggregate hours of work (2001–2022). *Source* Economic and Social Research Institute, Cabinet Office, Japan (2023c) and Statistics Bureau, Ministry of Internal Affairs and Communications, Japan (2023b). *Note 1* "GDP" is real GDP. "Employed" is the number of employed persons. "Productivity" is labor productivity, which is real GDP divided by aggregate hours of work. "Hours" is aggregate hours of work. *Note 2* Due to the Great East Japan Earthquake, data on aggregate hours of work in 2011 are not available. Therefore, the rates of increase in labor productivity and aggregate hours of work are blank in 2011, and annualized growth rates for the two-year period from 2010 to 2012 are shown in 2012

Since the 1997 financial crisis, the rate of increase in the number of employed persons has been mostly negative. The only exception was the period from 2004 to 2007 during the Izanami boom period. However, since the start of Abenomics, the rate of increase in the number of employed persons has been positive for most years. The only negative year was in 2020 when the COVID-19 pandemic broke out. Table 2.3 shows that the annual increase in the number of employed persons through 2019 is nearly 1%. Considering that the working-age population declined by an average of nearly 1% per year over the past seven years, this is a high level.

However, the economic growth rate during the Abenomics period was only 0.9%. Despite this low growth, one of the main reasons for the increase in the number of employed persons was the increase in the number of employed persons who worked only for short hours. In fact, the rate of increase in aggregate hours of work from 2012 to 2019 remained almost unchanged at an annual rate of 0.04%. However, as the aggregate hours of work decreased during the Izanami boom period, it can be said that aggregate hours of work improved, even though it was flat. However, another factor contributing to the increase in the number of employed persons is the decline in the rate of increase in labor productivity, which is only 0.9%. It fell by more than 1% compared to the Izanami boom period.

During the 1960s, Japan was amid a period of high economic growth. However, the rate of increase in the number of employed persons at that time was at the 2%

level, even during the strong growth years. Economic growth is usually supported by rising labor productivity. Therefore, even if the economy showed strong growth, as in Japan in the 1960s, it is normal for the number of employed persons not to increase accordingly. Conversely, if the rate of increase in labor productivity is low, low growth and an increase in the number of employed persons will be possible. Thus, the increase in the number of employed persons during the Abenomics period can also result from economic stagnation.

2.6 Theories and Strategies Based on Wishful Thinking and Assumptions

The strategy of both the BOJ under Kuroda and reflationists was to raise the CPI by the Japanese-style inflation target and supply a large monetary base. This would raise wages and revive the economy. In a speech in December 2013, less than a year after his inauguration, Kuroda (2013, p. 6) said, "[T]he Bank aims at creating and embedding an economic virtuous cycle of a moderate rise in prices, an increase in sales and profits, an increase in wages, a boost in consumption, and a moderate rise in prices."

These words were also quoted during a lecture in December 2022, shortly before Kuroda's retirement (Kuroda, 2022, pp. 6–7). In his speech in 2022, he continued, "In other words, in order to achieve the price stability target in a sustainable and stable manner, it is crucial that price rises are backed by increases in corporate sales and profits, and by growing wages. A simultaneous increase in both wages and prices was observed as a matter of course even in Japan until around the mid-1990s." As Kuroda said, "[U]ntil around the mid-1990s," he was perhaps aware that this mechanism disappeared. Therefore, it would be the goal of the BOJ under Kuroda to revive the mechanism to raise both prices and wages, which has now ceased to exist.

However, Kuroda did not explain in his 2013 or 2022 speech why monetary easing could create a mechanism for both prices and wages to rise. Perhaps he cannot explain it. In fact, the BOJ under Kuroda could not rebuild the mechanism for raising prices and wages together, even if it took ten years. The idea that monetary easing could raise prices and wages together was just wishful thinking without theoretical or empirical evidence.

This chapter clarifies the claim that the Japanese economy will revive if the BOJ succeeds in overcoming deflation through monetary easing, which is wishful thinking by reflationists and the BOJ under Kuroda. Firstly, what moves the CPI in Japan is import prices, not the monetary base or inflation expectations. Besides, even if the CPI grows due to soaring import prices, real wages and real income will decline, and so will consumption. Consumers will also experience the burden. This has occurred in a big way with imported inflation since 2022. However, since 2022, there is clarity because of the large rise in import prices, but this mechanism has continued since the 2000s.

Policies based on misguided economics will inevitably fail.

Appendix: Mathematical Model and Empirical Analysis of the Price Theory Determined by Costs

Mathematical Model

First, let us consider determining the market price (excluding indirect taxes minus subsidies) of Good 1 p_{d_1}.[4] Suppose that there are n kinds of domestic goods in the country. The vector indicating the market price of each good $\boldsymbol{p_d} = (p_{\mathrm{d}_1}, \ldots, p_{\mathrm{d}_n})$, and that indicating the amount of input is the vector $\boldsymbol{a}^1 = \begin{pmatrix} a_1^1 \\ \vdots \\ a_1^n \end{pmatrix}$. Then, the cost of domestic intermediate goods will be $\boldsymbol{p_d} \cdot \boldsymbol{a}^1$. Similarly, there are m types of goods in imported intermediate goods. The vector indicating each price is $\boldsymbol{p_m} = (p_{\mathrm{m}_1}, \ldots, p_{\mathrm{m}_n})$, and the vector indicating the input amount $\boldsymbol{m}^1 = \begin{pmatrix} m_1^1 \\ \vdots \\ m_1^m \end{pmatrix}$. Then, the cost of imported intermediate goods will be $\boldsymbol{p_m} \cdot \boldsymbol{m}^1$. Suppose that wage w and labor input l^1, wage cost is wl^1. As the market price is these costs multiplied by $1 +$ markup k^1, the market price of Good 1 is,

$$p_{\mathrm{d}1} = \left(1 + k^1\right)\left(\boldsymbol{p_d} \cdot \boldsymbol{a}^1 + \boldsymbol{p_m} \cdot \boldsymbol{m}^1 + wl^1\right). \tag{2.1}$$

The market prices of Good 2, …, Good n can be made into a formula in the same form. Summarizing this, we get a system of simultaneous equations.

$$\begin{aligned} p_{\mathrm{d}1} &= \left(1 + k^1\right)\left(\boldsymbol{p_d} \cdot \boldsymbol{a}^1 + \boldsymbol{p_m} \cdot \boldsymbol{m}^1 + wl^1\right) \\ p_{\mathrm{d}2} &= \left(1 + k^2\right)\left(\boldsymbol{p_d} \cdot \boldsymbol{a}^2 + \boldsymbol{p_m} \cdot \boldsymbol{m}^2 + wl^2\right) \\ &\vdots \\ p_{\mathrm{d}n} &= \left(1 + k^n\right)\left(\boldsymbol{p_d} \cdot \boldsymbol{a}^n + \boldsymbol{p_m} \cdot \boldsymbol{m}^n + wl^n\right). \end{aligned} \tag{2.2}$$

Suppose $A = \left(\boldsymbol{a}^1, \ldots, \boldsymbol{a}^n\right)$, $M = \left(\boldsymbol{m}^1, \ldots, \boldsymbol{m}^n\right)$, $\boldsymbol{l} = \begin{pmatrix} l^1 \\ \vdots \\ l^n \end{pmatrix}$, $K = \begin{pmatrix} k^1 & \cdots & 0 \\ \vdots & \ddots & \vdots \\ 0 & \cdots & k^n \end{pmatrix}$, these simultaneous equations can be written as an expression of the matrices and the

[4] Appendix is based on the analysis by Hattori (2024, pp. 43–47), with some modifications.

vectors below,

$$\boldsymbol{p}_d = (I + K)\left(\boldsymbol{p}_m A + \boldsymbol{p}_m M + w\boldsymbol{l}\right). \tag{2.3}$$

Therefore,

$$\boldsymbol{p}_d = (I + K)\left(\boldsymbol{p}_m M + w\boldsymbol{l}\right)[I - (I + K)A]^{-1}. \tag{2.4}$$

Actual price is the market price plus indirect taxes minus subsidies $\boldsymbol{t} = (t_1, \ldots, t_n)$. Therefore,

$$\boldsymbol{p} = \boldsymbol{p}_d + \boldsymbol{t} = (I + K)\left(\boldsymbol{p}_m M + w\boldsymbol{l}\right)[I - (I + K)A]^{-1} + \boldsymbol{t}. \tag{2.5}$$

Price changes from period to period $t - 1$ to t $\Delta\boldsymbol{p}_t$,

$$\begin{aligned}
\Delta\boldsymbol{p}_t &= \boldsymbol{p}_t - \boldsymbol{p}_{t-1} \\
&= (I + K_t)\left(\boldsymbol{p}_{m_t} M_t + w_t \boldsymbol{l}_t\right)[I - (I + K_t)A_t]^{-1} + \boldsymbol{t}_t \\
&\quad - (I + K_{t-1})\left(\boldsymbol{p}_{m_{t-1}} M_{t-1} + w_{t-1}\boldsymbol{l}_{t-1}\right)\left[I - (I + K_{t-1})A_{t-1}\right]^{-1} - \boldsymbol{t}_{t-1} \\
&= (I + K_t)\left(\boldsymbol{p}_{m_t} M_t - \boldsymbol{p}_{m_{t-1}} M_{t-1} + w_t \boldsymbol{l}_t - w_{t-1}\boldsymbol{l}_{t-1}\right) \\
&\quad [I - (I + K_t)A_t]^{-1} + \boldsymbol{t}_t - \boldsymbol{t}_{t-1} \\
&\quad + (I + K_t)\left(\boldsymbol{p}_{m_{t-1}} M_{t-1} + w_{t-1}\boldsymbol{l}_{t-1}\right) \\
&\quad \left[\{I - (I + K_t)A_t\}^{-1} - \{I - (I + K_t)A_{t-1}\}^{-1}\right] \\
&\quad + \left(\boldsymbol{p}_{m_{t-1}} M_{t-1} + w_{t-1}\boldsymbol{l}_{t-1}\right) \\
&\quad \left[(I + K_t)\{I - (I + K_t)A_{t-1}\}^{-1} - (I + K_{t-1})\{I - (I + K_{t-1})A_{t-1}\}^{-1}\right].
\end{aligned} \tag{2.6}$$

The subscripts $t - 1$ or t indicate the period $t - 1$ or t. Thus, price changes can be divided into those due to changes in the cost of imported intermediate goods, wage costs, indirect taxes − subsidies, changes in inputs of domestic intermediate goods, and changes in markups.

Markups vary greatly from industry to industry, company to company, and goods to goods. However, in the price theory determined by costs, such as Kalecki (1954) and Morishima (1984), markups do not change significantly in the time series. If indirect taxes and subsidies change, prices will also change, which is a special factor. Therefore, essential factors for price fluctuations are the cost of imported intermediate goods and the cost of wages.

However, *National Accounts* in Japan does not classify intermediate goods into domestic and imported intermediate goods. For this reason, the contributions of the rate of increase in the output deflator cannot be decomposed in the same way as shown in Eq. (2.5). Instead, Fig. 2.4 shows a different way of disassembling and illustrating.

Granger Causality Test

Granger causality is a statistical hypothesis test that examines if one time series is useful for predicting another. Although the word causality is used, it does not necessarily mean causality in the normal sense. Suppose there is an autoregressive model $y_t = a + y_{t-1} + \cdots y_{t-n} + u_t$. If the explanatory power of the new model tested by adding another time series to it as an independent variable,

$$y_t = a + y_{t-1} + \cdots + y_{t-n} + x_{t-1} + \cdots + x_{t-n} + u_t,$$

is significantly increased, x is said to have Granger causality for y.

We first tested the Granger causality test for CPI. The variables are all differences of logarithmic. The lag is 12 months. The period is from January 2000 to March 2023, with some exceptions. From 2020, amid the spread of COVID-19, cash-strapped companies such as the travel industry and restaurants surged borrowing from banks, which led to a sharp increase in M3. The BOJ also sharply increased the monetary base in response. The subsequent sharp increases in the monetary base and M3 are due to special factors, so both data are used through December 2019. For M3, continuous statistical data were obtained from May 2004. The consumption activity index is from February 2004 to March 2023, of which data are available.

Even if import prices and wages rise, if their inputs decrease, their costs may not change, or conversely, they may decline. Therefore, as shown in the mathematical model above, they are not import prices or wages that move CPI but the cost of imported intermediate goods and wages. However, as there is no input data, import prices and scheduled cash earnings of regular workers are used instead. Scheduled cash earnings, monetary base, M3, and real consumption activity index are seasonally adjusted.

The results are shown in Table 2.4. Import prices, energy, and food prices are significant at the 1% level. The yen-dollar exchange rate is significant at the 10% level. Scheduled cash earnings are also marginally significant at the 10% level. In contrast, neither the monetary base nor M3 is significant. Neither the business condition index (coincident index of the composite index) nor the consumer activity index is significant. The Granger causality test also supported import prices and wages that were influencing the CPI. Conversely, monetary factors such as the monetary base and M3, as well as demand factors such as the business condition and consumption, had no effect.

Table 2.4 Granger causality

CPI (January 2000–December 2023)

	Import prices (%)	Scheduled cash earnings (%)	USD-JPY rate (%)	Energy prices (%)	Food prices (%)
Cause	0.0	9.7	6.3	0.0	0.0
Result	12.3	54.9	83.3	51.0	2.8

	Monetary base (%)	M3 (%)	CI (%)	Consumption (%)
Cause	81.4	88.3	18.9	45.5
Result	70.1	39.6	20.4	46.7

Consumers' price expectations a year ahead (April 2004–December 2023)

	CPI (%)	Import prices (%)	Scheduled cash earnings (%)	Monetary base (%)	M3 (%)
Cause	15.9	2.8	5.4	72.8	13.7
Result	0.0	8.2	19.1	84.0	84.3

Source Statistics Bureau, Ministry of Internal Affairs and Communications, Japan (2023a), the Bank of Japan (2023a, 2023b), Ministry of Health, Labor and Welfare, Japan (2023) and Economic and Social Research Institute, Cabinet Office, Japan (2023a, 2023b)

Note 1 "USD-JPY rate" is the exchange rate between the U.S. dollar and the Japanese yen. "CI" is a coincident index among indexes of business conditions (composite index). "Energy prices" and "Food prices" are items in import prices. "Consumption" is the real consumption activity index

Note 2 M3 is from April 2003, when continuous data were available. Consumption is from February 2004, when data are available. Both the monetary base and M3 are through December 2019, attributable to a temporary spike during the COVID-19 crisis starting in 2020. Monetary base, M3 and "Consumption" are seasonally adjusted

Note 3 "CPI" is consumption tax-adjusted index less imputed rent. Scheduled cash earnings are index of regular workers (establishments with five employees or more)

Note 4 "Consumers' price expectations a year ahead" are consumers' expectations of an increase in the prices of goods that consumers commonly purchase over the next 12 months, including the portion due to the consumption tax hikes and other factors

Note 5 Difference from the previous month in the natural logarithm. However, "consumers' price expectations a year ahead" is the difference in consumers' price expectations a year ahead from the previous month. The data for the counterpart also shows the difference in the year-on-year rate of change from the previous month

Note 6 Since April 2013, the price expectations survey has changed from a home-visit detention survey to a mail-in survey; therefore, the figures are not necessarily consistent with the previous surveys

Note 7 Among the results for the price expectations survey, declines and increases are divided into three levels: less than 2%, between 2 and 5%, and more than 5%, respectively. In addition, there are "no change" and "don't know," comprising a total of eight levels. In the figure, both declines and increases are weighted averages as 1% for less than 2%, 3.5% for 2–5%, and 6% for 5% or more ("no change" and "don't know" are calculated with the weights as zero)

Next, we examined the Granger causality of inflation expectations. However, high accuracy in price forecasts and self-fulfillment of forecasts are completely different. For example, even if there is an accurate weather forecast, this means that the forecasts have high accuracy, and the weather is not determined according to the weather forecast. Most people not only do not know the value of the inflation expectations by the ESP forecast, but they probably also do not know its existence. In such a situation, it is impossible for the ESP forecast to affect actual prices. If there is such a thing as a self-fulfilling prediction, it would be the expected inflation rate of consumers or businesses.

We use consumers' price expectations one year ahead, as published by the Economic and Social Research Institute, Cabinet Office, Japan (2023a), as the expected inflation rate. However, the Economic and Social Research Institute categorizes consumers' price expectations into eight categories: three levels of increase, three levels of decrease, "no change," and "don't know." For this reason, the price expectations are weighted and averaged by assigning points to each of the three levels of increase and decrease (zero weighted for items "no change" and "don't know"). The price expectations are the difference from the previous month's expectations for the next 12 months. To match the scale, the paired variables are the differences from the previous month in year-on-year changes. The time period is from May 2005.

A questionnaire from the Economic and Social Research Institute asked about the rate of increase over the next 12 months in the prices of goods that consumers will commonly purchase, including the portion due to the consumption tax hike and other factors. Therefore, from April 2013 to March 2014, the consumption tax hikes should raise the price expectations by about 2% points. In fact, it is only a slightly higher degree. It is safe to assume that most people answered without considering the consumption tax.

The results show that import prices are causal at the 5% level and scheduled cash earnings of regular workers at the 10% level. Again, the monetary base or M3 is not causal. What affects consumers' price expectations are also fluctuations in costs, and the monetary base and money are irrelevant. Conversely, the price expectations are significant at the 10% level for import prices and 1% for CPI. As CPI fluctuates with a lag to changes in import prices, it would not be surprising if consumers could predict some changes in CPI in the near future. However, when reflationists discussed the self-fulfillment of inflation expectations, they assumed that consumers would be more active in their consumption if their inflation expectations increased. However, as mentioned earlier, Japan's consumption has stagnated since the 2000s, especially when prices were rising. Even if consumers could predict price increases in the near future, this does not mean that the self-fulfillment of inflation expectations, as described by reflationists, has occurred.

The results of the Granger causality test are consistent with the historical fact that the BOJ under Kuroda failed to overcome deflation and that soaring import prices have raised the CPI inflation rate to more than 4% since 2022.

Vector Error Correction Model (VECM)

The VECM is also a time-series model. It can simultaneously model cointegration, which indicates a long-term equilibrium relationship, and short-term variability. Here, our VECMs show that costs, especially import prices, drive Japan's CPI.

The variables are logarithms of import prices, scheduled cash earnings, CPI, and the monetary base. Of these, scheduled cash earnings and the monetary base are seasonally adjusted. The period is from January 2000 to March 2023. Real GDP in Japan fell sharply and, in response, increased significantly from 2008 to 2010 due to the global financial crisis and from 2020 to 2022 due to the pandemic crisis. However, as we believe that the effects of demand and production on CPI are small, these variables are not included in the model. The reason for including the monetary base in the variable is to demonstrate that it has little effect.

Before testing models, each variable should be tested for unit roots. The results are shown in Table 2.5. The result was that there are no stationarities at the levels but there are at the first differences. As mentioned earlier, imported raw material costs and wage costs drive the CPI and not import prices or wages. Therefore, assuming that the input of imported raw materials and labor is decreasing at a constant rate each period, the trend term of the VECM includes a time dummy that increases by one every quarter.

We first tested the VECM for import prices, scheduled cash earnings, and the CPI. As the Akaike Info Criterion (AIC) declined beyond the 12th period, we discontinued it at the 12th period. Johansen's cointegration test shows that at the 5% level, we have one cointegration for both the trace test and the maximum eigenvalue test (see Table 2.6). The results support our contention that both CPI and costs are linked in the long run. Conversely, the VECM of the monetary base and CPI did not yield a model with a cointegration relationship (as far as we have tested, because we cannot deny that a cointegration relationship may be obtained by changing the periods and lags).

Figure 2.9 illustrates the VECM results. The cointegration is one. Import prices have Granger causality at the 1% level to CPI and scheduled cash earnings. Scheduled cash earnings have Granger causality at the 5% level to CPI. The order of impulse responses, considering Granger causality, is import prices, scheduled cash earnings, and CPI. However, even if the order is reversed, the result does not change significantly. Shocks in import prices and scheduled cash earnings raise the CPI. In particular, the impact of import prices is very large. The effect of the shock on the scheduled cash earnings is small because the shock itself is small, and the effect per unit is large.

Table 2.5 Unit root test (January 2000–March 2023)

Levels				
Variable	Lag	*t*-value	Model	Significance
CPI	13	− 0.01439	Constant	None
	13	− 0.91802	Constants, trends	None
Import prices	1	− 2.12525	Constant	None
	1	− 3.01844	Constants, trends	None
Scheduled cash earnings	4	1.93480	Constant	None
	4	0.49935	Constants, trends	None
Monetary base	3	0.43644	Constant	None
	3	− 1.46646	Constants, trends	None
First differences				
Variable	Lag	*t*-value	Model	Significance (%)
CPI	12	− 2.81121	Without	1
	12	− 2.88935	Constant	5
Import prices	0	− 9.52357	Without	1
	2	− 8.53159	Constant	1
Scheduled cash earnings	3	− 7.47871	Without	1
	3	− 7.76216	Constant	1
Monetary base	4	− 3.89029	Without	1
	2	− 6.00508	Constant	1

Source Statistics Bureau, Ministry of Internal Affairs and Communications, Japan (2023a), the Bank of Japan (2023b) and Ministry of Health, Labor and Welfare, Japan (2023)
Note 1 "CPI" denotes consumption tax-adjusted index less imputed rent. Scheduled cash earnings are indexes of regular workers (establishments with five employees or more). Scheduled cash earnings and monetary base are seasonally adjusted
Note 2 The natural logarithm of each is used as the variable

Table 2.6 Johansen test

	Eigenvalue	Trace	Significance	Max-Eigen	Significance
None	0.10082	48.3448	5%	29.6497	5%
At most 1	0.03464	18.6951	None	9.83603	None
At most 2	0.03125	8.85907	None	8.85907	None

Source Statistics Bureau, Ministry of Internal Affairs and Communications, Japan (2023a), the Bank of Japan (2023b) and Ministry of Health, Labor and Welfare, Japan (2023)
Note Variables are import prices, scheduled cash earnings of regular workers (establishments with five employees or more), and CPI (consumption tax-adjusted index less imputed rent of owner-occupied houses). Scheduled cash earnings are seasonally adjusted. All the figures are natural logarithms

Consequences of cointegration

ln CPI=0.029870 ln IMPORT +1.22677 ln WAGE -0.000086 TIME-1.16608

(1.90) (7.55) (-2.76)

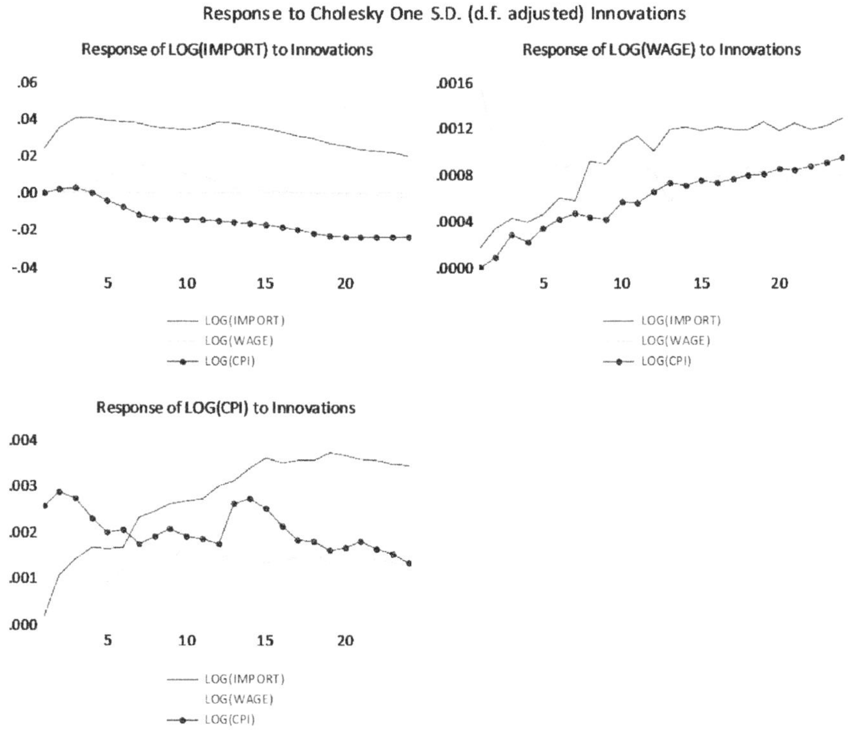

Granger causality

1% IMPORT→CPI, WAGE 5% WAGE→CPI

Fig. 2.9 VECM (January 2000–March 2023). *Source* Statistics Bureau, Ministry of Internal Affairs and Communications, Japan (2023a), the Bank of Japan (2023b) and Ministry of Health, Labor and Welfare, Japan (2023). *Note* "IMPORT" is the import price, "WAGE" is the scheduled cash earnings of regular workers (establishments with five employees or more), "CPI" is tax-adjusted index less imputed rent, and "TIME" is a dummy variable that takes the first quarter of 2000 as 0 and adds 1 for each quarter. Scheduled cash earnings are seasonally adjusted. All the figures are natural logarithms

Table 2.7 Johansen test

	Eigenvalue	Trace	Significance	Max-Eigen	Significance
None	0.13020	69.9986	5%	38.9181	1%
At most 1	0.05820	31.0805	None	16.7306	None
At most 2	0.03401	14.3499	None	9.65330	None
At most 3	0.01669	4.69659	None	4.69659	None

Source Statistics Bureau, Ministry of Internal Affairs and Communications, Japan (2023a), the Bank of Japan (2023b) and Ministry of Health, Labor and Welfare, Japan (2023)
Note Variables are import prices, scheduled cash earnings of regular workers (establishments with five employees or more), monetary base, and CPI (consumption tax-adjusted index less imputed rent). Scheduled cash earnings and monetary base are seasonally adjusted. All the figures are natural logarithms

Next, we created a VECM of import prices, scheduled cash earnings, monetary base, and the CPI. Johansen's cointegration test has one cointegration at the 5% level in the trace test and at the 1% level in the maximum eigenvalue test (see Table 2.7). Figure 2.10 illustrates the results of this VECM. Cointegration is one. As the AIC declined beyond the 12th period, we discontinued it in the 12th period. Import prices have Granger causality at the 1% level to CPI and at the 5% level to scheduled cash earnings. The order of impulse responses, considering Granger causality, was import prices, scheduled cash earnings, the monetary base, and CPI. However, even if the order is reversed, the result does not change significantly.

The effects of shocks in import prices and scheduled cash earnings on CPI are not significantly different from those shown in Fig. 2.9. In contrast, the shock of the monetary base has raised the CPI only slightly despite the large shock of the monetary base. Nor is Granger causality. Variance decomposition shows that the effect of import prices is overwhelmingly large. The shock of scheduled cash earnings can be said to have a great effect, considering the small shock. Conversely, the monetary base has little effect despite the magnitude of the shock.

The VECM results also support our contention that it is costs, especially import prices, and not the monetary base, that play a major role in Japan's CPI fluctuations.

Consequences of cointegration

$$\ln CPI = 0.025105 \ln IMPORT + 1.590956 \ln WAGE - 0.010701\, MB$$
$$(1.35) \qquad (8.29) \qquad (-1.46)$$
$$-0.0000263 TIME + 2.770086$$
$$(0.36)$$

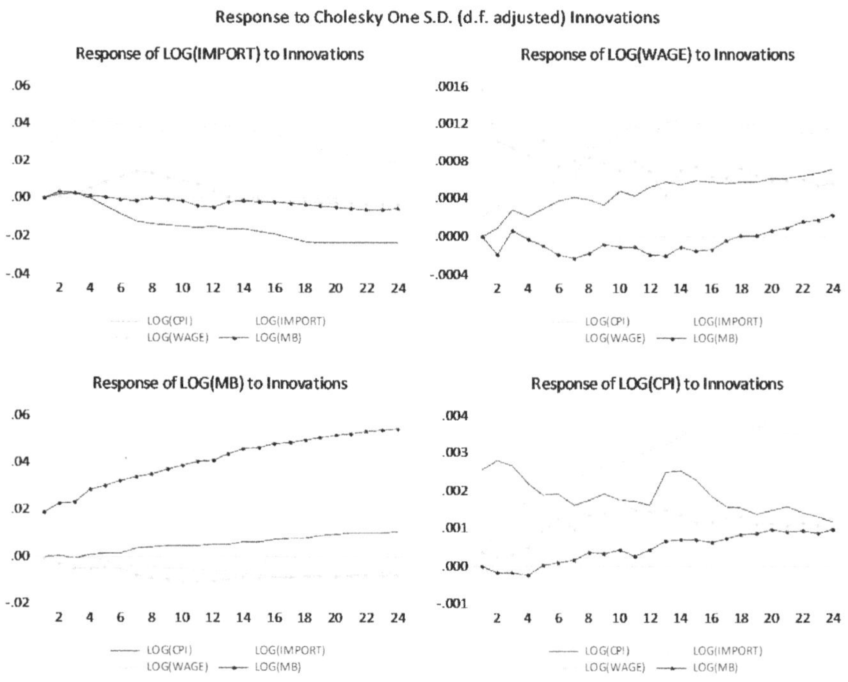

Granger causality

1% IMPORT→CPI 5% IMPORT→WAGE

Fig. 2.10 VECM (January 2000–March 2023). *Source* Statistics Bureau, Ministry of Internal Affairs and Communications, Japan (2023a), the Bank of Japan (2023b) and Ministry of Health, Labor and Welfare, Japan (2023). *Note* "IMPORT" is the import price, "WAGE" is scheduled cash earnings of regular workers (establishments with five employees or more), "MB" is the monetary base, "CPI" is tax-adjusted index less imputed rent, and "TIME" is a dummy variable that takes the first quarter of 2000 as 0 and adds 1 for each quarter. Scheduled cash earnings and monetary base are seasonally adjusted. All the figures are natural logarithms

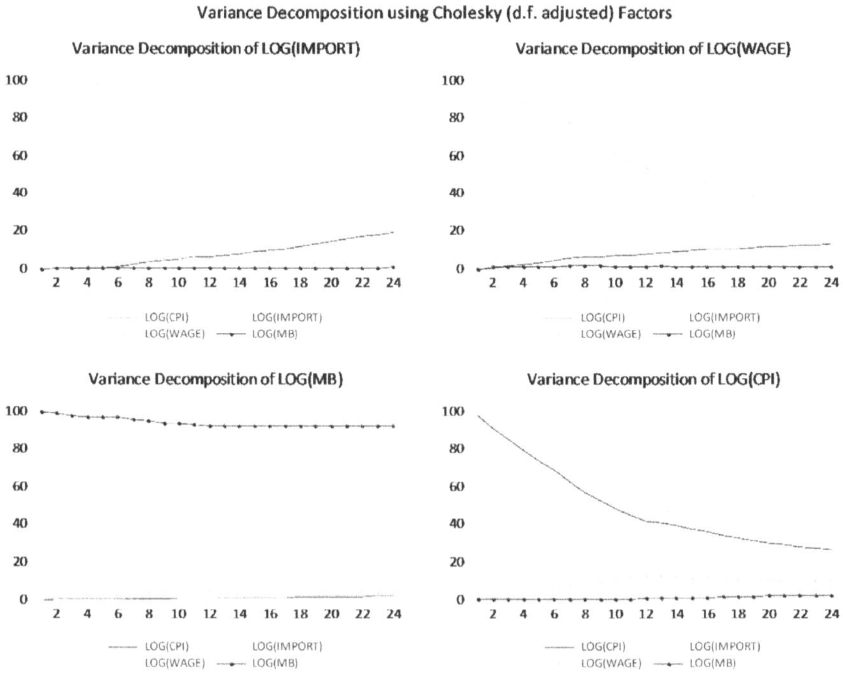

Fig. 2.10 (continued)

References

In Japanese

Asahi Shimbun (2013). Datsu Defure no Kōjunkan Mada: 'Yoi Bukka Jōshō' ga Kagi: Seifu Hōkoku 'Defure Nakunari tsutsu Aru' (Still no virtuous circle to end deflation: 'Good price inflation' is the key: Government report 'deflation is disappearing'). August 16.

Director General for Economic Research, Cabinet Office, Japan (Ed.). (2014). *Nihon Keizai, 2013–2014: Defure Dakkyaku e no Tatakai, Tsugi Naru Stēji e (Japanese economy, 2013–2014: The struggle to overcome deflation, moving to the next stage)*. Nikkei Printing.

Economic and Social Research Institute, Cabinet Office, Japan. (2023a). Consumer confidence survey. https://www.esri.cao.go.jp/jp/stat/shouhi/shouhi.html

Hamada, K. (2013). *Amerika wa Nihon Keizai no Fukkatsu o Shitte iru (America knows the revival of Japanese economy)*. Kodansha.

Hamada, K. (2017). 'Abenomikusu': Watashi wa Kangae Naoshita ('Abenomics': I have reconsidered). *Bungeishunju, 95*(1), 124–131.

Hattori, S. (2012a). Suitai Suru Sangyō: Beikoku Keizai no Chōki Teitai wa Rīman mae kara Hajimatte ita (Industries in decline: The secular stagnation of the U.S. economy began before the bankruptcy of Lehman). *Shūkan Ekonomisuto, 90*(39), 36–37.

Hattori, S. (2012b). Kommei Suru Kin'yū Seisaku: Sekai Keizai to Keizai gaku no 'Kiki' (Monetary policy in turmoil: World economy and the 'crisis' of economics). *Sekai, 835*, 246–253.

Hattori, S. (2014). *Abenomikusu no Shūen (The end of Abenomics)*. Iwanami Shoten.

Hattori, S. (2017). *Itsuwari no Keizai Seisaku: Kakusa to Teitai no Abenomikusu (Deceptive economic policy: Abenomics of inequality and stagnation).* Iwanami Shoten.
Hattori, S. (2023a). Chōki Teitai to Kommei Suru Keizai Seisaku (Secular stagnation and economic policies in turmoil). *Sekai, 965*, 116–123.
Hattori, S. (2023b). Chōki Teitai to Ikizumaru Kin'yū Seisaku (Secular stagnation and monetary policy at a stalemate). *Monthly Jichiken, 65*(761), 42–50.
Hattori, S. (2024). Nani ga Nihon no Bukka wo Kimeru no ka (What dives consumer prices in Japan). *Political Economy Quarterly, 61*(1), 37–48.
Iwata, K. (2012). *Nippon Ginkō : Defure no Ban'nin (The Bank of Japan: Keeper of deflation).* Nikkei Publishing.
Iwata, K. (2013). *Rifure wa Tadashii: Abenomikusu de Fukkatsu Suru Nihon Keizai (Reflation is correct: The Japanese economy revived by Abenomics).* PHP Institute.
Iwata, K. (2018). Rifure Riron mo Seisaku mo Tadashii, Daga Gyakuhū de Jikan ga Kakaru: Deguchi no Meikyū: Kin'yū Seisaku wo Tou (34) (Reflationist theory and policy are correct, but it takes time due to headwinds: Maze of exits: Questioning monetary policy, 34). *Shūkan Ekonomisuto, 96*(23), 82–85.
Morishima, M. (1984). *Mu Shigen Koku no Keizai gaku: Atarashii Keizai gaku Nyūmon (Economics of resource-poor countries: An introduction to the new economics).* Iwanami Shoten.
Noguchi, A. (2021). *Han Kinshuku no Keizai gaku (The economics of anti-austerity).* Toyo Keizai.
Noguchi, Y. (2022). *Nihon ga Senshin Koku kara Datsuraku Suru Hi: "En Yasu to iu Mayaku" ga Nihon wo Mazushiku Shita!! (The day Japan drops out of the developed countries : The "drug of a weak yen" made Japan poor!!).* President, Inc.
Policy Research Institute, Ministry of Finance, Japan. (2023). Financial statements statistics of corporations by industry. https://www.mof.go.jp/pri/reference/ssc/results/index.htm
Shiozawa, Y. (2014). *Rikādo Bōeki Mondai no Saishū Kaiketsu: Kokusai Kachi Ron no Fukken (The final solution of the Ricardo's trade problem: The revival of the international theory of value).* Iwanami Shoten.
The Bank of Japan. (2013). Sōsai fuku Sōsai Shūnin Kisha Kaiken Yōshi (Summary of the press conference of the inauguration of the governor and deputy governor, March 21). March 22.
The Bank of Japan. (2016a). Sōsai Kisha Kaiken Yōshi (Summary of the governor's press conference, September 21). September 23.
Watanabe, T. (2022). *Bukka to wa Nani ka? (What are prices?).* Kodansha.
Yoshikawa, H. (2013). *Defrēshion: "Nihon no Mansei Byō" no Zembō wo Kaimei Suru (Deflation: Elucidating the whole picture of "chronic diseases of Japan").* Nikkei Publishing.

In English

Bernanke, B. S. (2022). *21st century monetary policy: The Federal Reserve from the great inflation to COVID-19.* W. W. Norton.
Blinder, A. S. (1979). *Economic policy and the great stagflation.* Academic Press.
Blinder, A. S., Canetti, E. R. D., Lebow, D. E., & Rudd, J. B. (1998). *Asking about prices: A new approach to understanding price stickiness.* Russell Sage Foundation.
Blinder, A. S., & Rudd, J. B. (2013). The supply-shock explanation of the great stagflation revisited. In M. D. Bordo & A. Orphanides (Eds.), *The great inflation: The rebirth of modern central banking* (pp. 119–178). University of Chicago Press.
Bureau of Economic Analysis, the U.S. (2023). Gross domestic product. https://www.bea.gov/data/gdp/gross-domestic-product
Economic and Social Research Institute, Cabinet Office, Japan. (2023b). Indexes of business conditions. https://www.esri.cao.go.jp/en/stat/di/di-e.html
Economic and Social Research Institute, Cabinet Office, Japan. (2023c). National accounts for 2022. https://www.esri.cao.go.jp/en/sna/data/kakuhou/files/2022/2022annual_report_e.html

Economic and Social Research Institute, Cabinet Office, Japan. (2023d). Quarterly estimate for GDP. https://www.esri.cao.go.jp/en/sna/data/sokuhou/files/2023/qe233_2/gdemenuea.html

Federal Open Market Committee. (2012). Transcript of chairman Bernanke's press conference. January 25.

Federal Reserve Bank of St. Louis. (2023). FRED. https://fred.stlouisfed.org/

Hall, R. L., & Hitch, C. J. (1939). Price theory and business behaviour. *Oxford Economic Papers, 2*(1), 12–45.

Hauseman, J. K., Unayama, T., & Wieland, J. F. (2021). Abenomics, monetary policy, and consumption. In T. Hoshi & P. Y. Lipscy (Eds.), *The political economy of the Abe government and Abenomics reforms* (pp. 139–169). Cambridge University Press.

Hoshi, T., & Kashyap, A. K. (2021). The great discontent: The decoupling of wage and price inflation in Japan. In T. Hoshi & P. Y. Lipscy (Eds.), *The political economy of the Abe government and Abenomics reforms* (pp. 170–199). Cambridge University Press.

Iwata, K. (2014). Japan's economy and monetary policy. Speech at a meeting with business leaders in Ishikawa, September 10.

Japan Bond Trading Co., Ltd. (2023). BEI rate. We were personally provided with the data.

Japan Center for Economic Research. (2023). JCER ESP forecast. https://www.jcer.or.jp/en/esp-forecast-top

Kaldor, N. (1978 [1976]). Inflation and recession in the world economy. In N. Kaldor (Ed.), *Further essays on economic theory* (pp. 214–230). Duckworth.

Kalecki, M. (1954). *Theory of economic dynamics: An essay on cyclical and long-run changes in capitalist economy*. Allen and Unwin.

Kichikawa, Y., Iyetomi, H., Aoyama, H., Fujiwara, Y., & Yoshikawa, H. (2020). Interindustry linkages of prices—Analysis of Japan's deflation. *PLoS One, 15*(2).

Kuroda, H. (2013). Overcoming deflation and after. Speech at the meeting of Councillors of Nippon Keidanren (Japan Business Federation) in Tokyo, December 25.

Kuroda, H. (2022). Toward achieving the price stability target in a sustainable and stable manner: Accompanied by wage increases. Speech at the meeting of Councillors of Keidanren (Japan Business Federation) in Tokyo, December 26.

Krugman, P. R. (2015). Rethinking Japan. *The New York Times, October 20*.

Mian, A., & Sufi, A. (2011). House prices, home equity-based borrowing, and the US household leverage crisis. *American Economic Review, 101*(5), 2132–2156.

Ministry of Economy, Trade and Industry, Japan. (2023). Indices of industrial production. https://www.meti.go.jp/english/statistics/tyo/iip/index.html

Ministry of Health, Labour and Welfare, Japan. (2023). Monthly labour surveys. https://www.mhlw.go.jp/english/database/db-l/monthly-labour.html

Phillips, A. W. (1958). The relation between unemployment and the rate of change of money wage rates in the United Kingdom, 1861–1957. *Economica, 25*(100), 283–299.

Shiozawa, Y. (2017). The new theory of international value: An overview. In Y. Shiozawa, T. Oka, & T. Tabuchi (Eds.), *A new construction of Ricardian theory of international values: Analytical and historical approach* (pp. 3–73). Springer.

Shirakawa, M. (2012). Delevareging and growth: Is the developed world following Japan's long and winding road? Lectured at the London School of Economics and Political Science (co-hosted by the Asia Research Centre and STICERD, LSE), January 10.

Shirakawa, M. (2021). *Tumultuous times: Central banking in an era of crisis*. Yale University Press.

Sraffa, P. (1960). *Production of commodities by means of commodities: Prelude to a critique of economic theory*. Cambridge University Press.

Statistics Bureau, Ministry of Internal Affairs and Communications, Japan. (2023a). Consumer price index. https://www.stat.go.jp/english/data/cpi/index.htm

Statistics Bureau, Ministry of Internal Affairs and Communications, Japan. (2023b). Labour force survey. https://www.stat.go.jp/english/data/roudou/index.html

Statistics Bureau, Ministry of Internal Affairs and Communications, Japan. (2023c). Result of the population estimates. https://www.stat.go.jp/english/data/jinsui/2.html

The Bank of Japan. (2016b). Comprehensive assessment: Developments in economic activity and prices as well as policy effects since the introduction of quantitative and qualitative monetary easing (QQE): The background. September 21.

The Bank of Japan. (2023a). Consumption activity index. https://www.boj.or.jp/en/research/research_data/cai/index.htm

The Bank of Japan. (2023b). BOJ time-series data search. https://www.stat-search.boj.or.jp/index_en.html

Wakatabe, M. (2022). *The future of monetary policy: Lessons from the history of monetary economics*. Keynote speech at the 38th annual meeting of the Japan Association of Business Cycle Studies, December 3.

Yoshikawa, H. (2022). *Reconstruction of macroeconomics: Methods of statistical physics, and Keynes' principle of effective demand*. Springer.

Chapter 3
There Is No Monetary Policy Working on Inflation Expectations

Abstract Reflationists, including Kikuo Iwata, who was the Deputy Governor of the Bank of Japan (BOJ), have argued that monetary policy achieved success by working on inflation expectations. The theoretical problem with the monetary policy proposed by reflationists, which works on inflation expectations, is that no one can explain why inflation expectations and the actual inflation rate rise when the BOJ defines an inflation target with a deadline and declares commitment to achieving it, and rapidly expands the monetary base. The reflationist price theory has no theoretical basis. Next, reflationists argue that the monetary policy advocated is the standard of mainstream American economics. This is also false. On the contrary, mainstream economists in the United States, including Bernanke and Gertler, have seen the failure of the BOJ and insist that the BOJ is not capable of overcoming deflation. Instead, Iwata submitted what he called evidence. Ironically, we show that the BOJ under Kuroda and Iwata proved their own evidence false. It was inevitable that policies based on theories with no theoretical basis or evidence would fail.

Keywords Abenomics · The Bank of Japan under Kuroda · Deflation in Japan · Monetary base · Inflation expectations · Reflationists · Kikuo Iwata · Paul Krugman

3.1 Introduction

Kikuo Iwata argued that even if nominal interest rates were at the zero lower bound, the Bank of Japan (BOJ) could end deflation by working on inflation expectations.[1] In this chapter, we will critique the monetary policy that works on inflation expectations.

Krugman (1998) argued that even under the lower bound of interest rates, monetary policy would enable deflation to be overcome. He solved this problem by assuming that even if current monetary policy at the lower bound of interest rates is not effective, future monetary policy out of the lower bound of interest rates is. Logically, however, for future monetary policy to be effective, people in the future

[1] Chapters 3 and 4 explain Hattori's (2022) assertions in more detail and comprehensive.

S. Hattori, *Why the Bank of Japan Has Failed to Conquer Deflation in Japan*,
https://doi.org/10.1007/978-981-97-9408-9_3

must get out of the liquidity trap before then. Nevertheless, Krugman does not write about how people in the future will get out of the liquidity trap. The problem of getting out of the liquidity trap is solved by assuming that people will get out of the liquidity trap in the future. This is a circular argument.

Although the Krugman model is strange when logically pursued in this way, it had a great impact on the reflationists. As mentioned in the Preface and Sect. 2.2.2, Iwata's tools for raising inflation expectations are the Japanese-style inflation target and a massive supply of monetary base. However, the Krugman model does not argue that a large supply of monetary base will raise inflation expectations. Iwata, however, does not provide any theoretical basis for his argument.

Furthermore, reflationists claim that their monetary policy that works on inflation expectations is the standard in mainstream American economics. This is also false. Conversely, after seeing the failure of the BOJ under Kuroda, Bernanke (2017); Bernanke (2023, p. 12) and Gertler (2017) began to argue that the BOJ was not capable of overcoming deflation. Finally, Iwata argues that the BOJ and the Federal Reserve have proven their theory that a large supply of monetary base increases inflation expectations. We show that this does not generally hold, although the correlation between the monetary base and the expected inflation rate was positive in the period measured by Iwata.

Section 3.2 again clarifies that there is nothing monetary policy can do under a lower bound on interest rates. Section 3.3 provides a theoretical critique of the Krugman model and Iwata's monetary policy that works on inflation expectations. In Sect. 3.4, we show that a monetary policy that works on inflation expectations is a policy that does not exist in mainstream economics in the United States (U.S.). Section 3.5 shows that there is no basis for Iwata's purported evidence. Finally, Sect. 3.6 concludes the chapter.

3.2 Why the Reflationist Theory Does Not Work

3.2.1 No Means of Monetary Easing

The reflationist price theory emphasizes that "deflation is a monetary phenomenon" and claims that deflation can be overcome if the BOJ is determined to deal with it. The problem with this claim is its fallacy. Therefore, the BOJ under Kuroda failed to achieve its inflation target even after ten years. Conversely, when import prices soared from 2021 onward, the inflation rate exceeded 4% in 2022. Firstly, it was a fundamental mistake to think that it was monetary policy and inflation expectations rather than import prices and costs that were driving the consumer prices (CPI) in Japan. Moreover, since the 2000s, Japan's short-term interest rates have been near zero, and monetary policy tools have dried up. The terms liquidity trap or the zero lower bound of interest rates imply that monetary policy cannot be effective there.

However, even if short-term interest rates fall to zero, long-term interest rates, corporate bonds, and other interest rates do not necessarily decline to zero. Therefore, it may be possible to exert an effect by purchasing long-term Japanese government bonds (JGBs) and corporate bonds. However, when Kuroda was appointed governor of the BOJ, long-term interest rates were already very low. Even if lowered further, the CPI inflation rate would not be raised to 2%. In fact, under Kuroda, the BOJ brought long-term interest rates down to almost zero but failed to end deflation. With long-term interest rates at the zero lower bound, long-term interest rates could no longer be lowered, and Bernanke (2017, p. 30) referred to it as a "super liquidity trap."

However, monetarists like Milton Friedman have argued that prices rise as the money stock increases. According to Friedman, the severe deflation during the Great Depression after 1929 was caused by the collapse of the money stock brought about by the Federal Reserve, and the exit from the Great Depression was also caused by an increase in the money stock. Iwata (e.g., 1993, 2002, 2009, pp. 178–188, 201) followed Friedman's footsteps and argued for an increase in the money stock through an expansion of the monetary base until a certain time.

However, money can also be hoarded. Even if you need money to spend, having money does not necessarily mean you will spend. In the Appendix to Chap. 2, we show that M3 has no Granger causality for CPI in Japan. Yoshikawa (2009, pp. 147–152; 2013, Chap. 4, 97–148) shows that prices and money stock are not linked in Japan. In fact, it is often pointed out that large companies rapidly increase cash and deposits amid secular stagnation. Since the beginning of Abenomics, the profits of large corporations have skyrocketed. However, most of these profits were ultimately hoarded as cash and deposits. The hoarding of money manifested itself in an extreme form during the COVID-19 crisis. In 2020, the number of companies struggling with cash flow increased, mainly in the travel industry and restaurants, attributable to requests for business closures and people refraining from going out. At that time, the government and the BOJ supported cash-strapped companies so that they could borrow from banks. As a result, bank lending soared, and so did the money stock. However, consumption decreased, and the economy fell sharply due to requests for business closures and people's preventive behaviors, such as refraining from going out.

Watanabe (2022, pp. 110–117) argues that as central banks increase money stock, interest rates decline. When interest rates fall very low, money demand saturates, and the monetary policy framework loses its effectiveness. Therefore, monetary policy is effective in combating inflation, but it is asymmetrical as it has limitations in countering deflation. He points out that Keynes used the term "liquidity trap" for this condition.[2]

In addition, there are various monetary indicators, such as those limited to cash and demand deposits (M1), those that include time deposits (M2 and M3), and those that include other financial instruments (broadly-defined liquidity in Japan). A common

---

[2] The liquidity trap is an important concept in Keynes's (1973 [1936]) *General Theory*, but this term is not used in it.

criticism of monetarists is that they say money is important; however, they cannot define what money is.

In December 2022, Wakatabe (2022, pp. 4–5) stated that cost-push inflation would not last long. Furthermore, he (Wakatabe, 2022, p. 5) said that prices are determined by the relationship between the natural rate of interest and the market rate of interest. While the natural rate of interest fluctuates due to real factors, the market rate of interest is determined by the central bank, implying that prices are determined by the monetary policy. However, the fact that the natural rate of interest is determined by real factors indicates that real factors move prices through the natural rate of interest. More problematic is the fact that the market interest rate has a lower bound. Especially in Japan, the long-term interest rate has also reached its lower bound. The question for Japan is what monetary policy should do when the interest rate reaches the lower bound, but Wakatabe has not attempted to answer this question at all. He should not be able to answer this question.

Furthermore, Wakatabe (2022, pp. 13–14) also says that inflation expectations determine prices. He probably believes that even under the zero lower bound, monetary policy can raise prices by working on inflation expectations. The inflation target was Wakatabe's tool. The inflation target has not been achieved at all, even in 2022, almost ten years after the inflation target was set. As discussed in Chap. 4, the BOJ abandoned its Japanese-style inflation target. However, he does not explain how the inflation target can end deflation in the first place. This was probably because he could not explain it.

Wakatabe is unable to indicate what monetary policy should do when interest rates reach the lower bound or what monetary policy should do to raise inflation expectations. As the deputy governor of the BOJ, he would be very irresponsible. This in itself would indicate that there is nothing the BOJ can do.

3.2.2 *Monetary Base and Money Stock Are Different*

Moreover, when monetarists say that money is important, they are referring to the money stock, not the monetary base. The BOJ under Kuroda expanded its monetary base, but the rate of increase in its money stock remains sluggish. After the global financial crisis of 2008, central banks in the U.S. and Europe adopted the so-called QE policies, which sharpened the monetary base but did not lead to an increase in money stock. Under such circumstances, it is impossible to overcome deflation, even from a monetarist standpoint.

During the early 1990s, controversy over money supply ensued in Japan. After the bubble burst, Iwata (e.g. 1993) pointed out the sluggish rate of increase in money stock, arguing that if the BOJ increased the rate of money stock growth and resolved deflation, the Japanese economy would be revived. In contrast, Okina (e.g. 1993) argued that the BOJ supplies the monetary base in response to its demand. He further countered that in the absence of an increase in lending, money stock would not increase, notwithstanding the expansion in the monetary base. Chapter 5 clarifies why a large supply of the monetary base does not necessarily lead to an increase in the money stock (in fact, it leads to an increase in some cases).

Since then, the assertion that an increase in the monetary base does not lead to an increase in the money stock is a typical critique of reflationists. For example, Suzuki (2022, p. 134) stated that money stock must be inherently increased to revitalize the economy. However, an increase in the current account at the BOJ or the monetary base does not increase the money stock. He says using the current account at the BOJ or monetary base as policy targets, as they are controllable, is deceptive. Moreover, the BOJ has been reluctant to engage in quantitative easing (QE) because it is aware of this situation (see also Ito, 2022, pp. 209–210n).

Woodford (2012, pp. 49–56) distinguishes QE as pure QE that purchases short-term Treasury discount bills with zero interest rates and asset purchases that involve buying long-term bonds with positive interest rates because purchasing bonds with zero interest does not lower interest rates. Therefore, he claims that the success of pure QE depends on whether the money stock increases. He pointed out that Friedman agreed to the QE policy implemented in 2001 by the BOJ, as Friedman believed that it would increase money stock. However, Woodford argues that QE does not increase money stock because the demand for excess reserves becomes infinite under the zero interest rate. Logically, Woodford would agree with the anti-reflationist arguments in the controversy over money supply in Japan. If Friedman's approval was also due to his misunderstanding that QE in Japan would lead to an increase in the money stock, he may turn to his conclusion that it is invalid once his misunderstanding is cleared up. As for the policy of lowering long-term interest rates, Woodford (2012, p. 53) points out that if long-term government bonds are purchased and short-term government bonds are sold at the same time (this is called operation twist), there is no need to increase the monetary base. For this reason, Woodford does not consider a cut in long-term interest rates as the outcome of the QE.

Furthermore, Friedman (e.g., 1991, p. 16) argued that "*inflation is always and everywhere a monetary phenomenon*," but this did not mean that deflation would inevitably stagnate the economy. After the Civil War in the U.S., Friedman and Schwartz (1963, p. 15) pointed out that economic growth was high, even though prices were less than half by 1879.

Figure 3.1 shows the rate of increase in CPI, monetary base, and money stock in Japan. For CPI, the figure shows the index less imputed rent and the index less imputed rent and fresh food. As a result of Kuroda's policy, the monetary base surged at an annual rate of more than 50% at one point, but it did not lead to any increase in the money stock. It was not only the BOJ under Kuroda, but central banks in the U.S. and Europe also expanded their monetary base after the global financial crisis, but the sharp increase in the monetary base did not lead to an increase in the money stock.

Moreover, the rate of increase in the money stock and the rate of increase in the CPI are not closely linked. The relationship of the CPI with the monetary base is even weaker. After the end of the first round of the QE, the monetary base decreased sharply, but the CPI inflation rate did not decline. Thereafter, the monetary base leveled off, but the CPI rose and fell due to soaring and plunging global energy

Fig. 3.1 Consumer price inflation rate and rate of change in monetary base and money stock (January 2005–March 2023). *Source* Statistics Bureau, Ministry of Internal Affairs and Communications, Japan (2023) and The Bank of Japan (2023). *Note 1* "MB" is indicated on the right-hand side axis, while others are on the left side. *Note 2* Year-on-year change. *Note 3* "MB" is monetary base. "CPI" is less imputed rent. "Less fresh food" is CPI less imputed rent and fresh food

prices. After the BOJ under Kuroda adopted the QQE measures, the monetary base increased by more than 50% annually. The CPI rose during this period, but the rate of increase did not reach the 2% target. Thereafter, the rate of increase in the monetary base declined sharply because the rapid increase in the monetary base caused the denominator to soar. Nevertheless, the CPI inflation rate declined from mid-2014 onward, reversed at the end of 2016, and declined again from the beginning of 2018.

Incidentally, Iwata (2013a, pp. 32–37) once criticized the BOJ, stating that only Japan was in deflation because the BOJ was not expanding the monetary base rapidly. However, Iwata's criticism is not acceptable. On the contrary, the BOJ under Kuroda supplied the monetary base much more than central banks in the U.S. and Europe. If Iwata's criticism were correct, the rate of price hikes in Japan would be much higher than in the U.S. and Europe. The opposite is true. Japan has been unable to achieve its 2% inflation target forever and ever (excluding imported inflation since 2022). In fact, the BOJ under Kuroda and Iwata has shown that Iwata's criticism had no basis.

3.2.3 *Prices Do Not Rise by Inflation Expectations*

Monetary policy working on inflation expectations, which reflationists advocate, replaced these depleted tools. However, shortly after the BOJ under Kuroda began implementing the QQE, inflation expectations began declining.

Then, the BOJ under Kuroda (e.g., the Bank of Japan, 2016a, p. 8) emphasized that inflation expectations in Japan would not improve because they were more adaptive to the actual inflation rate. Gertler (2017) also models that when inflation expectations become more adaptive to actual inflation rates, the power of monetary policy to raise inflation expectations diminishes. Based on this, as we pointed out in Sect. 1.1, he suggested at the end of his lecture that luck is necessary to overcome deflation in Japan. An important point of this adaptive inflation expectations theory is that it rejects the core of the reflationist theory that monetary policy operates by raising inflation expectations.

The more fundamental question is whether inflation expectations will raise prices. The story that future forecasts drive current prices is an event in the world of speculation and bubbles. This is true of asset markets, especially financial markets. Most consumer goods, however, have nothing to do with speculation or bubbles. However, the markets for primary commodities, especially the futures markets for the primary commodities, now considered quasi-financial markets, are different. Hence, speculation occurring in the market for primary commodities may cause fluctuations in the prices of primary commodities, which in turn will affect the prices of consumer goods.

Watanabe (2022, pp. 271–274) states that when Abenomics began, the tavern, "Torikizoku," raised prices based on its forecast. However, "Torikizoku" lost customers, and its sales declined. This shows that the price increase based on the forecast is not profitable for the company itself. When a company raises prices when neither its own nor its rivals' costs are rising, it loses customers to rival companies. In the consumer goods market, (reasonable) companies do not raise prices based on their forecasts. Instead, if only one company does not raise prices when its own and its rivals' costs are rising, it will be able to lift customers from rival companies. However, if the price is not increased, the more it sells, the greater its losses. For this reason, companies raise prices when costs rise.

Watanabe says that the failure of the price increase of "Torikizoku" was due to the lack of interaction with other companies to follow suit. We agree with Watanabe. However, as we mentioned in Sect. 2.4.3, Watanabe's view is that the mechanism for determining individual prices in the restaurant industry and absolute price is different. Consistent with Watanabe's view, absolute price should rise even if prices did not rise in the restaurant industry because consumers should use their excess money to purchase other goods.

Figure 2.1 shows the CPI inflation rate as well as the ESP forecast. The forecasted values by the ESP forecasts generally change in tandem with the real inflation rate prevailing at that time (see also Ito, 2016, pp. 69–72). However, price movements are more stable in the ESP forecast because it is probably common for humans to base their forecasts on the actual inflation rate, but to a lesser degree when the actual value fluctuates. However, the benchmark for the CPI is revised every five years. It is not rigorous as it is not judged by data based on the benchmark of the time. Nonetheless, overall tendencies would not be wrong. Conversely, the correlation with the actual inflation rate one year later is insignificant. As experts in economic forecasting, their forecasts are adaptable, but their inflation forecasts a year from now are not so accurate.

As shown in Fig. 2.1, the rate of increase in CPI in Japan is highly correlated with the rate of increase in import prices six months ago. If we examine import prices, predicting the CPI a few months from now is possible. Besides, there are many consumer goods and imported goods. Therefore, some consumer goods may have a significantly higher price correlation with certain imported goods. Price forecasts for these consumer goods could be made with even greater accuracy. Even for some consumer goods for which price forecasting is highly accurate, you have probably never heard of a price increase being made because future prices are expected to be higher. Again, our answer is that if the price is raised ahead of time, customers will be lost to rivals. In fact, the Director General for Economic Research, Cabinet Office, Japan (2014, pp. 54–55) shows that it takes a maximum of nine months for the rise in import prices to be transmitted to the final prices of consumer goods.

As noted in Sect. 2.3.1, it is either consumers' or firms' price expectations that could be self-fulfilling. Figure 3.2 shows that consumers' price expectations are generally higher than the current inflation rates. However, fluctuations in consumers' price expectations are closely related to fluctuations in inflation rates at that time. It can be affirmed that the closeness exceeds that of the ESP forecast. Since 2022, the gap with the CPI inflation rate has narrowed and consumers' price expectations have been below in some periods. Although there was a sharp increase in the number of respondents who indicated that the rate of increase would be above 5% in the face of imported inflation, all these responses were treated as 6%. Therefore, the upper bound of the price expectation is 6%. Given this, it is likely that price expectations after 2022 were underestimated. However, the price expectations have little to do with the actual inflation rate one year from now. This indicates that consumer inflation expectations are adaptive to the actual inflation rate, but consumers' price expectations would not affect prices a year from now.

The figure also shows the consumer confidence index (CCI). The index deteriorated significantly during the global financial crisis and the COVID-19 crisis. Unsurprisingly, many consumers will feel that their situation deteriorated during severe crises. At the same time, the index deteriorated when consumers' price expectations and the CPI inflation rate were high. These results are consistent with the fact that imported inflation drives CPI inflation in Japan. Conversely, this contradicts reflationists' supposition that consumers become more optimistic about the future when inflation expectations rise. This also indicates that consumers' inflation expectations do not fluctuate in the way reflationists believe.

The fact that inflation expectations are adaptive does not mean that the BOJ under Kuroda was able to raise inflation expectations and overcome deflation if people had rationally expected inflation. Firstly, rational expectations mean to expect rationally using all the available information. Section 2.3.1 showed that when import prices rise, CPI also rises with a lag of six months. Therefore, it is rational for those who see import prices rising to expect CPI to rise. On the contrary, there is no relationship between the monetary base and CPI. A person who sees an increase in the monetary base and thinks that CPI will rise is, by definition, irrational.

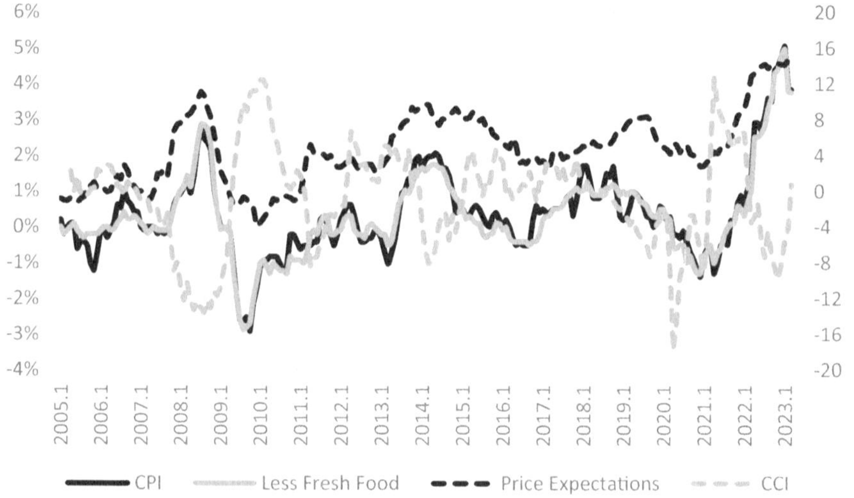

Fig. 3.2 Consumer price inflation rate, consumer's price expectations and consumer confidence index (January 2005–March 2023). *Source* Statistics Bureau, Ministry of Internal Affairs and Communications, Japan (2023) and Economic and Social Research Institute, Cabinet Office, Japan (2023). *Note 1* "CCI" is indicated on the right-hand side axis, while others are on the left side. *Note 2* "CPI" is less imputed rent, and "Less fresh food" is CPI less imputed rent and fresh food. Both exclude the impact of consumption tax hikes and other factors. "Price expectations" are consumers' expectations of an increase in the prices of goods that consumers will commonly purchase over the next 12 months, including the portion due to the consumption tax hikes and other factors. "CCI" is the year-on-year difference. *Note 3* The price expectations and CCI are not necessarily consistent with the previous ones because the surveys were changed from a home-visit detention survey to a mail-in survey in April 2013. *Note 4* Among the results for price expectations, declines and increases are divided into three levels: less than 2%, between 2 and 5%, and more than 5%. In addition, there are "no change" and "don't know," creating a total of eight levels. In the figure, both declines and increases are weighted averages as 1% for less than 2%, 3.5% for 2–5%, and 6% for 5% or more ("no change" and "don't know" are calculated with the weights as zero)

As the only information available to humans is past information, rational expectations are based only on past information. Information that was not available in the past will become available over time. The critical information that the BOJ under Kuroda failed to achieve its inflation target even after ten years and that the CPI has surged since 2022 as soaring import prices were not available in 2013 but are currently available. People like reflationists who continue to say that deflation can one day be overcome if the BOJ continues to ease monetary policy without adapting to this vital information are not rational but simply stupid.

3.3 Theories with No Theoretical Basis

3.3.1 Krugman Model

In 1998, Krugman's paper argued that monetary policy could be effective even under the liquidity trap. This paper has had a tremendous impact on reflationists. Since the mid-1990s, short-term interest rates have been almost zero in Japan. Under the zero lower bound, interest rates can hardly be lowered. The challenge of Krugman's model is to show that monetary policy can be effective under these circumstances.

Krugman (1998, pp. 157–158) argued that an increase in the monetary base may not expand the money stock because money and bonds can be perfectly substituted at the zero lower bound of interest rates. When the BOJ purchases JGBs from a bank, the BOJ pays the bill to the bank. If the interest rate is positive, the bank can buy bonds with the bill and make a profit. When a bank buys bonds, money is supplied throughout the market; thus, the money stock increases. When the interest rate on the bond is zero, a bank may not buy the bond because it will not earn a profit. Or even if the interest rate on the bond is positive, a bank will not buy one if it is too risky. This will only increase excess reserves.

Krugman (1998, Fig. 3, p. 155) indicates that even during the Great Depression of 1929–1933, the U.S. money stock was declining despite the expansion in the monetary base. We noted earlier that it is a typical criticism of reflationists that a sharp increase in the monetary base does not lead to an increase in lending but only to an increase in excess reserves and not to an increase in the money stock. Krugman argues that this situation also occurred in the U.S. during the Great Depression.

Krugman (1998) argues that monetary policy can be effective by working on expectations even at the lower zero bound. The point is to assume that, in the future, Japan will be out of the liquidity trap. Subsequently, in the future, Japan's monetary policy can raise prices. Therefore, if monetary easing is implemented in Japan in the future, future prices can be increased. If future prices increase, current prices will increase due to an increase in the demand for current goods because it will be profitable to sell them in the future. Thus, the future monetary policy will retroactively raise current prices. A literal understanding of the conclusions based on the Krugman model suggests that the BOJ under Kuroda's failure to end deflation is not its fault but rather the failure of its successor, the BOJ under Ueda, to conduct sufficient monetary easing. Alternatively, the BOJ under Ueda could have gone further back and raised prices during the Shirakawa era. This is science fiction and cannot be found in the real world.

In the world of abstract mathematical models, there is little difference between a two-period model comprising the present and future (which can have three or more periods) and a two-country model consisting of the home and foreign country, in which the exchange rate is not in the two-period model, and the interest rate is not in the two-country model. However, apart from these minor differences, the model structure remains basically the same.

In the two-country model, it is possible that what happens in a foreign country, whether in monetary policy or otherwise, will raise prices in the home country in a roundabout way. In fact, Russia's war with Ukraine led to soaring global energy and food prices, and Japan's CPI rose due to soaring import prices. Therefore, even in the two-period model, where the structure of the model is basically the same as the two-country model, it is possible in a mathematical model that future events will increase the current prices. Current events can affect the future in the real world, but there is no reverse. This is the critical difference between space and time. Abstract mathematical models lead to science fiction-type results by ignoring the difference between space and time.

In the Krugman model, expectations solve this problem. Humans expect future events and determine their current actions. While the future monetary policy cannot affect current prices, current expectations of the future monetary policy may affect the prevailing prices. It is unclear to what extent Krugman was aware, but in this way, he can give reality to a science fiction-like story. However, this solution does not clarify what can be done to raise people's inflation expectations.

Krugman's 1998 paper concludes with comments on his paper, which acknowledged the novelty of his idea but were negative about the reality of his idea. Robert Gordon (Krugman, 1998, p. 201) shows that while inflation expectations adapt to actual inflation, people do not experience any rise in inflation unless they come under the pressure of goods, services, and labor markets. Blinder (Krugman, 1998, p. 201) agreed with Gordon. Krugman's inflationary policy will work if implemented, but it will require the BOJ to create inflation expectations. However, he said that it would have to convince people that the future would be different from the past and that it would be difficult to create the 4% inflation forecast proposed by Krugman based on past experiences in Japan. Thus, the skepticism that the BOJ would fail to realize its inflation target, even if it set one, has existed from the beginning.

Yoshikawa (2009, p. 143) also commented on the Krugman model, saying, "Anyone can argue that 'even if the nominal interest rate goes to zero, if the inflation expectations rates increase, the real interest rate will decline, and the economy will recover.'" Noguchi (2021, pp. 160–161) also wrote in the Krugman model, "What means can be used to 'work on expectations' is not a question that can be answered so easily." We agree with him. We only add that the ten years of the BOJ revealed that even reflationists, including Kuroda and Noguchi, were not aware of the measures that could be used to raise inflation expectations.

Another important and related problem is that Krugman assumes that the Japanese economy will not experience the liquidity trap at a point in the future. This is essential because if the Japanese economy experiences a liquidity trap in the future, the monetary policy will be ineffective. Nevertheless, he does not describe how the Japanese economy can escape the liquidity trap. For monetary policy to take effect at some point in the future, it will need to get out of the liquidity trap. However, to escape the liquidity, monetary easing must be implemented further in the future, and so on. Krugman solves this by simply assuming that the future is not under a liquidity trap. The question is how to get out of the liquidity trap; the answer is solved based on assumptions. This is circular reasoning.

Summers (2015) also describes Krugman's assumption that Japan is out of the liquidity trap at a future point as "It has always seemed to me be a classic example of economists' tendency to 'assume a can opener.'" "Assume a can opener" refers to a famous joke that ridicules the unreality of assumptions of economics. Three people drifted on an uninhabited island: a physicist, a chemist, and an economist. They had canned food and no can opener. Hence, each of them proposed a method to open the can. At that time, the economist proposed, "Assume there is a can opener here." Summers said that Krugman suggested unrealistic assumptions to draw a convenient conclusion.

In a 2014 paper, however, Krugman (2014, p. 66) wrote, "[N]ow we are talking seriously about secular stagnation in Europe and the U.S. as well, which means that it could be a very long time before 'normal' monetary policy resumes." Conversely, his 1998 paper may have assumed that liquidity traps could heal spontaneously within a relatively short period of time without using the monetary policy.

As another problem, Yoshikawa (2009, pp. 144–147) points out the model's unreality. First, as future prices are determined by a future monetary policy, the lower the prices now, the higher the future inflation rate will be. In other words, the higher the deflation is now, the higher the inflation expectations are. Second, it assumes that the interest elasticity of demand is high. Due to the low elasticity of interest rates, Japan fell into a liquidity trap. Even if nominal interest rates are zero and 2% inflation can be achieved, real interest rates will only be − 2%. There is no basis for whether demand can be expected to end stagnation at a − 2% interest rate. The second criticism also applies to the U.S. and Europe. After the global financial crisis, interest rates fell to zero in the U.S. and Europe, and the so-called QE was implemented, but this did not lead to a V-shaped recovery in the economy.

Moreover, even if it is possible to exit the liquidity trap in the future, the question of when will remain a problem. In extreme cases, for example, if inflation is expected to occur one or two decades later, no one would think that it would raise prices today. Furthermore, if there is room for expansion of production in the future, even if demand increases, it can be solved by expanding production in the future. In such a case, there is a possibility that the current inflation will not be affected. Even if Krugman's assumptions are relaxed slightly, there is a possibility that Krugman's thinking mechanism will not work.

3.3.2 Reflationist Theory that Cannot Explain Its Theoretical Basis

The Krugman model received much skepticism but profoundly influenced Iwata and other reflationists. Iwata's policy tool for raising inflation expectations was the Japanese-style inflation target and the large supply of the monetary base.

However, an inflation target is a target and not a policy. Even children understand and identify that certain things can be achieved and some other things cannot be achieved and that even if they themselves set an unreasonable target, they will not be able to achieve it. There is no basis for the claim that the BOJ can achieve its targets if it sets them, shows a willingness to do so, and is prepared to take responsibility when it fails. This "no basis" was demonstrated by the BOJ under Kuroda. The critical mistake is to ignore the wolf-boy effect. This is a term derived from Aesop's fable "The Boy Who Cried Wolf," which refers to the fact that if someone keeps spreading false information, their credibility will decline, and people will stop believing the information.

Although the BOJ under Kuroda set an inflation target of 2%, it failed to achieve it even once in ten years. Moreover, although the BOJ said it would take responsibility if it failed to achieve the target, it shifted the blame for the failure to everything other than monetary policy, and in the end, no one took responsibility. No reasonable person would take the word of such an incompetent and irresponsible institution. Subsequently, when deflation really does seem to be ending in the near future, no one will believe the BOJ when it says that the end of deflation is subliminally near.

As mentioned earlier, in the Krugman model, the future monetary easing raises prices today, not the current massive supply of the monetary base. Therefore, the argument that the large supply of the monetary base will raise inflation expectations does not emerge from the Krugman model. However, Iwata (e.g., 2012, 2013a) also does not explain why supplying a large amount of the monetary base at the current time would raise inflation expectations.

After he was appointed the deputy governor, Iwata (2013b, pp. 7–9) explained during a speech in 2013 that an increase in expected inflation would lower real interest rates and increase demand. As Yoshikawa pointed out, it is self-evident that even if the nominal interest rates are zero, real interest rates will decline when inflation expectations rise. However, he does not explain why an increase in the monetary base raises inflation expectations. His 2013 lecture was titled "Quantitative and Qualitative Monetary Easing and its Transmission Mechanism: Logic behind the First Arrow." However, strangely enough, Iwata refuses to explain the first and most important part of the transmission mechanism. Probably, he just cannot explain it.

Firstly, most people living in Japan will not know what the monetary base is (as will people in other countries). Most people who know the monetary base are perhaps not aware of how much it is in real-time, nor are they interested in how much it is. Furthermore, no convenience store or supermarket will raise prices because the monetary base has increased. Some people may buy a house because interest rates are low, but no one will buy it because the monetary base has increased. We also do not know how much the monetary base is in real-time, and we have never used it for anything other than research.

According to Noguchi (2021, pp. 164–168), the answer to Krugman's problem is a change in the policy regime. In fact, since the start of Abenomics, there has been a shift in the policy regime in exchange rates and stock prices. However, Noguchi also admitted that inflation expectations did not have a clear effect in the end. He attributes this to the stickiness of prices and wages. He also argues that the consumption tax hike in 2014 prevented the end of deflation. The truth is that the rise in prices since 2013 has been the result of a surge in import prices, as mentioned in Sect. 2.3.1.

Figure 2.1 shows that the decline in the rate of increase in CPI since 2014 is also the result of the decline in import prices. Furthermore, Noguchi also did not explain why the BOJ set the Japanese-style inflation target and expanded the monetary base, causing a regime shift and raising inflation expectations.

Instead, Iwata (2012, Figs. 4–7, 4–8, p. 110) shows that the correlation between the monetary base and breakeven inflation (BEI) is positive in both Japan and the U.S. As explained in Sect. 3.5, the positive correlation only holds for the period Iwata made his figures, but not in general. Ironically, under Kuroda, the correlation was negative for most of the period.

Iwata (2012, pp. 200–203) calculates the amount of monetary base required to achieve the 2% inflation target. In the case of the QE period, it was ¥211 trillion. In contrast, in the aftermath of the Lehman Brothers' collapse, the inflation rate became more sensitive to inflation expectations in the monetary base, resulting in a figure of ¥162 trillion. He added that if the BOJ is committed to achieving its inflation target, the amount of the monetary base needed would be even smaller. However, the monetary base (seasonally adjusted) in March 2023 was ¥665 trillion. Even in December 2019, shortly before the spread of COVID-19, the monetary base was ¥517 trillion, surpassing Iwata's calculations. Nevertheless, excluding imported inflation, there is probably no prospect of achieving the 2% inflation target. Iwata's calculations were utterly misguided.

The BOJ under Kuroda (The Bank of Japan, 2016b, p. 5) indicates that there is a long-run relationship between the monetary base and inflation expectations but does not explain why. In a speech at Oxford University, Kuroda (2017, pp. 6–7) stated that to raise inflation expectations, the BOJ adopted an inflation target, demonstrating its commitment to do whatever it takes to end deflation and lower long-term interest rates by purchasing long-term government bonds. However, he does not clarify why inflation expectations rise when the BOJ adopts these policies. Moreover, it will be explained in Chap. 4 that when Kuroda referred to this, the BOJ ceased its commitment to the inflation target, and long-term interest rates were near zero, having reached their lower bound. In 2022, as indicated earlier, Wakatabe (2022, pp. 13–14) stated that monetary policy works by working on inflation expectations. He cited inflation targeting as a tool for achieving this target. However, he did not explain how a policy that has failed for almost ten years can achieve this target.

Adachi (2013, pp. 117–119), a member of the Policy Board at the BOJ since March 2020, states that it is impossible to think with common sense that even if the BOJ purchases all JGBs equivalent to 200% of GDP, the economy will not change. While it is true that the monetary base expands when the BOJ purchases JGBs, he does not explain why the monetary base, which amounts to 200% of GDP, will end deflation. Even if JGBs actually exist, the BOJ cannot force potential sellers to sell JGBs to the BOJ. Therefore, as discussed in Sect. 4.2.1, it seems impossible for the BOJ to purchase 200% of GDP. Nonetheless, the BOJ has already purchased JGBs roughly equal to GDP. Even so, there is no prospect of overcoming deflation. The "common sense" that Adachi and reflationists refer to is not only not common sense but also a bias that does not match facts.

3.3.3 Do Excess Reserves Raise Inflation Expectations?

Most of the monetary base supplied in large quantities by the BOJ under Kuroda and the central banks of the U.S. and Europe are in excess reserves. It is a standard criticism of reflationists that an increase in the monetary base will only create excess reserves. However, Iwata (e.g., 2012, pp. 109–112) argues that excess reserves effectively raise inflation expectations. It is financial institutions that hold excess reserves. Households and businesses will not know how much excess reserves financial institutions have. Even if they knew, households and firms would not be able to use the excess reserves to buy goods. Nevertheless, Iwata does not explain why excess reserves raise inflation expectations. Instead, he presents figures showing a correlation between excess reserves and expected inflation in both Japan and the U.S. (Iwata, 2012, Figs. 4–4, 4–5, p. 106). However, as described in Sect. 3.5, this empirical analysis is also incorrect.

In some situations, excess reserves may have a consequential effect. The first is the case of the lender of last resort. Under normal circumstances, a bank that is short of funds can borrow from a bank that is overstocked. The central bank should supply liquidity so that there is no excess or shortage across the banking system. However, during a financial crisis, a bank with excess funds may recall its funds for fear of non-performing loans. Banks with insufficient liquidity will not be able to manage their funds. Therefore, the central bank must lend to banks experiencing insufficient liquidity and try to prevent them from failing. As a result, banks with sufficient funds will have excess reserves. However, when Kuroda was the governor of the BOJ, the financial system was normal. Moreover, even during a financial crisis, providing liquidity to banks that have enough will have no effect. Theoretically, a central bank could also sell securities to banks with enough money to absorb the excess funds. Therefore, in theory, it may be possible to become a lender of last resort without increasing the monetary base.

Second is the case of the portfolio rebalancing effect. Risky assets have higher interest rates by the amount of the risk premium. Therefore, even if short-term interest rates fall to zero, the interest rate on risky assets remains positive. If the central bank purchases risky assets, the seller's risky assets will decrease, and the amount of loss suffered from risky assets will decrease. As a result, the interest rate on risky assets falls as the risk premium falls (King, 2018, pp. 27–28). This policy corresponds to the qualitative aspects of the QQE in the BOJ under Kuroda. In this case, the funds paid by the BOJ will also result in excess reserves. As Woodford (2012, p. 53) mentions, however, if the operation twist is implemented, there is no need to increase the monetary base. Also, for example, if pension funds purchase large amounts of risky assets, the risk premium will decline. Essentially, policies that reduce the risk premium belong to policy-based finance, which is fiscal policy in the broad sense.

However, there is also a lower bound to the risk premium. In Japan, long-term interest rates are now near zero. Strictly speaking, interest rates other than those on long-term JGBs are positive near zero, but we can consider that they have almost reached the lower bound. This situation, which Bernanke (2017, p. 30) describes as a super liquidity trap, was mentioned in Chap. 1.

The last is funding for lending schemes. This is a preferential measure for increasing bank lending in certain sectors. As discussed in Sect. 4.2.6, the BOJ established the interest scheme to promote lending in March 2021. When banks borrow from the BOJ, the monetary base increases, and when banks lend to firms, money stock also increases. This is also a policy-based finance. Moreover, no matter how much preferential treatment BOJ offers, bank lending will not increase unless firms and households want to borrow. Except for the period when COVID-19 was widespread, the use of the interest scheme to promote lending was negligible.

Thus, in some cases, meaningful policies could result in excess reserves. However, policy does not exert its impact through a rise in inflation expectations. Currently, there is no consensus among scientists about what theory is. However, there is no disputing that anything that cannot explain why it works is not a theory. Therefore, the reflationist price theory cannot be called a theory.

3.4 Policies that Do Not Exist in Mainstream U.S. Economics

3.4.1 Mainstream Economics Changed by the Global Financial Crisis and the BOJ Under Kuroda

Reflationists posit that the monetary policy they propose is the standard in mainstream American economics. However, mainstream economics changed after the 2008 global financial crisis.

Theoretically, the 2008 global financial crisis was impossible in mainstream American economics. Before the financial crisis, Bernanke (e.g., 2002), who was chair of the Federal Reserve during the 2008 financial crisis, and his predecessor Chair Greenspan (e.g., 2008 [2007], pp. 200–202) declared that pricking a bubble with a monetary policy would damage the economy. Instead, they proposed that monetary easing, specifically when the economy deteriorates after a bubble burst, would be sufficient because the economy would recover quickly. Bernanke (2000) said that the BOJ's failure was not to burst the bubble. He criticized the BOJ for not easing monetary policy sufficiently after the bursting of the bubble and leaving deflation unattended. Reflationists in Japan also criticized the BOJ and agreed with Bernanke's criticism of the BOJ at that time.

If his criticism of the BOJ were precise, then even if the U.S. housing bubble burst, thereby creating a financial crisis, the U.S. and other global economies would not be on the verge of collapse as long as Bernanke was easing monetary policy appropriately. It was possible that some sloppy financial institutions, such as Lehman Brothers, would collapse. If his monetary policy had been appropriate, it could not have led to the economic collapse. When financial institutions began to fail in 2008, the U.S. government contained the crisis by injecting public funds into financial institutions. If Bernanke were right, there would be no need for any fiscal action at all. Bernanke himself proved that his criticism of the BOJ was unfounded.

After the crisis, mainstream economists argued that conventional macroeconomics was wrong (e.g., The Economist, 2009). The consensus on measures against bubbles shifted to a classification of bubbles into those accompanied by credit expansion and those not accompanied by credit expansion, and that bubbles should be prevented when accompanied by credit expansion (e.g., Mishkin, 2011b). However, it is debatable if financial regulation is sufficient to prevent a bubble or, as in some cases, monetary policy should be used.

The bursting of Japan's bubble economy in the early 1990s coincided with my graduate school years. When the bubble burst, Mitsuharu Ito[3] taught us that a bubble is not an increase in asset prices, citing Miyazaki's (1992) *Fukugō Fukyō* (*Compound Recession*) and Galbraith's (1988 [1954]) *Great Crash*. In a bubble, some people borrow money and buy assets in anticipation of a rise in asset prices. When the bubble bursts, asset prices fall, but debt does not decrease. Thus, financial institutions collapse due to non-performing loans. Mainstream economics in the U.S. caught up with the levels proposed by Ito and Miyazaki for more than two decades.

Furthermore, despite the Federal Reserve's QE and fiscal stimulus, the recovery of the U.S. economy has been disappointing. This has led to controversy about secular stagnation in the U.S. (e.g., Teulings & Baldwin eds., 2014). The main theme of this debate is not only if the U.S. is in secular stagnation but also if monetary easing will end this stagnation. This indicates that it is no longer the consensus of mainstream American economics after the global financial crisis that monetary easing can easily restore the economy after a bubble burst.

After the global financial crisis, Bernanke (2011, 2012) also said that monetary policy was not a panacea. Nevertheless, he also said that monetary policy can be a powerful tool (Bernanke, 2011). This is a contradiction because a tool that cannot solve economic stagnation is not called a powerful tool. We believe that these contradictory claims are made for organizational defense. The Federal Reserve, led by Bernanke, stated that the economy will recover after the bubble burst as soon as monetary easing is implemented. In reality, however, the bursting of the bubble caused one of the largest financial crises in human history, and the Federal Reserve failed to resolve the secular stagnation that followed. This was a historic debacle. Yet, no amount of monetary easing would solve the secular stagnation. He stated that he was doing all he could but that there are certain limits, which in itself is not wrong.

---

[3] Mitsuharu Ito was my supervisor at university and graduate school, but he had retired from Kyoto University at the time of this lecture.

When the investment bank Lehman Brothers went bankrupt in September 2008, people worldwide wondered why U.S. policymakers allowed the bankruptcy. Policymakers, such as Bernanke in the U.S., responded by saying that they were aware that bankruptcies would trigger crises, but they did not have the authority (e.g., Bernanke et al., 2020, pp. 1–2).

However, the day after the Lehman collapse was the day of the Federal Open Market Committee (FOMC) meeting that set the Federal Reserve's monetary policy. According to the transcript of the Federal Open Market Committee (2008a), several participants approved that allowing Lehman to fail was about re-establishing market discipline. One participant said this judgment was premature, but none directly argued that a historic financial crisis was inevitable. Even the day after the collapse of Lehman, the Federal Reserve, as an organization, did not believe that the collapse of Lehman would lead to the financial crisis that would shake the world. After retiring as chair of the Federal Reserve, Bernanke wrote his memoir. Bernanke (2015, pp. 278–280) also mentions this FOMC but does not indicate that several participants agreed that allowing Lehman to fail was the right strategy. It is unlikely that policymakers, such as Bernanke, would say anything contrary to the facts except to obscure the historic fiasco and use the disaster to expand their powers.

Conversely, Mishkin (2011a, pp. 52–53), one of the governors of the Federal Reserve at the time, admitted that the FOMC had made a mistake in its policy decisions. However, he also stated that the Federal Reserves had no authority. It is true that policymakers had no authority. Hence, after the collapse of Lehman Brothers, policymakers lobbied Congress to enact legislation to bail out financial institutions. This shows that authority can be created by making laws, and the lack of such authority is not a reason in the first place (for the above, see Hattori, 2023, pp. 77–81).

3.4.2 Policies for Lowering Long-Term Interest Rates

As we made clear in Chap. 1, Bernanke (2017, pp. 30–31) also states that the BOJ under Kuroda's monetary policy did not affect either price increases or inflation expectations. Furthermore, Bernanke (2017, p. 31) also shows that there is no basis for the BOJ under Kuroda to shift blame to others. Thus, Bernanke judged that the BOJ under Kuroda had failed to raise the CPI in Japan at least. Examining monetary easing by the BOJ under Kuroda, Gertler (2017) concluded that the argument of attributing monetary policy as the cause of Japan's economic stagnation does not hold. Besides, he argues that monetary easing cannot solve deflation in Japan (the fact that the monetary policy of the reflationists is not the standard policy of Bernanke and other mainstream American monetary policymakers, see also Hattori, 2022, pp. 22–23). If one defines anti-reflationists as those who believe that Japan's deflation cannot be solved by the BOJ alone, then both Bernanke and Gertler have now converted to anti-reflationists.

Bernanke (2022, Chaps. 11 and 12, pp. 281–329) cites QE in the sense of purchasing long-term government bonds, lowering long-term interest rates, and providing forward guidance as unconventional monetary policies adopted by the Federal Reserve after the global financial crisis. The effect is equivalent to a policy rate of 3% in the Fed/U.S. model (Bernanke, 2022, p. 316. See also Bernanke, 2020 for a discussion on the unconventional monetary policy in the U.S. and its impact). Bernanke does not include the QE that the BOJ has conducted since 2001 in the QE here. (The reason will be shown in the next section.) He also noted two types of forward guidance: those that merely forecast and those that involve a commitment.

However, in the first place, it is said that long-term interest rates cannot be controlled from the mainstream view. Theoretically, the long-term interest rate for ten years will be as follows.

$$
\begin{aligned}
&\text{10-Year Long-Term Interest Rate}\\
&\quad = \text{Average of Expected Short-Term Interest}\\
&\qquad \text{rates for 10 years} + \text{Term Premium}\\
&\quad = \text{Average Inflation Expectations for 10 Years}\\
&\qquad + \text{Average of Expected Short-Term Real}\\
&\qquad \text{Interest Rates for 10 Years}\\
&\qquad + \text{Term Premium.}
\end{aligned}
$$

If a borrower continues to refinance a loan with next-day repayment for ten years, it is similar to a 10-year loan. Theoretically, the long-term interest rate is the average of short-term interest rates over ten years. In addition, the nominal interest rate can be decomposed into the inflation rate and the real interest rate. However, as short-term interest rates for the next ten years are not recognized at this point, they are considered a forecast. Moreover, the forecast can go wrong; therefore, a term premium is included as a margin of safety when it is incorrect.

If the central bank purchases a large amount of long-term government bonds, the risk of losses due to price fluctuations of long-term government bonds will decrease because the amount of government bonds held by financial institutions will decline rapidly. The premium will also decline; however, the decline will be limited because the premium on safe government bonds is not large. Consequently, if the expected inflation rate rises and the market expects future short-term interest rates to rise, the market believes that long-term interest rates will also rise. Conversely, the reduction in long-term interest rates indicates that the market deems that the central bank has failed to end deflation.

If the central bank issues forward guidance that short-term interest rates will remain abnormally low for a long period of time, it means that the central bank has admitted that it cannot solve the problem of deflation for a long period of time. If the market really believed this, deflationary expectations would be strengthened. Even more problematic is if the market believes what the BOJ says. As we will show in Sect. 4.3.2, the BOJ under Kuroda continued to forecast that the 2% inflation target could be achieved in the near future. However, these forecasts were always wrong. It would be foolish for anyone to believe the central bank's incorrect forecasts simply because the central bank says so.

Kohn (Kohn and Sack, 2020, p. 449), vice chair of the Federak Reserve during the global financial crisis, wrote: "Asset purchases worked through their effects on the prices of the assets acquired. The amount of high-powered money provided seems, by itself, to have little consequence for inflation or inflation expectations." The vice chair, who implemented the Federal Reserve's QE policy, was also pessimistic about the impact of the QE on inflation, even though the policy had a portfolio rebalancing effect.

3.4.3 Federal Reserve Rejects Quantitative Easing of Japan

After the global financial crisis, the Bernanke-led Federal Reserve is supposed to have implemented three QE programs. However, Bernanke (2022, pp. 282–283) excludes easing particular asset purchases aimed at stabilizing specific financial markets in a narrow sense from QE (This corresponds to the lender of last resort). Besides, he (Bernanke, 2022, p. 282) also excludes QE conducted by the BOJ since 2001. According to him (Bernanke, 2022, pp. 141–144), QE in Japan was based on the concept of monetarism, which is intended to increase the money stock. He then stated that at the FOMC of December 2008, the majority, including Bernanke, did not agree with this BOJ's view. However, he said that as a form of forward guidance, it made sense. He adds that its effectiveness was undermined by the fact that the BOJ officials questioned its efficacy. The controversy on money supply was mentioned earlier. We do not know if Bernanke is aware of this controversy, but he effectively admitted that Okina is correct. In his speech in 2017, Bernanke (2017, p. 24n) said that the Federal Reserve's policy was different from the BOJ's QE since 2001. Bernanke also said that he wanted to identify the program as Credit Easing, but this name never stuck.

Tanaka (2023, pp. 8–9) also rejects the concept of the simple theory of monetary multiplier and monetarism. The simple theory of monetary multiplier holds that when the monetary base increases, banks increase the money stock by increasing their lending. However, in order to increase lending, borrowers must increase their borrowing. To do so, the interest rate must be lowered. However, since interest rates cannot be lowered under zero interest rates, the money stock cannot be increased more.

Bernanke (2020, 2022) does not mention the policy of raising the expected inflation rate by increasing the monetary base, as claimed by reflationists. If a large monetary base supply were able to raise CPI through an increase in the expected inflation rate, then no other unconventional monetary policy would be more effective. However, none of the mainstream American economists, including Bernanke, mention this policy. This shows that the monetary policy that works on inflation expectations, which Iwata and other reflationists have been advocating as common sense, is considered a "nonsense" policy by even mainstream American economists.

At the FOMC of December 2008, QE, which had been implemented in Japan since 2001, was also considered. Mayer (Federal Open Market Committee, 2008b, pp. 17–18), who was on the staff of the Federal Reserve at that time, explained three policies similar to QE. The first is the Japanese-style of the QE, which purchases short-term assets (with near-zero interest rates) and expands the monetary base and reserves. The second is to purchase long-term financial assets and lower long-term interest rates. This policy aimed at a portfolio rebalancing effect. The last is the provision of special liquidity and lending, which is the equivalent of the lender of last resort. As noted earlier, the latter two programs do not necessarily require any increase in the monetary base.

Chair Bernanke (Federal Open Market Committee, 2008b, pp. 25–27) said that the BOJ's QE focuses on central bank debt, especially bank reserves and the monetary base. However, he said that providing a large amount of liquidity to banks did not increase lending or the money stock. Bernanke recommended Mayer's second policy of purchasing long-term financial assets. In the case of the Federal Reserve, it also bought large quantities of mortgage-related securities.

Janet L. Yellen (Federal Open Market Committee, 2008b, p. 46), the then president of the Federal Reserve Bank of San Francisco and Bernanke's successor as Chair of the Federal Reserve and Treasury Secretary in the Biden administration, said that money is linked to prices in the very long term. However, under the liquidity trap, changes in the monetary base have insignificant economic effects in the short and medium term. Moreover, "[a]s Japan found during its quantitative easing program, increasing the size of the monetary base above levels needed to provide ample liquidity to the banking system had no discernible economic effects aside from those associated with communicating the Bank of Japan's commitment to the zero-interest rate policy" (Federal Open Market Committee, 2008b, p. 46).

Laker was relatively favorable toward the BOJ's QE. Bernanke said to Laker that the BOJ had increased the monetary base by a large amount, but there was no increase in M1 or inflation. Laker responded that the BOJ was eager to raise the interest rate because it believed that raising the interest rate would discipline the bank and promote restructuring. Therefore, he did not " view that experience as providing the best evidence about what a firm commitment to preventing deflation could be" (Federal Open Market Committee, 2008b, p. 35). Fundamentally, Laker's response is similar to that of reflationists in Japan. Therefore, some members of the Federal Reserve favored the Japanese-style of QE. However, many members, led by Bernanke and Yellen, believed that the policy of a sharp increase in the monetary base was meaningless because it would not increase lending or money stock. In addition, no one, including Laker, has said that a sharp increase in the monetary base would raise inflation expectations.

As mentioned earlier, Adachi wrote in 2013 that it was common sense that inflation would occur if the BOJ bought JGBs. However, in 2019, Adachi (2019, p. 155) contended that standard macroeconomic models do not consider anything other than the interest rate policy. Therefore, when the policy interest rate reaches zero, monetary policy becomes the limit; nothing can be done after that. Furthermore, he wrote that QE has been implemented, and demonstrating its effectiveness has become a requirement of our times; however, it is difficult to find an effective answer. That is the opposite of what he used to do.

Adachi (2019, pp. 145–149) considered exchanging JGBs with zero interest rates for cash as an exchange of money. Based on this, Adachi created the Divisia index, a theoretical construct to measure monetary easing by considering interest rates on JGBs. The Divisia index rose sharply from 2013 onward but declined sharply in 2016 when long-term government bond yields became negative with the introduction of a negative interest rate policy (briefly discussed in Sect. 4.2.2). After that, it was expected to recover rapidly due to yield curve control (YCC), but it declined sharply in 2019 due to a downturn in long-term government bond yields. Therefore, Adachi stated that monetary easing effects could not be expected much in a situation where yields on long-term JGBs approached zero. We doubt if the Divisia index is an appropriate indicator of monetary easing. However, if this is an appropriate indicator, then when long-term interest rates are negative, the more the BOJ buys JGBs, the tighter the monetary policy. The purchase of JGBs tightens monetary conditions multiplicatively by further lowering negative interest rates.

Since the Meiji Restoration, Japan has learned to build nations from the West. With the U.S. occupation after World War II, Japan became strongly influenced by the U.S. It is common for reform advocates to refer to their reform proposals as the American standard even today. However, the so-called American standard is often quite different from the American original. Monetary policy that works on inflation expectations, as recommended by reflationists, was one among them. Moreover, some reflationist economists are now beginning to reject (at least in part) monetary policies that work on inflation expectations.

3.5 Iwata's "Evidence" Is the Magic of Statistics

3.5.1 Monetary Base and Breakeven Inflation Rate

However, Iwata showed what he called evidence. His *Nippon-Ginkō* (*The Bank of Japan*) (Iwata, 2012, Fig. 4–7, p. 110) shows that changes in the monetary base positively correlate with inflation expectations. Moreover, the number is extremely high, from 0.8 to about 0.9. He used semi-annual data from September 2008, when the global financial crisis began, to February 2012, and the expected inflation rate is the seven-year BEI in his figure. However, he used less than ten data points. Surprisingly, he claims that his theory has been proven with such a small amount of data.

If Iwata's argument were acceptable, the BOJ under Kuroda, which expanded the monetary base much faster than the BOJ under Shirakawa, would raise BEI even further. Figure 3.3 illustrates the relationship between the monetary base and BEI. This figure shows monthly data, and BEI is the 10-year rate. The BOJ releases data on the monetary base at the beginning of the following month. Therefore, in our analysis, we used data from the monetary base one month earlier and BEI data on the 10th day of each month. However, if data were not available for the 10th day, data for the next available day were used. Since October 2013, BEI has been replaced by a new index, namely the inflation-linked bond with a principal guarantee.

The first figure in Fig. 3.3 covers the period from March 2004, when BEI data are available, to March 2013, just before the start of the QQE. The figure distinguishes between the period from September 2008 to February 2012, illustrated in Iwata's Fig. 4–7, and the rest of the period. For the period shown by Iwata, the monetary base and BEI are generally positively correlated even in monthly data. However, for the entire period shown in the figure, it seems doubtful that the correlation is linear. The decisive period was the era of the BOJ under Kuroda. BEI switched to a new index in October 2013. Even if the sharp decline in BEI at that time was excluded as a special factor, the correlation was overall negative since switching to the new index. Contrary to Iwata's assertion, inflation expectations declined as the monetary base increased. However, since mid-2020, the correlation has changed positively.

Why did this happen? As Fig. 2.1 shows, BEI can either rise or fall over a four-year period. Therefore, even if there is no relationship between the monetary base and the BEI, it is possible that over a period of about four years, the BEI will increase as the monetary base expands. Therefore, what Iwata calls evidence is not evidence. On the contrary, if Iwata were correct, it would be impossible for BEI to keep declining at the same time as a large supply of monetary base by the BOJ under Kuroda. This should be logical to anyone who understands the basics of statistics.

In time-series data, when there is a trend of going up or down, correlation occurs even if there is no causal relationship between the two datasets. It is common to use the rate of change or difference in data to eliminate these problems. The third figure illustrates the relationship between the monetary base and BEI based on the year-on-year differences. The figure presents old index and new index separately. By examining this figure, we can observe that there is nothing to do with the two.[4]

In hindsight, Iwata simply assumed that his theory had been proven by using a method and data from a period that produced results consistent with his theory. What Iwata called evidence was the magic of statistics. Ironically, Kuroda and Iwata themselves exposed the flaws in this magic.

Iwata and Harada (2013) claim to have demonstrated that an increase in the monetary base raised inflation expectations using the vector autoregressive (VAR) model. Again, we (Hattori, 2020) show that even if the VAR model and VECM are created using the same variables, the conclusions will be overturned if they are re-estimated, including the period of the BOJ under Kuroda. Moreover, if the estimation period is changed, the impact of the monetary base could be negative. Matsuura and Maeda (2014) also used the VAR model to derive a similar conclusion.

---

[4] Hattori (2022, Table 2, p. 25) clarifies that there is no relationship between the year-on-year change in the monetary base and the year-on-year difference in BEI, and between the month-on-month change in the monetary base and the month-on-month difference in BEI.

Level

March 2004 to March 2013

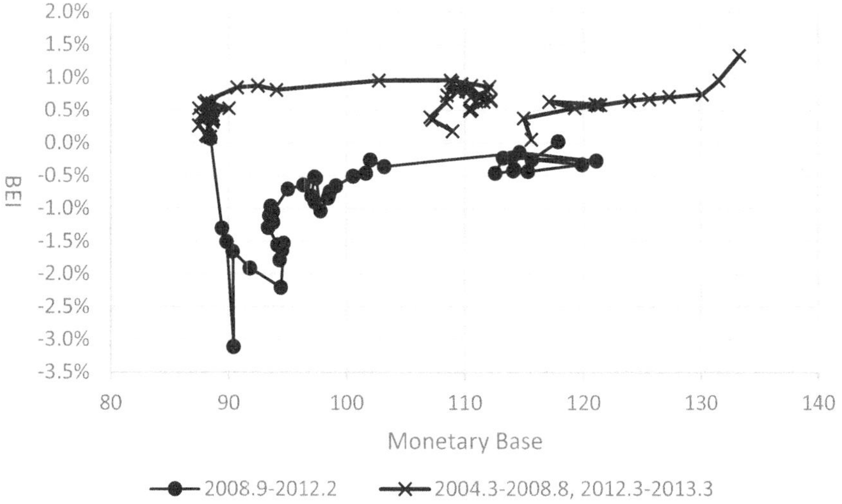

April 2013 to March 2023

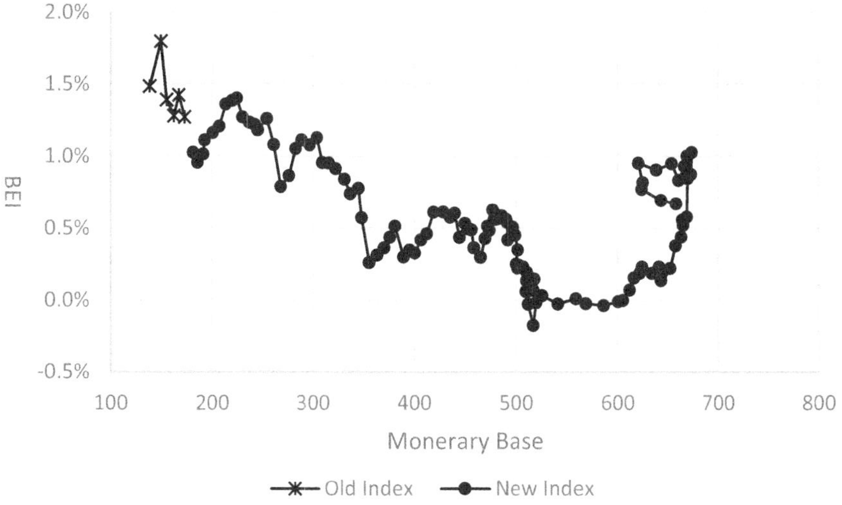

Fig. 3.3 Relationship between the monetary base and the breakeven inflation rate. *Source* The Bank of Japan (2023) and Japan Bond Trading Co., Ltd. (2023). *Note 1* The monetary base is seasonally adjusted one month ago. Those in the figures of year-on-year difference are not seasonally adjusted. The "BEI" is a 10-year BEI. The seven-year BEI used by Iwata was missing some data, so the figure uses the 10-year BEI provided by Japan Bond Trading, Co., Ltd. Data from March 2004. A new index from October 2013. The old index has no principal guarantee for inflation-linked bonds, and the new index has a principal guarantee. BEI data are for the 10th of each month in the figure. However, if data were not available for the 10th, the next available day of data was used. *Note 2* The figure of year-on-year difference omits data for one year after the switch to the new index. *Note 3* Japan Bond Trading Co., Ltd. personally provided us with the data on the BEI. We would like to express our gratitude to Japan Bond Trading Co., Ltd.

Year-On-Year Difference
March 2005–September 2013; October 2014–March 2023

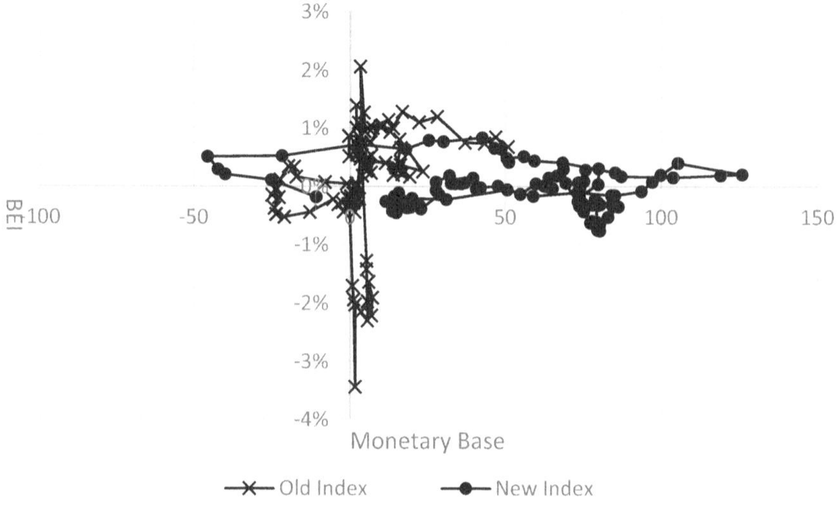

Unit: trillion yen

Fig. 3.3 (continued)

We also mentioned earlier that Iwata (e.g., 2012, pp. 109–112) argued that excess reserves raise inflation expectations. He does not provide the theoretical basis for this argument; instead, he provides evidence that the relationship between excess reserves and BEI is positive. Figure 3.4 illustrates the relationship between excess reserves and BEI in Japan. Again, excess reserves are data from one month ago. Since the 2000s, most of the increase in Japan's monetary base is attributable to excess reserves. Therefore, the relationship between excess reserves and BEI is not much different from the relationship between the monetary base and BEI. As can be seen from the figure, the correlation with BEI was generally positive in the old index, but the correlation with the new index was generally negative. Concisely, when the BOJ was under Kuroda, excess reserves increased, and BEI was lower, shattering Iwata's claim that excess reserves also have the effect of raising inflation expectations.

3.5.2 *Bernanke Did Not Raise Breakeven Inflation Rates*

In "*Nippon-Ginkō* (*The Bank of Japan*)," Iwata (2012, pp. 104–109) assesses that after the global financial crisis, Bernanke, chair of the Federal Reserve during that time, raised inflation expectations by rapidly increasing the monetary base and prevented

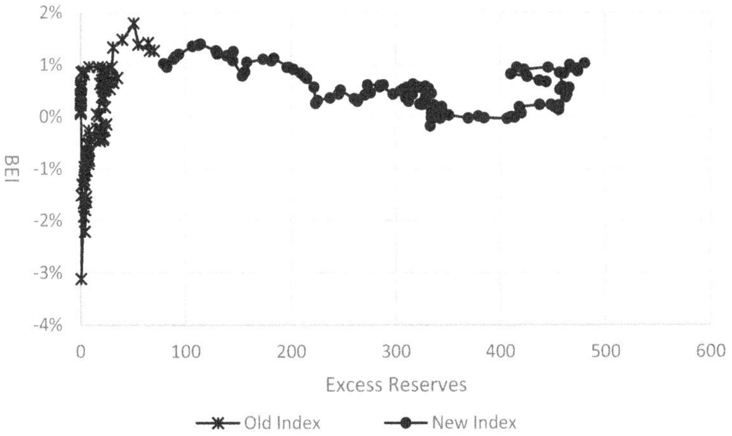

Unit: trillion yen

Fig. 3.4 Relationship between excess reserves and breakeven inflation rate (March 2004–March 2023). *Source* The Bank of Japan (2023) and Japan Bond Trading Co., Ltd. (2023). *Note 1* Excess reserves data are from one month ago. The "BEI" is a 10-year BEI. The seven-year BEI used by Iwata was missing some data, so the figure uses the 10-year BEI provided by Japan Bond Trading Co., Ltd. Data from March 2004. A new index from October 2013. The old index has no principal guarantee for inflation-linked bonds, and the new index has a principal guarantee. BEI data are for the 10th of each month in the figure. However, if data were not available for the 10th, the next available day of data was used. *Note 2* Data on the BEI was provided by Japan Bond Trading Co., Ltd. We would like to express our gratitude to Japan Bond Trading Co., Ltd.

the U.S. from falling into deflation. The proof of this, as in the case of Japan, is that in the U.S., seven-year BEI rose alongside an increase in the monetary base, according to several semi-annual data. However, if the Federal Reserve intended to increase the expected inflation rate through a massive supply of monetary base, it would have said so. In fact, the parties involved (at least as far as we know) deny this.

Bernanke's so-called QE was implemented thrice: from November 2008 to June 2010, November 2010 to June 2011, and from September 2012 to October 2014. However, in September 2008, when the financial crisis broke out, the Federal Reserve rapidly increased its monetary base by acting as the lender of last resort. Iwata believes that the sharp increase in the monetary base began in September 2008.

Figure 3.5 illustrates the relationship between the U.S. monetary base and the BEI from September 2008 to October 2014. In this figure, the monetary base is from one month ago. In the U.S., BEI declined sharply after the global financial crisis. However, once the financial crisis subsided, BEI started to rise. As the monetary base increased rapidly due to the QE, the correlation between the two is positive if we consider this part alone. However, BEI peaked in early 2013 and declined thereafter.

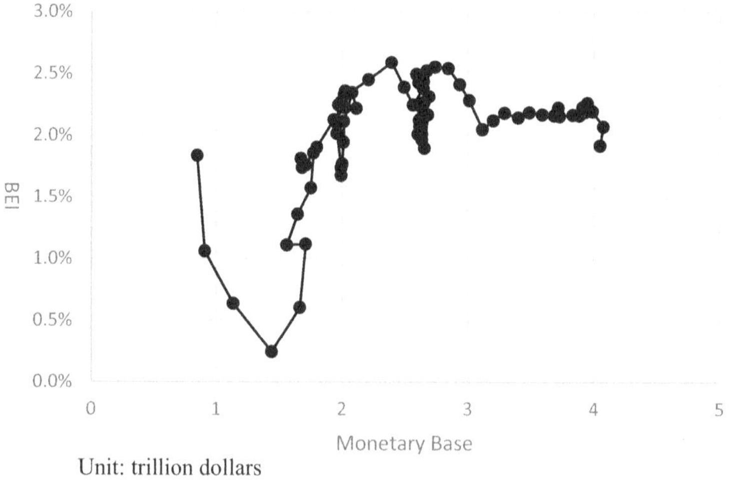

Fig. 3.5 Relationship between monetary base and breakeven inflation in the U.S. (September 2008–October 2014). *Source* Federal Reserve Bank of St. Louis (2023). *Note* Monetary base is seasonal adjustment value one month ago. BEI denotes 10-year BEI, monthly average

After 2013, the correlation is thus negative. We can conclude that Iwata's argument does not hold for the U.S. if the period is extended.[5]

We mentioned in Sect. 3.4.3 that Bernanke and other officials of the Federal Reserve did not believe that an increase in the monetary base would raise inflation expectations. The so-called QE in the U.S. was not intended to raise inflation expectations. As mentioned earlier, Kohn himself stated that the effect of the so-called QE on inflation was small. The results of this book support the assertions of policymakers at the Federal Reserve after the global financial crisis of 2008.

Firstly, both in Japan and the U.S., BEI fell sharply after the global financial crisis. Naturally, low BEI will rise when the financial crisis subsides. If Iwata's theory were correct, BEI would continue to rise if the large supply of the monetary base had continued. In fact, BEI in both Japan and the U.S. reversed. If the data are analyzed correctly, Iwata's theory is disproved in Japan and the U.S.

[5] Hattori (2022, Table 3, p. 29) clarifies that there is no relationship between the year-on-year change in the monetary base and the year-on-year difference in BEI, and between the month-on-month change in the monetary base and the month-on-month difference in BEI also in the U.S.

3.6 Assumptions that Have No Theoretical Basis or Evidence

Iwata argued that a large supply of the monetary base and excess reserves would raise inflation expectations. This chapter proves that there is no theoretical basis or evidence to support his claim.

First, Iwata and other reflationists could not theoretically explain why a large supply of the monetary base and excess reserves raise inflation expectations. The reflationist theory cannot explain its theoretical basis. Such a theory does not deserve to be acknowledged as a theory. Furthermore, reflationists argue that their theories and policies are standard for mainstream American economics. These claims are also unfounded. No mainstream economist in the U.S. alleges that increasing the monetary base would raise inflation expectations. Bernanke's so-called QE was not intended to raise inflation expectations through a large supply of the monetary base. Finally, Iwata's alleged evidence was a mere result of taking data from a period consistent with Iwata's claims. Coincidentally, using data from the time of the BOJ under Kuroda, the result is contrary to Iwata's claims.

After the global financial crisis and the failure of the BOJ under Kuroda, mainstream U.S. economists now understand that there is a limit to monetary policy: the lower bound of interest rates. Even Bernanke (2023, p. 12) now clearly states that the BOJ is not capable of overcoming deflation. However, the fact that monetary policy cannot function under the liquidity trap has already been pointed out by Keynes (1973 [1936]) in his *General Theory*. It is a historical necessity that a theory devoid of a theoretical basis or evidence will fail.

References

In Japanese

Adachi, S. (2013). Kin'yū Seisaku Kettei Purosesu to Kin'yū Seisaku Ronsō no Keifu (The genealogy of the monetary policy decision-making process and the monetary policy debate). In K. Iwata (Ed.), *Mazu Defure wo Tomeyo: Nihon Keizai Saisei (Stop deflation first: Revitalization of the Japanese economy)* (pp. 71–125). Nikkei Publishing.

Adachi, S. (2019). *Shōhi Zei 10% go no Nihon Keizai (Japanese economy after 10% consumption tax)*. Subarusha.

Bernanke, B. S. (2023). Nihon Go Ban e no Jobun (Preface to the Japanese edition). *21 Seiki no Kin'yū Seisaku: Dai Infure kara Korona Kiki made no Kyōkun (Japanese edition of 21st century monetary policy: The Federal Reserve from the great inflation to COVID-19)* (pp. 7–12). Nikkei Business Publications and Nikkei Publishing.

Director General for Economic Research, Cabinet Office, Japan (Ed.). (2014). *Nihon Keizai, 2013–2014: Defure Dakkyaku e no Tatakai, Tsugi Naru Stēji e (Japanese economy, 2013–2014: The struggle to overcome deflation, moving to the next stage)*. Nikkei Printing.

Economic and Social Research Institute, Cabinet Office, Japan. (2023). Consumer confidence survey. https://www.esri.cao.go.jp/jp/stat/shouhi/shouhi.html

Hattori, S. (2020). Manetarī Bēsu to Infure Yosō: Refure ha Keizai gaku no Gensō (Monetary base and inflation expectations: Delusion of reflationists). *Doshisha Shogaku, 71*(5), 145–179.
Hattori, S. (2022). Kuroda Nichigin wa Naze Defure Dakkyaku ni Shippai Shita no ka (Why the Bank of Japan under Governor Haruhiko Kuroda failed to overcome deflation). *Doshisha Shogaku, 74*(3), 1–41.
Hattori, S. (2023). *Gurōbaru Kin'yū Shihon Shugi no Kiki: Kommei no Sekai to Keizai gaku (Crisis of the global financial capitalism: The world in turmoil and economics).* Koyo Shobo.
Ito, O. (2016). *Nihon Keizai "Warui Kinkō" no Shōtai: Shakai Heisoku no Wana wo Yomi Toku (The true nature of the Japanese Economy's "bad equilibrium": Deciphering the social blockage trap).* Akashi Shoten.
Ito, O. (2022). *Baburu go no Kin'yū Kiki Taiō: Zen Kiseki, 1990–2005 (Responses to financial crisis after the bubble: The complete trajectory, 1990–2005).* Yuhikaku Publishing.
Iwata, K. (1993). *Kin'yū Seisaku no Keizai gaku: "Nichigin Riron" no Kenshō (Economics of monetary policy: An examination of the Bank of Japan's theory).* Nikkei, Inc.
Iwata, K. (2002). Yoshō Keisei ni Hatarakikakeru Kin'yū Seisaku wo: Komiya Rombun Hihan (1) (Monetary policy working on the formation of the inflation expectations: A critique of Komiya (1)). In R. Komiya & Center for Japan Economic Research (Eds.), *Kin'yū Seisaku Rongi no Sōten: Nichigin Hihan to sono Hanron (Issues in the monetary policy debate: Criticism of the Bank of Japan and its rebuttal)* (pp. 391–418). Nikkei, Inc.
Iwata, K. (2009). *Sekai Dōji Fukyō (Simultaneous world recession).* Chikuma Shobo.
Iwata, K. (2012). *Nippon Ginkō: Defure no Ban'nin (The Bank of Japan: Keeper of deflation).* Nikkei Publishing.
Iwata, K. (2013a). *Rifure wa Tadashii: Abenomikusu de Fukkatsu Suru Nihon Keizai (Reflation is correct: The Japanese economy revived by Abenomics).* PHP Institute.
Iwata, K., & Harada, Y. (2013). Kin'yū Seisaku to Seisan: Yosō Infure ritsu no Keiro (Monetary policy and production: A channel of expected inflation rate). [Working Paper, No. J1202] Waseda Institute of Political Economy, Waseda University, March.
Matsuura, K., & Maeda, K. (2014). Manetarī Bēsu to Keizai (Monetary base and macro economy). *The Hiroshima Economic Review, 38*(1), 47–76.
Miyazaki, Y. (1992). *Fukugō Fukyō: Posuto Baburu no Shohōsen wo Motomete (Compound recession: In search of prescriptions for the post-bubble).* Chuokouronsha.
Noguchi, A. (2021). *Han Kinshuku no Keizai gaku (The economics of anti-austerity).* Toyo Keizai.
Okina, K. (1993). *Kin'yū Seisaku: Chūō Ginkō no Shiten to Sentaku (Monetary policy: Perspectives and choices of a central bank).* Toyo Keizai.
Suzuki, A. (2022). *Defure to no 20 Nen Sensō (The 20-year war against deflation).* Kinzai Institute for Financial Affairs.
Tanaka, T. (2023). *Kin'yū Seisaku no Dai Tenkan: Chūō Ginkō no Mosaku to Kadai (The great transformation of monetary policy: Quests and challenges for central banks).* Keio University Press.
The Bank of Japan. (2016a). Sōsai Kisha Kaiken Yōshi (Summary of the Governor's Press Conference, September 21). September 23.
Watanabe, T. (2022). *Bukka to wa Nani ka? (What are prices?).* Kodansha.
Yoshikawa, H. (2009). Defrēshion to Kin'yū Seisaku (Deflation and monetary policy). In H. Yoshikawa (Ed.), *Defure Keizai to Kin'yū Seisaku (Deflationary economy and monetary policy).* In Economic and Social Research Institute, Cabinet Office, Japan Supervision. *Baburu/Defure Ki no Nihon Keizai to Keizai Seisaku (Economy and economic policy in the Japanese economy during the bubble and deflationary period)* (Vol. 2, pp. 117–154). Keio University Press.
Yoshikawa, H. (2013). *Defrēshon: "Nihon no Mansei Byō" no Zembō wo Kaimei Suru (Deflation: Elucidating the whole picture of "chronic disease in Japan").* Nikkei Publishing.

In English

Bernanke, B. S. (2000). Japanese monetary policy: A case of self-induced paralysis? In R. Mikitani & A. S. Posen (Eds.), *Japan's financial crisis and its parallels to U.S. experience* (pp. 149–166). Institution for International Economics.
Bernanke, B. S. (2002). Asset-price 'bubbles' and monetary policy. Before the New York Chapter of the National Association for Business Economics, October 15.
Bernanke, B. S. (2011). Economic outlook and recent monetary policy actions. Testimony before the Joint Economic Committee, US Congress, October 4.
Bernanke, B. S. (2012). US monetary policy and international implications. At a high-level seminar 'Challenges of the global financial system: Risks and governance under evolving globalization'. Sponsored by the Bank of Japan and the International Monetary Fund, October 14.
Bernanke, B. S. (2015). *The courage to act: A memoir of a crisis and its aftermath.* W.W. Norton and Company.
Bernanke, B. S. (2017). The Mayekawa lecture: Some reflections on Japanese monetary policy. *Monetary and Economic Studies, 35*, 23–37.
Bernanke, B. S. (2020). The new tools of monetary policy. *American Economic Review, 110*(4), 943–983.
Bernanke, B. S. (2022). *21st century monetary policy: The Federal Reserve from the great inflation to COVID-19.* W. W. Norton.
Bernanke, B. S., Geithner, T. F., & Paulson, H. M., Jr. (2020). The financial crisis and its lessons for the future. In B. S. Bernanke, T. F. Geithner, & H. M. Paulson, Jr. (Eds.), *First responders: Inside the U.S. strategy for fighting the 2007–2009 global financial crisis* (pp. 1–48). Yale University Press.
Federal Open Market Committee. (2008a). Transcript. September 16.
Federal Open Market Committee. (2008b). Transcript. December 15–16.
Federal Reserve Bank of St. Louis. (2023). FRED. https://fred.stlouisfed.org/
Friedman, M. (1991). The counter-revolution in monetary theory. In M. Friedman (Ed.), *Monetarist economics* (pp. 1–20). Basil Blackwell.
Friedman, M., & Schwartz, A. J. (1963). *A monetary history of the United States, 1867–1960.* Princeton University Press.
Galbraith, J. K. (1988 [1955]). *The great crash, 1929.* Houghton Mifflin.
Gertler, M. (2017). Rethinking the power of forward guidance: Lessons from Japan. *Monetary and Economic Studies, 35*, 39–57.
Greenspan, A. (2008 [2007]). *The age of turbulence: Adventures in a new world.* Penguin Books.
Iwata, K. (2013b). Quantitative and qualitative monetary easing and its transmission mechanism: Logic behind the first arrow. Speech at a meeting held by the Kyoto Chamber of Commerce and Industry (KCCI), August 28.
Japan Bond Trading Co., Ltd. (2023). BEI rate. We were personally provided with the data.
Keynes, J. M. (1973 [1936]). *The general theory of employment, interest and money, the collected writings of John Maynard Keynes* (Vol. VII). Macmillan.
King, M. (2018). Money: How could economists do without it. In P. Hartmann, H. Huang, & D. Schoenmaker (Eds.), *The changing fortunes of central banking* (pp. 21–31). Cambridge University Press.
Kohn, D., & Sack, B. (2020). Monetary policy during the financial crisis. In B. S. Bernanke, T. F. Geithner, & H. M. Paulson, Jr. (Eds.), *First responders: Inside the U.S. strategy for fighting the 2007–2009 global financial crisis* (pp. 421–450). Yale University Press.
Krugman, P. R. (1998). It's Baaack: Japan's slump and the return of the liquidity trap. *Brookings Papers on Economic Activity, (2)*, 137–205.
Krugman, P. (2014). Four observations on secular stagnation. In C. Teulings & R. Baldwin (Eds.), *Secular stagnation: Facts, causes and cures* (pp. 61–68). CEPR Press.
Kuroda, H. (2017). The role of expectations in monetary policy: Evolution of theories and the Bank of Japan's experience. Speech at the University of Oxford, June 8.

Mishkin, F. S. (2011a). Over the cliff: From the subprime to the global financial crisis. *Journal of Economic Perspectives, 25*(1), 49–70.
Mishkin, F. S. (2011b). Monetary policy strategy: Lessons from the crisis. [NBER Working Paper, No, 16755], February.
Statistics Bureau of Japan, Ministry of Internal Affairs and Communications. (2023). Consumer price index. https://www.stat.go.jp/english/data/cpi/index.htm
Summers, L. (2015). Larry Summers: Where Paul Krugman and I differ on secular stagnation. *The Washington Post*, November 2.
Teulings, C., & Baldwin, R. (Eds.). (2014). *Secular stagnation: Facts, causes and cures.* CEPR Press.
The Bank of Japan. (2016b). Comprehensive assessment: Developments in economic activity and prices as well as policy effects since the introduction of quantitative and qualitative monetary easing (QQE): The background. September 21.
The Bank of Japan. (2023). BOJ time-series data search. https://www.stat-search.boj.or.jp/index_en.html
The Economist. (2009). What went wrong with economics: And how the discipline should change to avoid the mistakes of the past. 392(8640), 9–10.
Wakatabe, M. (2022). The future of monetary policy: Lessons from the history of monetary economics. Keynote speech at the 38th annual meeting of the Japan Association of Business Cycle Studies, December 3.
Woodford, M. (2012). Methods of policy accommodation at the interest-rate. September 16 (Revised draft of a paper presented at the Federal Reserve Bank of Kansas City Symposium on 'The changing policy landscape', Jackson Hole, Wyoming, August 31).

Chapter 4
The Bank of Japan Under Kuroda Has Abandoned the Reflationist Theory

Abstract Although the Bank of Japan (BOJ) under Kuroda initiated quantitative and qualitative easing policy, it failed to achieve its inflation target. While reflationist theory requires a more massive supply of monetary base, the BOJ reduced this supply and ceased its commitment to the inflation target. Instead, the BOJ introduced yield curve control, in which the monetary base and the amount of long-term government bonds purchased are supplied in response to demand under a fixed interest rate, which reflationists have criticized, calling it "the BOJ theory." Kikuo Iwata, the deputy governor of the BOJ, criticized the BOJ's explanation that deflation was caused by something other than monetary policy, calling it "the BOJ's theory of deflation." However, Iwata and the BOJ under Kuroda pin the reason for the BOJ's inability to achieve the inflation target on everything but monetary policy. In effect, both the theories and the policies of the reflationists have been abandoned. Nevertheless, to save their positions and reputations, the BOJ under Kuroda and reflationists pretended that monetary policy based on the reflationist theory continued and the Japanese economy was on its way out of deflation. Thus, wrong policy gave way to deceptive policy.

Keywords Abenomics · The Bank of Japan under Kuroda · Deflation in Japan · Quantitative and qualitative monetary easing · Japanese-style inflation target · Yield curve control · The Bank of Japan's theory · The Bank of Japan's theory of deflation · Reflationists · Kikuo Iwata

4.1 Introduction

The Bank of Japan under Kuroda has supplied a large amount of the monetary base through its quantitative and qualitative monetary easing (QQE) policy since April 2013. Ten years later, Kuroda stepped down without achieving the inflation target, excluding imported inflation. Inflation expectations also reversed midway. Based on the reflationist theory, the Bank of Japan (BOJ) under Kuroda should have supplied an even larger monetary base to rebuild the reflation regime emphasized by reflationists.

S. Hattori, *Why the Bank of Japan Has Failed to Conquer Deflation in Japan*,
https://doi.org/10.1007/978-981-97-9408-9_4

However, the supply of a large amount of the monetary base requires the purchase of a large amount of Japanese government bonds (JGBs). Under Kuroda, the amount of JGBs to be purchased exceeded to an extent that made it impossible to find JGB sellers. Thus, the massive supply of the monetary base—one of the policy tools of the reflationists—ended.

In September 2016, the BOJ under Kuroda adopted a new monetary policy: yield curve control (YCC). Under this policy, long-term interest rates would be kept close to zero. Reflationists such as Kikuo Iwata (e.g., 1993) and Noguchi (2021, pp. 222–237) criticized the BOJ's monetary policy framework until Governor Shirakawa, calling it "the BOJ's theory," which supplies a monetary base in response to demand. However, the YCC accommodates both the amount of JGBs purchased and the monetary base supplied according to the sales of JGBs under fixed short- and long-term interest rates, ultimately reviving the much-criticized the BOJ's theory. Iwata (2018b, p. 419) also acknowledges that YCC does not have the power to raise inflation expectations—a de facto declaration of defeat.

Upon failing to achieve its inflation target, the BOJ under Kuroda was caught in a vicious cycle of postponing the target and failing to achieve the postponed target. These repeated postponements attracted ridicule against Abenomics and the BOJ under Kuroda. Ultimately, the BOJ stopped announcing the outlook for achieving the inflation target to avoid accountability. This marks the end of another policy tool used by reflationists.

Before becoming the deputy governor, Iwata criticized the BOJ's theory of deflation, which stated that the cause of deflation was something other than monetary policy. Upon his appointment as deputy governor, Iwata declared that he would take responsibility for any failure of the BOJ to overcome deflation. Nevertheless, when failure did strike, Iwata and the BOJ under Kuroda blamed all else above monetary policy, reviving the BOJ's theory of deflation, which Iwata had once criticized.

In about three years, monetary policy based on the reflationist theory was abandoned. However, admitting that policies advocated by reflationists have failed undermines the positions and reputations of the BOJ under Kuroda as well as the reflationists. Despite abandoning the reflationist theory, both the BOJ under Kuroda and reflationists continued to justify the existing monetary policy on the basis of the policy and theory they had once criticized.

The remainder of this chapter is structured as follows. Section 4.2 addresses how the BOJ was no longer able to supply a large amount of the monetary base and eventually introduced the YCC. Section 4.3 explains how the inflation target could not be achieved for any length of time, and in response, the BOJ stopped announcing its inflation target outlook. Section 4.4 reveals that, even after abandoning the monetary policy advocated by reflationists, the BOJ and the reflationists blamed the failure on everything but monetary policy and continued to tout the so-called success of reflationist policy. Finally, Sect. 4.5 concludes the chapter.

4.2 Stealth Tapering

4.2.1 *"Kuroda Bazooka" Runs Out of Its Bullets*

The reflationists' tools for overcoming deflation were Japanese-style inflation targeting and the massive supply of the monetary base. Initially, the BOJ under Kuroda stated that the monetary base would increase at an annual pace of about ¥60 trillion to ¥70 trillion, and the amount of outstanding long-term JGBs would increase at a yearly pace of about ¥50 trillion. As the inflation rate began to decline after the consumption tax hike in April 2014, the BOJ under Kuroda started to rapidly increase the monetary base and the amount of outstanding long-term JGBs to about ¥80 trillion per year in October. The average remaining maturity of long-term JGBs was also extended from seven to ten years. Until the first half of 2016, these measures were also implemented in practice.

Figure 4.1 shows the increase (year-on-year difference) in the monetary base and the BOJ's holdings of some assets, such as long-term JGBs. As Fig. 4.1 illustrates, the increase in the monetary base and purchases of long-term JGBs had been proceeding as announced. However, the pace of increase in both the monetary base and outstanding JGBs began to slow down in 2016—this change might not have been noticeable at first, but it became apparent in 2017. By the end of 2019, the pace of increase was less than ¥20 trillion per year for both.

By the end of 2018, the Japanese economy entered a recession, and in 2019, it was in the midst of a recession. Harada (2021, pp. 18–21), then a member of the Policy Board, writes in his post-retirement memoir *Defure to Tatakau* (*Fighting Deflation*) that the rate of increase in the monetary base affects nominal GDP growth with a lag.

This claim by Harada is itself questionable. Figure 4.2 illustrates the growth rates of the monetary base, nominal GDP, and real GDP. The growth rate of the monetary base is the rate from four quarters before. At first glance, it appears that the growth rate of the monetary base and nominal GDP are not linked. The linkage between the rate of increase in the monetary base and real GDP is even weaker. The figure also illustrates the real GDP growth rate of the United States (U.S.). The figure shows that Japan's real GDP growth rate is much more closely related to the U.S. real GDP growth rate. Given the difference in the size of the economies and the low dependence of the U.S. on exports to Japan, the impact of Japan's economic situation on the U.S. is unlikely to be very large. Furthermore, the global economy may affect both Japan and the U.S. Given the magnitude of the correlation, one could conclude that the economic situation in the U.S. and the world is far more important than the supply of the monetary base by the BOJ.

Even more problematic was the situation after 2014. The growth rate of the monetary base peaked at over 50% in the first quarter of 2014, followed by a sharp decline. One factor was the sharp increase in the denominator balance owing to the large supply of monetary base. Thereafter, the numerator also declined owing to a decrease in the supply of monetary base. In conjunction, nominal and real GDP growth rates fell, and the Japanese economy entered a recession in 2018. From the first quarter

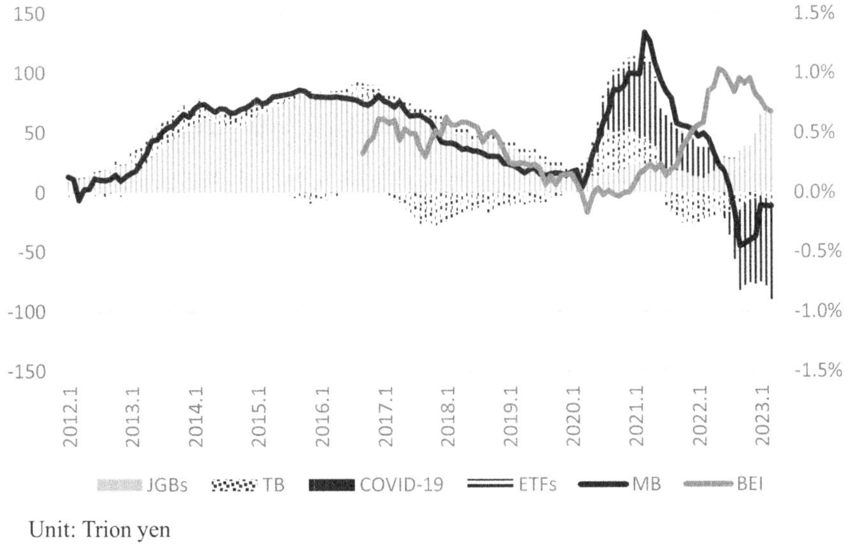

Fig. 4.1 Increase in the monetary base and assets of the BOJ (January 2012 to March 2023). *Source* The Bank of Japan (2023) and Japan Bond Trading, Co. Ltd. (2023). *Note 1* year-on-year difference except BEI. *Note 2* "MB" is monetary base. "TB" is treasury discount bills. "COVID-19" is the special funds-supplying operations to facilitate financing in response to the COVID-19. "ETFs" are exchange-traded funds. "BEI" stands for 10-year BEI. Data for the 10-day period is used in the figure. If there is no data for the 10th, the next available date is used. It has been indicated since September 2016. Data on the BEI were provided by Japan Bond Trading Co., Ltd. We would like to express our gratitude to Japan Bond Trading Co., Ltd

of 2015 to the fourth quarter of 2019, we observed a high correlation between the growth rate of the monetary base and the growth rate of nominal GDP or real GDP; however, given the paucity of data, this high correlation cannot be relied upon at all.

We believe that the sluggish monetary base growth rate since 2015 and the decline in the economic growth rate or the plunge into recession since 2018 have no causal relationship. Therefore, we also do not believe that the BOJ under Kuroda is responsible. However, according to Harada's argument, the post-2018 entry into recession was caused by the BOJ under Kuroda, which decided to reduce the growth rate of the monetary base. Inexplicably, Harada (2021, pp. 18–21) not only fails to criticize the BOJ under Kuroda for adopting policies contrary to his theoretical claims and plunging the Japanese economy into recession but also claims that the BOJ under Kuroda revived the Japanese economy.

Table 4.1 presents the cumulative transactions of JGBs and fiscal investment and loan program (FILP) bonds[1] from the second quarter of 2013 to the first quarter of 2023, as well as their outstanding assets and liabilities in the first quarter of 2023. In the ten years since 2013, the Japanese government has issued about ¥300 trillion of JGBs and FILP bonds in net. However, the cumulative purchases of JGBs by the

[1] FILP bonds are government bonds issued to finance the Fiscal Investment and Loan Program.

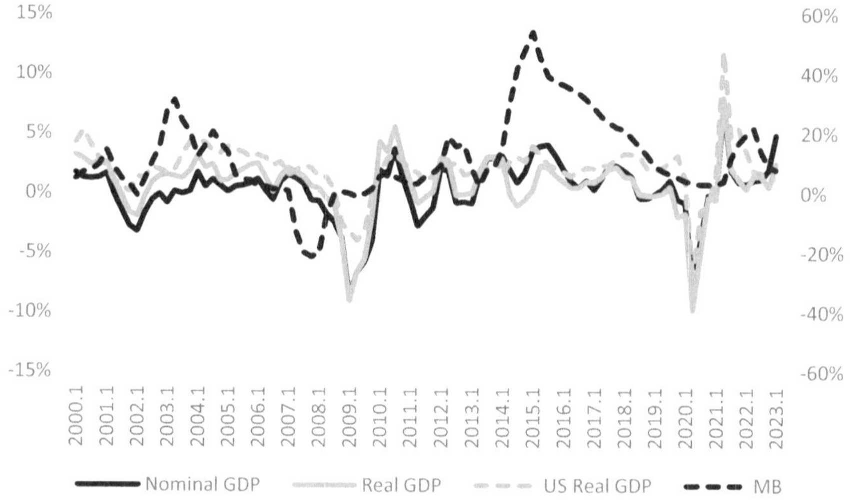

Fig. 4.2 Growth rates of monetary base, nominal GDP, and real GDP (2000.Q1 to 2023.Q1). *Source* Economic and social research institute, cabinet office, Japan (2023b), the Bank of Japan (2023) and Bureau of Economic Analysis, the U.S. (2023). *Note 1* "MB" is indicated on the left-hand side axis, while others are indicated on the right-hand side. *Note 2* Year-on-year growth rate. *Note 3* "MB" is the monetary base. It was four quarters ago

BOJ amounted to ¥480 trillion—far more than the amount issued by the government. However, depository institutions had sold over ¥190 trillion of JGBs. Per statistics, the BOJ had increased the monetary base by purchasing JGBs issued by the government and those held by depository institutions. In reality, the BOJ did not purchase JGBs from the government directly; instead, financial institutions bought JGBs issued by the government and then resold them to the BOJ.

Insurance and pension funds also hold a large amount of long-term JGBs and FILP bonds. However, during the BOJ under Kuroda, insurance and pension funds

Table 4.1 Net purchases and assets in government bonds and fiscal investment and loan program bonds

	Central government	Bank of Japan	Depository institutions	Insurance and pension fund	Others
Net purchases	(Net issuances) 302.1	476.3	−194.2	22.9	−7.5
Assess	(Net debts) 977.2	576.1	92.3	238.6	70.3

Unit trillion yen

Source The Bank of Japan (2023)

Note "Net purchases" are the sum of those from the second quarter of 2013 to the first quarter of 2023. "Net purchases" are the purchase minus redemption minus sale. "Net issuances" of the central government are issuances minus redemptions minus its own purchases. "Assets" are the amount held at the end of March 2023. "Net debts" of government are debts minus its own holdings

increased their holdings slightly. If the BOJ is not expected to purchase long-term JGBs from sources other than depository institutions, the BOJ would be able to purchase only ¥90 trillion plus the newly issued amount. The BOJ might even be able to buy in large quantities for two or three years. However, there was little prospect of overcoming deflation within two or three years. The more the BOJ proceeded with the large-scale purchases of long-term JGBs in accordance with the reflationist theory, the more the massive supply of the monetary base that the reflationists had advocated would come closer to its end.

In 2016, Kazumasa Iwata et al. eds. (2016, pp. 85–100) revealed that, if the current trend continued, JGB purchases would reach a dead end by mid-2017. From April 2015, Kiuchi (2015, p. 10–11), a member of the policy board at the time, proposed to slow the pace of increase in the monetary base and the amount outstanding long-term JGBs to about ¥45 trillion per year. He continued to propose the same until his last monetary policy meeting in July 2017, but all of them were rejected. Before his retirement, the supply of the monetary base began to decline in practice, and in December 2017, the increase in the monetary base compared with the same month of the previous year declined to ¥43 trillion. The BOJ effectively adopted the proposal to oppose the reflationists' policies while officially rejecting it. When the BOJ under Kuroda launched the QQE policy, it was called the "Kuroda Bazooka" because of its enormous scale, but it also ultimately ran out of "bullets" (see also, Hattori, 2017, pp. 117–122). By the time the COVID-19 pandemic spread in 2020, this situation changed temporarily, as discussed in Sect. 4.2.6.

4.2.2 From Negative Interest Rate Policy to Yield Curve Control

The BOJ under Kuroda introduced a negative interest rate policy in February 2016 as an alternative to the QQE policy. Current accounts at the BOJ accumulated by banks do not normally bear interest. However, in October 2008, the BOJ paid interest of 0.1% on excess reserves (no interest is paid on the legal reserves) to prevent interest rates in the interbank market from falling too low. This decision was also meant to facilitate the BOJ's purchases of JGBs by making it possible to profit from the current accounts at the BOJ that were accumulated as proceeds from the sale of JGBs.

However, in February 2016, the BOJ divided the current account of the BOJ into three categories and set interest rates of 0.1% (basic balance), 0% (macro-added balance), and −0.1% (policy-rate balance). By lowering interest rates to negative, the BOJ sought to encourage banks to use their current accounts for lending and securities investment. For this purpose, it is sufficient to have a negative interest rate only on a marginal portion. Conversely, if the interest rate were set to negative to the whole excess reserves, it would put pressure on financial institutions' profits. Thus, such a decision was avoided. Given that interest has been paid to excess reserves since October 2008, the BOJ decided to pay interest on this part as before.

The monetary policy advocated by reflationists was to raise inflation expectations through a large supply of the monetary base. However, owing to the impossibility of supplying a large amount of the monetary base, the monetary policy advocated by the reflationists was abandoned within three years. The BOJ under Kuroda supplied a large amount of the monetary base only because there was little room for interest rate cuts. While some negative interest rates are possible, significant negative interest rates are impossible; a negative interest rate policy would have stalled sooner or later.

The negative interest rate policy also turned negative interest rates on long-term JGBs. Long-term JGBs are stable investment destinations for mutual funds. Some mutual funds were suspended because they were not profitable. In addition, banks profit by borrowing money in the short term and lending in the long term. The decline in long-term interest rates further pressured banks, which had already undergone poor profits. Therefore, financial institutions did not receive the negative interest rate policy well. On the televised NHK *Supesharu* (NHK *Documentary*), Iwata (Nihon Hōsō Kyōkai, 2023) candidly admitted that the negative interest rate policy was a failure.

In September, the BOJ under Kuroda introduced YCC and an inflation-overshooting commitment (forward guidance) as new policies. Forward guidance is a policy that enhances the effectiveness of monetary policy by referring to future economic conditions and monetary policy. What the BOJ made in September 2016 was an overshooting commitment. Specifically, to raise inflation expectations, even if the inflation target of 2% is achieved in the future, monetary easing will continue until the 2% target stabilizes. However, the BOJ under Kuroda promised to ease monetary policy until the inflation target was achieved. The problem was that this promise had not been fulfilled. What the BOJ should really be thinking about is what it should do to achieve the target and what it should do after achieving it would be something to think about after achieving it. Eventually, the BOJ under Kuroda did not achieve its inflation target, and there is no guarantee that Kuroda's successor, Ueda, will adhere to the Kuroda-era decisions. In addition, there is no guarantee that the BOJ under Ueda will achieve the target.

YCC is a policy measure to control both short- and long-term interest rates. Specifically, the long-term interest rate should be kept near zero. As mentioned in Sect. 3.2.2, Woodford (2012, p. 53) believes that policy for lowering long-term interest rates is different from quantitative easing (QE) policy because the former can be done without an increase in the monetary base. It can also be achieved by institutions other than the BOJ—that is, it is a type of policy-based finance. We noted in Sect. 2.2.2 that Iwata had argued against the BOJ engaging in policy-based finance. We also noted in Sect. 3.4.2 that, regarding the so-called QE in the U.S. that was intended to lower long-term interest rates, the then Federal Reserve Vice Chair Kohn (Kohn & Sach, 2020, p. 449) said that the QE raised asset prices but had little effect on inflation expectations and inflation.

After stepping down as deputy governor of the BOJ, Iwata (2018b, p. 419) stated that the YCC was the best decision of the BOJ but admitted that it would not boost inflation expectations. Reflationists such as Iwata initially argued that monetary policy could be made effective through inflation expectations, only to admit that no such policy exists—a de facto declaration of defeat.

4.2.3 "Tenshin" (Change of Course) by the BOJ Under Kuroda

After the introduction of YCC, the pace of the purchases of JGBs and supplies of the monetary base slowed down further. This is not surprising because the real purpose of its introduction was a slowdown. In September 2016, the BOJ under Kuroda raised long-term interest rates from negative to near zero. Monetary easing continues, as both short-term and long-term interest rates are almost zero, which is a historic low, and the increase in the monetary base of over ¥10 trillion per year is also large. Nevertheless, reducing the supply of the monetary base and raising long-term interest rates is at least tapering of monetary easing. However, at a press conference, Kuroda (The Bank of Japan, 2016a, p. 3) stated, "Under the new policy framework, the Bank of Japan will pursue more aggressive monetary easing than before to achieve the 2% 'price stability target.'" Nakaso (2022, pp. 521–524), who supported Kuroda along with Iwata as the deputy governor at the time, later wrote that he was careful to communicate in a way that this policy change would not be misinterpreted as tapering of easing.

It is an undeniable fact that the BOJ under Kuroda had tapered monetary easing. Claiming to strengthen monetary easing and trying to convince the listener is nothing short of deception. During World War II, the Japanese government and military described the crushing defeats as "tenshin" (changes of course). The new policy was proclaimed the "tenshin" of the BOJ under Kuroda in this context (e.g., Asahi Shimbun, 2016. See also Hattori, 2019, p. 33–34; Suzuki, 2022, pp. 216–218). As stated in Sect. 2.2.2, Hamada (2013, p. 26) argued that saying the "medo" (goal) was different from the target is sophistry. However, this may not necessarily be sophistry; calling tapering of easing as strengthening of easing is genuine sophistry, which Hamada fails to criticize.

Nakaso (2022, p. 533) writes that YCC is "the ultimate evolution of monetary policy" that has been modified to withstand "long-lasting war." We believe this to be deliberate misleading by Nakaso. The policy of purchasing ¥80 trillion per year in long-term JGBs cannot be implemented unless financial institutions willing to sell ¥80 trillion worth of long-term JGBs per year are found. In the case of the YCC, if no financial institutions were willing to sell long-term JGBs, the BOJ would simply not purchase them. In this sense, it is a sustainable policy even if deflation continues, as surmised by Kiuchi. Moreover, if negative long-term interest rates were putting pressure on banks' profits, it is natural that raising long-term interest rates to zero would somewhat improve profits. Nonetheless, banks' profits have continued to deteriorate since fiscal year 2017, and this problem has not been fundamentally resolved.

The top priority of the BOJ under Kuroda is to overcome deflation. No economist would think that reducing the amount of long-term JGBs purchased and raising long-term interest rates would lead to an end to deflation. The YCC is a monetary policy framework that can be sustained even if deflation persists for a long time. Nakaso is right in this sense, but it is not monetary policy that solves deflation, which is the target of the BOJ under Kuroda and the reflationists.

We know that interest rates in both the short and long term were near zero, and there was little room for a cut. Iwata further admitted that the YCC is powerless to work on inflation expectations. The supply of the monetary base was decreasing as well. Monetary policy had reached its limits in terms of quantities of the monetary base, short- and long-term nominal interest rates, and real interest rates owing to the raising of inflation expectations. As indicated in the quotation at the beginning of Chap. 1, Bernanke was among those who demonstrated the limits of the BOJ under Kuroda's monetary policy. Therefore, the YCC can rightly be called "the ultimate limit of monetary policy." However, the phrase "ultimate evolution" can imply that the BOJ under Kuroda has nothing more to do. In this sense, Nakaso's assertion is not wrong.

Suzuki (2022, pp. 176–200) also points out that the new policy framework of September 2016 was intended to prevent the BOJ from expanding its front without removing the sign that it was fighting deflation. Suzuki also noted that overshooting commitment was important to make it appear that the signboard of overcoming deflation was being maintained. It is impossible to believe that deflation can be overcome based on the BOJ's verbal promises of monetary easing *after* the end of deflation—an end that no one can predict. We believed that an inflation-overshooting commitment was just lip service and meaningless. However, after reading Suzuki, we realize that, as quantity, nominal interest rates, and real interest rates are all reaching their limits, the use of monetary easing by paying lip service to an inflation-overshooting commitment has become even more important for the BOJ under Kuroda and reflationists. Conversely, Hamada (2013, p. 36) and Iwata (2012, p. 179) argued that deflation would persist because the BOJ until Shirakawa was "all take and no action," and refused to take responsibility for failures.

Suzuki (2022, 216–218) also notes that, while the BOJ under Kuroda rejected Kiuchi's proposal to purchase long-term JGBs to ¥45 trillion after the YCC was controlled, purchases of long-term JGBs decreased at a pace that exceeded Kiuchi's proposal. The supply of monetary base would have to be reduced for the simple reason that a large supply of monetary base was not possible. However, accepting Kiuchi's proposal exactly as it was would have made it clear that the BOJ tapered monetary easing; hence, Kiuchi's proposal was rejected. The BOJ created a new mechanism of YCC and overshooting commitment, allowing itself to claim that there was not tapering of monetary easing. Then, it would effectively carry out Kiuchi's proposal. Conversely, the BOJ, until Shirakawa implemented the QE policy in March 2001, set the "medo" (goal) in February 2012 and an inflation target in January 2013 while believing that these policies were ineffective. This seems contradictory, but it still occurred because of political pressure.

This approach was described as stealth tapering from the beginning (e.g., Takashima, 2016). At the governor's press conference in September 2016 (The Bank of Japan, 2016a, p. 18), the question of whether this was tapering was already raised, and Kuroda denied that. Iwata (2018a, p. 84) also denied stealth tapering but stated that it made exiting easier to accomplish. However, suppose one defines stealth tapering as a slowdown in the pace of increase of the monetary base and long-term JGBs, which the BOJ does not officially acknowledge. In that case, the decision of the BOJ under Kuroda is clearly stealth tapering. In the first place, the decision to use the supply of the monetary base as a policy tool was based on the BOJ and Iwata's belief that a large supply of the monetary base would effectively overcome deflation. To argue that a reduction in the supply of monetary base is not tapering is a contradiction in terms. Iwata's statement on easier exits indicates that the BOJ under Kuroda reduced the supply of the monetary base that is, tapering! However, as the reflationists believe that an exit is not possible until the inflation target is achieved, tapering would be a step further away from exit.

Hamada (2013, p. 36) criticizes the "medo" (goal) as a policy of deflection of criticism. The YCC and inflation-overshooting commitment was the policy of deflection, which was implemented on a much larger scale because of the sheer size of the monetary easing of different dimensions.

4.2.4 Yield Curve Control Succeeded Owing to Failure to Overcome Deflation

The mainstream view is that monetary easing will lead to higher expected inflation and higher long-term interest rates (see Sect. 3.4.2). Short-term interest rates in Japan are already negative, leaving little room for reduction. While there is a risk of losses from a rise in short-term interest rates (some financial institutions may profit from a rise), there is almost no risk of losses from a decline. However, the term premium would be low, because the risk of interest rate hike would be low under the BOJ under Kuroda, which was not able to solve deflation. Under these circumstances, term premium could rise, if monetary easing rises inflation and increases the risk of future short-term interest hike. Monetary easing should result in a further increase in long-term interest rates. In reality, long-term interest rates have remained stable at approximately zero. This is evidence that the market expects the BOJ to fail to end deflation in the long term and that short-term interest rates will remain near zero in the long term. In other words, the fact that the YCC is under control proves that the BOJ under Kuroda has failed to end deflation.

The BOJ under Kuroda's massive purchases of JGBs has also been criticized as fiscal monetization. In response, the BOJ and the reflationists argue that the purchase of JGBs is not to cover the government's budget deficit but to overcome deflation. As the purchase of JGBs is one of the basic tools of central banks' monetary policy, the purchase of JGBs cannot be prohibited in itself. However, we need to consider why fiscal monetization is banned: Fiscal monetization is expected to lead to extreme inflation. As long as deflation continues, the BOJ under Kuroda is allowed to continue purchasing JGBs indefinitely. This also means that it has failed to overcome deflation, which is its original purpose.

QQE had become unsustainable because they required large purchases of long-term JGBs. Instead, YCC is a policy that can be sustained as long as deflation continues (conversely, if deflation is overcome, it does not need to be sustained). This is an advantage, but the decisive disadvantage is that real interest rates correspondingly rise as deflation progresses. Therefore, according to the reflationist theory, YCC is a pro-deflationary policy. Nonetheless, while introducing policies once criticized by reflationists, Kuroda insisted that monetary easing would been strengthened.

September 2016 was a decisive turning point as monetary policy reached its ultimate limit. Tanaka (2023, pp. 197–201) also divided the BOJ under Kuroda's monetary policy into two stages in September 2016. The first period was when the BOJ reduced the long-term interest rates. In the second period, after the long-term interest rates were lowered to the lower bound, the BOJ talked about strengthening monetary easing; however, it proceeded with tapering. In practice, the negative interest rate policy is different from the QQE policy. We believe that if the negative interest rate policy had continued, stealth tapering would have started under negative interest rates, both short-term and long-term. Thus, Kuroda's monetary policy should be divided into three phases (i.e., by including the negative interest rate policy). However, the negative interest rate policy ended after six months, resulting in a transitional period.

After the introduction of YCC, the BOJ under Kuroda effectively adopted one policy after another, each of which had once been criticized by the reflationists. The BOJ under Kuroda "officially" made it appear as if it was continuing policies based on the reflationist theory, thereby creating the illusion that the economy was making steady progress in overcoming deflation. In this sense, September 2016 was also a major turning point.

4.2.5 Revival of "the Bank of Japan's Theory"

Whether money is exogenous or endogenous has been one of the most important issues in the disputes in the history of monetary theory. Noguchi (2021, pp. 222–237) argues that this dispute is unimportant because it is merely a question of whether the central bank chooses the interest rate or the quantity of money as its policy variable.

As we will discuss in Chap. 5, Iwata (1993) and Okina (1993) clashed over controversies over money supply in the early 1990s. Iwata argued that the BOJ should increase the money stock based on the idea of monetarism. He was contemptuous of the BOJ's theory and criticized the assertion by Okina, the BOJ, and others that the central bank supplies the monetary base in response to demand. However, the BOJ's theory is identical to the scarce reserve regime described by Bernanke (2022, p. 248), which the Federal Reserve and other central banks used *before* the introduction of QE. We believe that the BOJ's theory can also be called the Federal Reserve's theory. If the BOJ's theory was adopted by the U.S. and European Central Banks, the criticism by reflationists could not be untenable. Therefore, we can evaluate that Noguchi redefines the BOJ's theory.

The notion that interest rates and the money stock are alternative policy instruments is a mistake. The controversy on the money supply was also about whether the money stock could be controlled. Bernanke (2022, pp. 141–144) also acknowledges that the QE policy implemented by the BOJ since 2001 did not lead to an increase in the money stock. The QQE of the BOJ under Kuroda also led to a sharp increase in the monetary base, but it did not lead to an increase in the money stock (see Sect. 5.2.2). After the global financial crisis of 2008, central banks in the U. S. and Europe also increased their monetary bases rapidly, but this did not lead to an increase in the money stock. In the late 1970s and early 1980s, so-called "experiments in monetarism" were conducted in the U.S. and the U.K. Eventually, both countries succeeded in controlling inflation at the time but failed to control the rate of money-stock growth. A variable that the central bank is unable to control cannot be a policy variable.

The monetary base is also one of the quantities of money, but it is not a policy variable in and of itself. In the monetarist view, an increase in the monetary base is supposed to move the money stock, a policy variable, through the money multiplier. However, in the current mainstream monetary policy theory, the policy variable is the short-term interest rate. Under the scarce reserve regime, changes in the monetary base have policy effects through changes in the short-term interest rate. However, under the ample reserve regime, the interest rate on excess reserves determines the short-term interest rate. Under the ample reserve regime, the monetary base has no policy effect, and thus, policy variables and non-policy variables should not be treated equally. Reflationists such as Iwata argue that the monetary base has the policy effect of working on the expected inflation rate. This is a peculiar idea, as no one but reflationsts—even mainstream economists in the U.S.—makes such a claim. As we showed in Chap. 3, there is no theoretical basis or evidence for this assertion.

If the interest rate is the policy tool, then once the interest rate reaches the lower bound, there is nothing more that monetary policy can do. Particularly in Japan, long-term interest rates have also reached their lower bound. Bernanke (2017, p. 30) calls this a super liquidity trap. In this respect, there is an important difference between interest rates and the quantity of money as a policy tool. Conversely, until short-term rates reached the lower bound, the BOJ also manipulated interest rates. If, as Noguchi says, the choice between interest rates and the quantity of money as a policy tool taken were meaningless, the BOJ should not theoretically be blamed for using interest rates as its policy tool—even with criticism that interest rates should be lowered further.

The grave problem is that the YCC is a variant of the BOJ's theory. The YCC fixes both the short and long-term yields at near zero and is intended to accommodate the purchase of long-term JGBs. Nakaso (2022, pp. 526–527) also writes that under YCC, the amount of long-term JGBs purchased is endogenously determined. Theoretically, the BOJ could increase the monetary base by buying Treasury discount bills and other assets. However, except for the period when the COVID-19 pandemic spread, the increase in the monetary base was largely determined by purchases of long-term JGBs. The monetary base was also determined almost, if not completely, endogenously. The BOJ's theory was more complete under the YCC, which fixed interest rates, not only in the short term but also in the long term.

Under the YCC, when deflation progresses, real interest rates automatically rise in both the short- and long-term based on the amount of deflation. *Ceteris paribus*, deflation will lower nominal interest rates in both the short and long term. Then, to maintain nominal interest rates, purchases of long-term JGBs must be reduced. Figure 4.1 also illustrates the 10-year breakeven inflation rate (BEI). Since the introduction of the YCC, BEI was on a downward trend, and in tandem with this, the purchase rate of long-term JGBs also declined. Conversely, the consumer price (CPI) inflation rate has exceeded 2% since 2022, putting upward pressure on long-term interest rates. To control this rise in long-term interest rates, the BOJ increased its purchases of JGBs. While we do not believe that the monetary base significantly impacts CPI and inflation expectations, according to the reflationist theory, a monetary policy that reduces purchases of JGBs when deflation is in progress is a pro-deflationary policy.

However, Nakaso (2022, p. 532) points out that, as one of the flexibilities of the YCC, if the same shape of the yield curve is maintained, the degree of monetary easing will increase through a decline in real interest rates when inflation expectations rise. This in itself is logically correct. However, when deflation progresses, monetary conditions are tightened through a rise in real interest rates for the same reason. Generally speaking, it is a mistake for policymakers to formulate policies based on the assumption of situations that are convenient for them. Moreover, Nakaso (2022, p. 655) further writes to "prepare for the worst and pray for the best" as a principle of crisis response. The goal of the BOJ under Kuroda is to end deflation. He must consider the possibility of intensified deflation. Nakaso disguised the flaws in the policy by assuming a situation that was convenient for policymakers. This is also sophistry.

Harada (2021, p. 166) argues that the YCC amplifies the stimulus effect when there is a positive shock to the economy, but in the case of a negative shock, it would simply let interest rates fall, in the sense that they would not be forced back to zero by approximately ("medo") ¥80 trillion in JGB purchases. Therefore, YCC is somewhat reliant on another policy. Harada accurately understood the problems of the YCC. As the economy deteriorated and the expected inflation rate declined, the BOJ under Kuroda implemented policies that, according to the reflationist theory, would have promoted deflation by reducing the amount of long-term government bond purchases and the supply of the monetary base. Harada inexplicably does not oppose a policy that is directly opposed to the doctrine he and other reflationists espoused.

Fiscal austerity will worsen the economy by its amount. However, Kuroda cannot cut interest rates to offset the effects of fiscal austerity. If the issuance of JGBs decreases, nominal interest rates will decline if other conditions are held the same. Then, the BOJ under Kuroda must reduce the supply of the monetary base to contain this decline in interest rates. In theory, under the YCC, given that all conditions remain the same, monetary policy will passively react to austerity and worsen the economy.

The BOJ under Kuroda simply revived the BOJ's theory—once criticized by Noguchi and the reflationists—under the name of the YCC. According to the reflationist theory, the YCC is a policy that promotes deflation. There was no deflationary spiral. Conversely, the CPI inflation rate has exceeded 2% since 2022, owing to imported inflation. However, there is no virtuous spiral to overcome deflation, in which prices rise owing to negative real interest rates, and price rises further lower the real interest rate, as Nakaso suggests. This is consistent with our assertion that monetary policy has little impact on prices.

4.2.6 *Revival of the Bank of Japan's Theory on the Quantitative Easing*

The passive nature of the supply of monetary base after the introduction of YCC by the BOJ under Kuroda was evident when the COVID-19 pandemic spread. Several companies, primarily in the travel industry and restaurants, suffered a sharp decline in sales, leaving many cash-strapped. To help with the financial positions of these companies, in March 2020, the BOJ created the Special Funds-Supplying Operations to Facilitate Corporate Financing regarding the Novel Coronavirus (COVID-19). In April, the content was strengthened and renamed to the Special Funds-Supplying Operations to Facilitate Financing in Response to the Novel Coronavirus (COVID-19). The BOJ decided to pay a 0.1% interest rate on the BOJ's current account, which is equal to the outstanding amount of this operation, to the financial institutions that borrow from the BOJ through it. The interest rate on the BOJ's current account was set at 0% for twice the outstanding of these operations (thus reducing the portion of the current account that would be at a negative interest rate). In effect, the BOJ sought to increase bank lending through subsidies.

As Fig. 4.1 shows, the monetary base has surged significantly by more than ¥100 trillion on a year-on-year difference. Bank lending also surged, and as Fig. 3.1 shows, the money stock jumped approximately 10% growth year-on-year. However, as Fig. 3.4 shows, financial institutions' excess reserves easily exceed ¥400 trillion. We believe that it is a good policy to provide subsidies to increase bank lending. However, subsidies are fiscal policy, and it is essentially something that the government should do. Additionally, we believe that the current account at the BOJ was already excessively supplied and that further supply was unnecessary. However, this was only a temporary measure during the COVID-19 crisis. In 2022, the amount outstanding of the Operations in Response to COVID-19 declined sharply, and the supply of the monetary base declined accordingly. The rate of increase in money stock was also sluggish. Finally, in March 2023, the BOJ terminated its Operations in Response to COVID-19.

In March 2021, the BOJ established the Interest Scheme to Promote Lending. The BOJ provided the interest on the balance of eligible loans. In March, interest was granted at 0.2% or 0.1% for the Special Funds-Supplying Operations to Facilitate

Financing in Response to COVID-19, and at 0% for the Fund-Provisioning Measure to Support Strengthening the Foundations for Economic Growth Conducted through the Loan Support Program, the Fund-Provisioning Measure to Stimulate Bank Lending Conducted through the Loan Support Program, and the Funds-Supplying Operation to Support Financial Institutions in Disaster Areas. In September, the BOJ also created the Funds-Supplying Operations to Support Financing for Climate Change Responses. However, these initiatives had little impact owing to their small amounts, even if there is a growing proactive response of central banks to climate warming—for the BOJ and in the world.

Few would oppose helping businesses suffering from the COVID-19 pandemic, giving interest to financial institutions to encourage lending, or providing financial support for climate change. However, this is a matter of policy-based finance. As mentioned in Sect. 2.2.2, Iwata (2012, pp. 125–126) opposed the BOJ in conducting such a policy. As Iwata and others have criticized before, the BOJ before Kuroda believed that increasing the supply of funds in a situation where there was no demand for borrowing would not be effective. This includes the belief that, in situations where there is demand for borrowing, it is the BOJ's responsibility to supply funds in response to demand. Hence, during the Great East Japan Earthquake, the BOJ temporarily and rapidly increased the monetary base as a response to the crisis but quickly retracted it once the crisis subsided. Iwata criticized this move as the BOJ's theory on QE (see Sect. 2.2.2). However, during the COVID-19 crisis, the BOJ implemented the policies that Iwata (2013, pp. 81–86) had criticized on a much larger scale. Thus, we witness a revival of policy-based finance by the BOJ and the BOJ's theory on QE that Iwata had once criticized.

4.3 Abandonment of the Japanese-Style Inflation Target

4.3.1 There Was No Japanese-Style Inflation Target from the Beginning

The BOJ under Kuroda had announced its outlook for when the inflation target could be achieved. Table 4.2 shows the outlook for achievements. When it became clear that the target could not be achieved, the BOJ under Kuroda postponed the outlook. Although it is tautological, even with postponement, what was not able to be achieved was not able to be. The BOJ had no choice but to postpone the outlook again—this cycle repeated seven times, and each time, both the market and media ridiculed the failures of Abenomics. The only and biggest problem with the BOJ's outlook is that it cannot be achieved according to the outlook. Iwata (e.g., 2012, 2013) stated that the inflation target must be accompanied by the BOJ's responsibility for achieving it. However, no one, including Iwata, took responsibility. Once again, the BOJ under Kuroda did what Iwata and other reflationists had criticized.

Table 4.2 Outlook for the timing of achieving the inflation target of the BOJ

April 2013 (first)	With a time horizon of about two years
October, 2014	Around the fiscal year 2015
April, 2015	Around the middle of the projection period (first half of fiscal year 2016)
October, 2015	Around the second half of fiscal year 2016
April, 2016	During fiscal year 2017
October, 2016	Second half of the projection period (second half of fiscal year 2018)
July 2017	Around fiscal year 2019
April 2018	Stopping the announcements of outlook

Source The Bank of Japan (2013–2020)

Kuroda was reappointed as governor in April 2018 (however, Kuroda had taken over Shirakawa's remaining term when he took office in March 2013 and was reappointed in April). At the monetary policy meeting shortly thereafter, the BOJ under Kuroda withdrew the announcement of the outlook for when the target could be achieved. Reflationists such as Iwata have argued that even if an inflation target is set, it cannot be achieved unless the BOJ sets a deadline and is committed to achieving it. From the perspective of reflationist theory, this means that the BOJ under Kuroda has abandoned overcoming deflation. The cancellation of the announcements was widely trumpeted as a declaration of defeat by the BOJ under Kuroda (see Kodama, 2018).

Until the Shirakawa era, the BOJ did not believe that it had the power to achieve its inflation target; hence, it avoided setting an inflation target that it could not undertake. Governor Shirakawa succumbed to political pressure and introduced an inflation target, but even in doing so, the responsibility was shared with the government. Iwata and Hamada criticized the BOJ's attitude, saying that deflation could not be overcome indefinitely. Kuroda's cancellation of its announcement of the outlook for achieving its inflation target is also an admission that Iwata and Hamada's criticism was groundless and that thinking of the BOJ up to the Shirakawa era was correct.

Cancelling a policy tool owing to failure is different from having no policy at all. Setting unattainable targets indicates incompetence by the BOJ under Kuroda and reflationists while rejecting responsibility for failure demonstrates their irresponsibility. At present, credibility is considered one of the most important things for a central bank. No one can trust an incompetent and irresponsible group. The Japanese-style inflation target, which was unattainable and espoused no accountability, was the worst policy and undermined the BOJ's credibility.

At the governor's regular press conference, Kuroda (The Bank of Japan, 2018a, p. 4) stated, "In April 2013, when the Bank decided to achieve the 2 percent price stability target as soon as possible, it started 'Quantitative and Qualitative Monetary Easing' with about two years in mind, but thereafter, it has not been conducting monetary policy with such a specific achievement date in mind. This point became even clearer at the 'Quantitative and Qualitative Monetary Easing with Yield Curve

Control' in September 2016." This statement surprised us: Based on Iwata's and the reflationists' previous assertions, the outlook for achievement seemed to be a *commitment* by and *responsibility* of the BOJ under Kuroda.

Upon re-reading the "Summary of the Governor's Press Conference" (The Bank of Japan, 2013b, p. 1) in April 2013, when the BOJ started the QQE policy, we find that "the Bank of Japan decided today to introduce 'quantitative and qualitative monetary easing' in order to achieve the 'price stability target' of a 2 percent year-on-year increase in consumer prices as soon as possible, with a time frame of about two years." As Kuroda said, monetary policy was conducted with 2% in mind, but 2% was not a commitment that had to be taken responsibility for when it could not be achieved. There was no Japanese-style inflation target from the beginning. Incidentally, it was Iwata (2012, p. 179) who had criticized the "medo" (goal) of the BOJ under Shirakawa, stating that no deadline for achieving the inflation target was set; hence, there is no blame for its failure. However, the inflation target, which has no deadline for achievement and does not require taking the blame for its failure, is the same as the "medo" (goal) that Iwata criticized. Once again, the BOJ under Kuroda had begun to do what Iwata had criticized.

Karube (2022, pp. 76–81) writes that the removal of the outlook occurred because Abe was irritated at criticism over repeat failures and postponements. While we assumed that removal was decided by the BOJ under Kuroda, considering the power relationship, it is likely that such a decision would not have been made without Abe's approval, *at least*. Karube (2022, pp. 69–72) says that Abe had already lost interest in monetary policy in 2015. In response, the BOJ gradually changed its inflation target to a long-term measure. If this is true, then the monetary policy of reflationists has been abandoned in just over two years.

Stopping the commitment to the inflation target was such a major event that it could be described as a total rejection of the reflationist theory. Nevertheless, the BOJ under Kuroda pretended as if it had not abandoned the reflationist approach but treated it as a minor adjustment. Here, too, the BOJ under Kuroda pretended that it was continuing its reflationists' monetary policy while introducing theories and policies previously criticized by reflationists.

4.3.2 Price Outlook that Always "Rises Toward the Inflation Target"

The BOJ issued a semi-annual report, "Outlook for Economic Activity and Prices," which provides outlooks for economic conditions and prices. It has been issued every quarter since 2016. The Appendix shows the price outlook for each milestone period. Although there were differences in the wording, until the COVID-19 pandemic in 2020, the price outlooks were consistent with a rise toward the 2% inflation target. In April 2018, the government stopped announcing an outlook for the achievement of the inflation target. Since then, the outlook has remained consistent, rising to 2%.

The Appendix cites only some periods, but the outlooks are the same for the periods when they are not cited (we will not quote all reports for brevity). These outlooks had been consistently wrong, but the BOJ under Kuroda still repeated the same outlooks.

At the press conference in September 2018, when the BOJ stopped announcing an outlook on the inflation target, Kuroda (The Bank of Japan, 2018a, p. 5) said, "I think it will most likely reach around 2% around fiscal year 2019." However, the inflation rate in the CPI less fresh food in fiscal year 2019, excluding the consumption tax hike, was 0.4%, which is not only far from the target but also lower than those in fiscal years 2017 and 2018. Again, Kuroda refused to accept blame for the personal outlook being off the table and completed his term.

Since October 2016, the risk balance has also been included in the "Outlook" and consistently skewed toward downside risks. Although not included in the Appendix the balances of risks in the economic activity were not necessarily the same. Most who know that the BOJ's price outlooks were consistently higher than actual inflation may believe that the outlook for prices is too high rather than the downside risks being high.

Though economic outlooks rarely come true, it can be said that it is incompetent to miss them so consistently. Harada (2021, p. 272) argues that "perceptions of the economic conditions are randomly wrong, but conceptual errors are always wrong." The price outlook of the BOJ under Kuroda is not merely part of its perception of the economic condition; it is also a test of whether the concept of the reflationist theory is correct. If the perceptions of the economic conditions based on the erroneous idea of the reflationist theory are always wrong, then this would be consistent with Harada's assertion.

However, we believe that the erroneous price outlooks were likely not owing to incompetence. Remember that the BOJ under Kuroda has stopped its commitment to achieving its inflation target, and stealth tapering began in September 2016. The BOJ effectively abandoned monetary policy based on the reflationist theory. Even if it is based on the wrong theory of the reflationists, it is impossible to overcome deflation.

We consider the following two hypotheses as reasons for continuing to issue price outlooks that the BOJ under Kuroda deemed to be false. For one, publicly stating that the inflation target cannot be achieved means that the BOJ under Kuroda and the reflationists are wrong. They repeated the false price outlooks only to protect their positions and reputations. Second, admitting that the inflation target cannot be achieved in the near future means that further monetary easing will have to be conducted. However, monetary easing has reached its ultimate limit. To avoid further monetary easing, the BOJ under Kuroda repeated false outlooks. However, a person of average intelligence would not believe the BOJ's consistently incorrect outlooks. The false price outlook was also a policy that undermined the credibility of the BOJ under Kuroda.

Conversely, it would have been more believable had the BOJ under Kuroda forecasted that the 2% inflation rate was unattainable. Such asymmetry exists in the formation of expectations. However, the overwhelming majority of the public is not interested in the BOJ's price outlook, and many are unaware of its existence. The overwhelming majority of people will not increase their distrust simply because they simply do not know. However, there is no way for the BOJ to work with such people's inflation expectations.

In a speech in September 2018, Kataoka (2019, p. 4), a core reflationist, said, "Price projections have continued to be revised downward, reflecting the weak price developments, but the Bank's view is that the momentum of prices toward the 2% price stability target will be maintained. However, I dissented from the relevant description in the January Outlook Report as I think the possibility of the inflation rate rising toward 2% is low at the moment and that the momentum of inflation has not been strengthened. There are four main reasons behind my position."

In his *Nichigin Nikki* (Diary in the Bank of Japan), Iwata (2018b, p. 398) also points out in his record of January 18, 2018, shortly before his retirement, that the rate of increase in the CPI less fresh food and energy declined after peaking in November 2015 and reached zero in March 2017. The negative interest rate policy and the YCC policy implemented during this period have not stopped the decline in the CPI inflation rate, less fresh food and energy, and the BOJ cannot claim that the momentum of inflation has steadily been rising. Kataoka and Iwata, who are known as core reflationists, also admitted that the CPI had not risen toward the inflation target. They have come to agree with us on this point. We believe that this is also evidence that the policies advocated by reflationists are ineffective.

4.3.3 "Rhetoric of the Bank of Japan"

Eventually, even monetary policy based on the reflationist theory could no longer be implemented by the BOJ under Kuroda. Infallible, rigid, and irresponsible politicians, bureaucrats, and economists do not admit their failures. They also refuse to acknowledge deadlocks of their policy. The BOJ's technique of hiding inconvenient truths is called the rhetoric of the BOJ. Fujishiro (2019) says that this rhetoric of the BOJ was further strengthened under Kuroda. Incidentally, Suzuki (2022, p. 188) calls it "Hongoku-Chō rhetoric" after the location of the BOJ.

The official name of the negative interest rate policy introduced in March 2016 is the Quantitative and Qualitative Monetary Easing with Negative Interest Rate Control, and that of the YCC and an inflation-overshooting commitment introduced in September is the Quantitative and Qualitative Monetary Easing with Yield Curve Control. Both the negative interest rate policy and the YCC were merely improvements to the QQE, even though their frameworks were completely different.

When the negative interest rate policy was introduced, the BOJ's official announcement that the increase in outstanding long-term JGBs would be ¥80 trillion per year was unchanged. When the YCC was introduced, the BOJ changed from ¥80 trillion to ¥80 trillion at most ("medo" in Japanese). However, after the introduction of YCC, the amount of long-term JGB purchases declined, falling below ¥40 trillion per year at the end of 2018. At the end of 2019, it was less than ¥20 trillion per year (see Fig. 4.1). In addition, the common English translation of the Japanese word "medo" is "goal," and in this case, it can be translated as "approximately." The BOJ translates it as at most, but that is incorrect. This incorrect English translation would indicate that BOJ under Kuroda did not intend to purchase approximately ¥80 trillion.

The word "medo" can be written in three different letters in Japanese. Usually, the difference between the letters has no meaning. However, Suzuki (2022, pp. 188–190) says that the BOJ uses three different letters of "medo" with different meanings. One does not have a profound meaning, but it makes policy positioning clear. When the QE policy was introduced in March 2001, the BOJ set a "medo" (guideline) until the CPI inflation rate should remain stable at zero or above. The next is about the image of an effort target or something with a meaning similar to that of a target. This was the "medo" (goal) introduced by the BOJ under Shirakawa in February 2012. The last one is almost meaningless. The term "medo," meaning "at most," was used by the BOJ under Kuroda when it adopted the YCC in September 2016 and was concerned with the pace of increase in outstanding long-term JGBs. To summarize, the "medo" by the BOJ under Kuroda shows that the BOJ was ostensibly buying ¥80 trillion in long-term JGBs to make it look like it was continuing policies advocated by reflationists, but it had no intention of doing so. In this sense, "medo" had a significant meaning.

In April 2020, when the COVID-19 crisis spread, the BOJ (The Bank of Japan, 2020, p. 2) stated instead that "the Bank will conduct further active purchases of both JGBs and T-Bills for the time being." The Bank also abolished the upper limit on purchases of long-term JGBs. As Fig. 4.1 shows, Treasury discount bills temporarily increased by more than ¥30 trillion year-on-year at their peak. While the amount of increase in long-term JGBs has increased, even at its peak, it will remain at a pace of a little more than ¥20 trillion per year. The elimination of the quota was simply a matter of taking advantage of the COVID-19 crisis to eliminate the meaningless "medo" notation. Suzuki (2022, pp. 254–256) also notes that the increase in long-term JGBs was converted into purchases at this time. The increase in outstanding is the purchases minus the redemptions minus sales of government bonds. Therefore, the amount of JGBs purchases will be larger than the increase in outstanding JGBs. By doing so, he said, the BOJ made it appear that it was actively easing monetary policy.

Japanese economy entered a recession in October 2018 (the beginning of the recession was officially provisionally certified in July 2020). As Fig. 4.1 shows, BEI and inflation expectations by ESP forecasts also continued to decline after mid-2018. In July, the BOJ under Kuroda (The Bank of Japan, 2018b) announced the "Strengthening the Framework for Continuous Powerful Monetary Easing." Looking at this alone, it seems that the BOJ under Kuroda has taken preemptive measures against the recession and the decline in inflation expectations.

However, among the policies decided at that time, forward guidance and asset purchase policy remain unchanged. The YCC was to be more elastic, with a wider range of ups and downs. At that time, this was understood to be an increase in long-term interest rates, and indeed it was. This is monetary tightening or tapering of easing at most. It also decided to halve the portion of its excess reserves that would be at negative interest rates from the current level of about ¥10 trillion. Reducing the portion of negative interest rates applied was probably intended to ensure profits for struggling banks. However, from a normal perspective, reducing the portion of negative interest rates applied is raising interest rates and thus tapering monetary easing.

It also decided to increase exchange-traded funds (ETFs) purchases. If this had been realized, it could have been said to strengthen easing. However, the actual pace of purchases remained unchanged. Note that ETF purchases are inherently small. As Fig. 4.1 shows, since 2016, the BOJ under Kuroda has slowed the pace of increase in the monetary base, mainly by reducing the amount of JGBs it purchases. This has not changed since July 2018. The monetary easing of July 2018 was also a lip service and a tapering of monetary easing. Hamada (2013, p. 36) and Iwata (2012, p. 179) once criticized the BOJ for not implementing monetary easing while talking about monetary easing until the Governor Shirakawa era.

As we have mentioned, after the introduction of the YCC, the BOJ introduced policies opposed by reflationists and effectively abandoned the goal of overcoming deflation but made it appear that monetary easing based on the reflationist theory was continuing. Reflationists have insisted that their policies are global standards. However, transparency is also one of the current global standards of monetary policy. In practice, the BOJ under Kuroda is far from the global standard just because of its lack of transparency.

4.4 Revival of "The Bank of Japan's Theory of Deflation"

4.4.1 Iwata Makes Excuses Without Taking Blame

In Nippon-Ginkō (The Bank of Japan), Iwata (2012, Chap. 3, pp. 55–89) criticized the BOJ until Shirakawa for shifting the blame for deflation to everything except monetary policy. He called this the BOJ's theory of deflation and criticized it. Iwata (2013, p. 112) further states, "The BOJ is the one that keeps giving orders to people and never takes blame itself. Essentially, it says, 'We are not responsible for anything, but the government and corporations are.' The Diet members and the government are being forced to take the blame by the BOJ, but do they not understand that?".

When Iwata became deputy governor of the BOJ in 2013, he boasted that he would achieve the inflation target within two years. As we mentioned in Sect. 2.2.2, he (The Bank of Japan, 2013a, p. 5) also said he wouldn't make excuses if the BOJ missed its target. As he said, if the BOJ under Kuroda failed to achieve the target owing to other factors, then whether its next effort will achieve the target or not will depend on other factors.

Even after ten years, let alone after two years, Kuroda failed to achieve the inflation target, which Iwata (2018a) blamed on the consumption tax hike and the sharp decline in crude oil prices. These are excuses. When they failed, either Iwata, Kuroda, or Wakatabe would shift the blame away from monetary policy, make excuses, and refuse accountability. Here again, Iwata did what he had once criticized to avoid blame, thus compromising his credibility.

When asked whether the share of monetary policy in the reflation regime was smaller than expected, Iwata (2018a, p. 82) replied, "No, it was not little." This is because the percentage of periods with a positive CPI increase under the BOJ under Kuroda has increased more than before. Iwata says that, in the first year, he was able to switch to the reflation regime as expected, but that the consumption tax hike and the sharp fall in oil prices disrupted the reflation regime. This is not true. The rise in the CPI in 2013 was owing to the rise in import prices and not a surge in the monetary base (see Sect. 2.3.1 and Appendix of Chap. 2).

According to Iwata's explanation, monetary policy would be effective if CPI and inflation expectations rise even temporarily. If they do not rise, it would be blamed on headwinds such as a consumption tax hike and a sharp drop in oil prices. Thus, Iwata's theory would be correct whether or not CPI and the expected inflation rate rise. Iwata's false theory can never be proven, but he uses this trick to make it appear correct. In *Itsuwari no Keizai Seisaku* (Deceptive Economic Policies), we (Hattori, 2017, pp. 5–9) called this method the economic theory of Abenomics. According to falsificationism, the proposition that "monetary policy based on the reflationist theory makes it possible to end deflation by raising inflation expectations" can be disproved but cannot be verified. However, according to Iwata, this proposition can always be verified but never disproved, leading Hattori (2022, pp. 32–33) to term it "reverse falsificationism."

Iwata (2018a, p. 85) further states, "If monetary policy continues to maintain the 'reflation regime,' it will take time, but there is no doubt that the inflation rate will approach 2%." Conversely, he states that volume and commitment alone will not easily raise the expected inflation rate. This is tantamount to saying that the policies proposed by Iwata have failed. The YCC is a monetary policy based on the BOJ's theory, which Iwata and other reflationists have criticized. If this policy, once criticized by Iwata, succeeds in overcoming deflation, Iwata will be proven wrong again. Moreover, Iwata (2018b, p. 419) himself has admitted that the YCC has no power to raise inflation expectations and acknowledged that the momentum of inflation did not rise (Iwata, 2018b, p. 398).

Iwata admitted that monetary policy working on inflation expectations had failed and thus abandoned and that the momentum of inflation did not rise. We agree, too. The monetary policy advocated by reflationists clearly failed, but Iwata refuses to acknowledge this to protect his position and reputation. While admitting that monetary policy that works on inflation expectations has been abandoned and that the momentum of inflation did not rise, he incoherently asserts that monetary policy by the BOJ under Kuroda will surely overcome deflation someday. In April 2023, approximately five years after Iwata guaranteed that the BOJ could surely conquer deflation, Kuroda left the BOJ without achieving this goal. As Harada says, (Iwata's) conceptual errors are always wrong.

Notably, Iwata cited the improvement in economic conditions and said that it is a mistake to say that monetary policy has failed just because the 2% inflation target was not able to be achieved. Hamada (2017, p. 125) made a similar claim (see

Sect. 2.5.1). Yet again, under the economic theory of Abenomics, all improvements in the economy are attributed to the BOJ under Kuroda and Abenomics, while all lack of price increases are attributed to headwinds. The economic growth rate during the Abenomics period was not only far short of the 2% target but was even lower than before the Abenomics period (see Sect. 2.5.1). The rate of increase in the monetary base is not related to nominal or real GDP growth (See Fig. 4.2).

The basis of the reflationist theory is the price theory. Iwata and others argue that deflation is a monetary phenomenon and that prices would inevitably rise owing to the BOJ, terming it "common sense" economics. The fact that prices do not rise means that this common sense of reflationist was a delusion. The reflationist analysis of the current situation is that the Japanese economy cannot be revived unless deflation can be resolved. The argument that prices do not need to rise also means that the reflationists' analysis of the current situation is wrong. Iwata (2013, pp. 80–81) and Hamada (2013, pp. 55–57) stated that good deflation is impossible. Therefore, they also revived the good deflation theory that reflationists previously criticized.

Finally, the monetary policy of the reflationists that works on the inflation expectations is to lower the real interest rate by increasing prices, assuming that the nominal interest rate has reached its lower bound. As we show in "Preface," Harada's (2021, p. 54) definition of the reflationist school also includes the phrase "lowering real interest rates." To say that prices do not have to rise is also to abandon the policy advocated by reflationists. As building the reflation regime means that prices must rise, allowing prices not to rise also means that it is unnecessary to build the reflation regime.

Iwata (as did other reflationists) dismissed failure as if it were a minor problem. This logically means that Iwata and the reflationists have admitted that their price theory and analysis of the current situation are wrong and that their proposed monetary policy is unfeasible. In this way, Iwata began to self-deny the theories and policies of reflationists.

When asked about his resignation, Iwata (2018a, p. 84) replied that he never said he would resign immediately, whatever the reason. He also said that if there were a mistake in policy choice, he would have chosen to resign if it was the best way to take the blame. This is also trickery, given that Iwata himself decides whether a policy choice was a mistake.

In our opinion, Iwata misjudged the idea that deflation could be overcome by the Japanese-style inflation target and an increase in the monetary base. Moreover, the Japanese-style inflation target and the rapid increase in the monetary base, which Iwata advocated, were abandoned after only about three years. The YCC, which has been adopted since 2016 instead, is the policy based on the BOJ's theory, which Iwata once criticized and even admitted has not affected raising inflation expectations. After introducing the YCC, the BOJ, contrary to Iwata's claim, has reduced the increase in the monetary base. After 2016, although the BOJ under Kuroda introduced one policy after another once criticized by Iwata, he neither opposed the policies nor resigned but chose to defend them. Five years have passed since 2018, but the BOJ under Kuroda has not overcome deflation. As Harada indicates, predictions based on Iwata's erroneous concept are always wrong.

4.4.2 Accounting Theory in Revival

The view that a consumption tax hike will hinder overcoming deflation is widely spread. Noguchi (2021, p. 168) also argues that the consumption tax hike prevented overcoming deflation. If deflation is truly a monetary phenomenon, the consumption tax hike should not lower prices. The claim that the consumption tax hike prevented the end of deflation itself rejects the reflationist theory. More problematic is that the consumption tax hike did not lower prices but raised prices through higher costs. The current mainstream theory of prices states that rising costs do not raise prices. Conversely, a decline in demand will lower prices. Mainstream economists are trapped in a false theory of prices and, accordingly, distort reality.

Even if the portion of the consumption tax hike is omitted, the consumption tax hike has not lowered the CPI inflation rate. Table 4.3 compares the inflation rate between the time when Abe became prime minister (December 2012), just before the consumption tax hike (March 2014), and March 2016. The rate of increase in the CPI (less fresh food) in March 2016 was −0.3, which is lower than when Abe took office as prime minister. However, the negative inflation rate was owing to a sharp decline in energy prices. The index less fresh food and energy rose by 0.9%, which is higher than just before the consumption tax hike. A consumption tax hike cannot plummet energy prices alone. The decline in the CPI inflation after the consumption tax hike was not owing to the consumption tax hike. However, the sharp decline in global oil prices at the time caused energy-related prices in Japan to plummet.

The effect of a decrease in demand on the price of consumer goods is actually limited. A consumption tax hike raises prices through higher costs, while the price decline owing to lower demand is limited. A sharp drop in global oil prices will thus lower prices through lower costs, while improved terms of trade in Japan will increase demand, albeit with a limited impact on prices. Overall, if we omit the price increases owing to the consumption tax hike, CPI does not decline. Again, our argument that costs (not demand) have the decisive meaning for the CPI in Japan is supported.

The BOJ at the time was aware that the decline in the CPI resulted from the sharp decline of global energy prices. For example, the BOJ's (The Bank of Japan, 2015, pp. 4–5) Outlook Report for October 2015 states, "The year-on-year rate of change in the CPI for all items less fresh food has been about 0 percent, due to the effects of the decline in energy prices, but the underlying trend in inflation has steadily been

Table 4.3 Consumer price inflation rate by item

	Less fresh foods (%)	Less fresh food and energy (%)	Energy (%)
December, 2012	−0.2	−0.5	3.4
Mar 2013	1.4	0.8	6.1
March 2016	−0.3	0.9	−13.4

Source Statistics Bureau, Ministry of Internal Affairs and Communications, Japan (2023)
Note Year-on-year change

improving, as indicated, for example, by the year-on-year rate of change in the CPI for all items less fresh food and energy, which exceeds 1 percent" (on the 2020 base, the rate of increase in the CPI less fresh food and energy was 1.2% in September 2015).

Iwata (e.g., 2015, pp. 5–7) argued that the decline in the CPI inflation rate was owing to the sharp decline in energy prices and that the underlying trend in inflation was improving. However, on NHK Supesharu (NHK Documentary), Iwata (Nihon Hōsō Kyōkai, 2023) stated that, at the time he was the deputy governor, he believed the consumption tax hike was in danger of preventing the end of deflation. He only did not express this belief publicly because it would disagree with the governor and hinder the ability of monetary policy to influence inflation expectations. In summary, his statement was not his belief.

Takatoshi Ito (2016, pp. 218–219) also stated:

> Excluding energy, inflation is now over 1%. It has reached the level of 1.1% or 1.3%, so in that sense, it can be said that it is already approaching more than half way to 2%.

He continued:

> Of course, critics say, "You said the same thing one or two years ago. You said that oil prices should not fall any further two years ago." Well, the BOJ's view is that crude oil prices have fallen more than expected, so it comes down to which one to trust.

He seemed embarrassed that the price outlooks of the BOJ and its supporters continued to be wrong, adding that:

> Certainly, prices were rising slower than expected. However, if you look at labor market indicators, the unemployment rate has declined to almost 3%.

According to the price theory, which posits that the output gap raises prices, prices rise by themselves when the labor market approaches full employment. As we believe that rising costs are overwhelmingly important, a decline in the unemployment rate may indirectly raise prices through wage increases, but its direct effect will be insignificant. Since the start of Abenomics, the problem has been that wages have not risen much, even though the Japanese economy is approaching full employment. In such a situation, prices do not rise as much.

Until 2016, the BOJ, Iwata, and Ito all claimed that the decline in the CPI inflation rate resulted from a sharp decline in global energy prices and that the momentum of inflation was rising. In other words, they also admitted that the consumption tax hike did not lower prices, even excluding the consumption tax hike. However, the idea that a sharp decline in global crude oil prices will lower prices is an "accounting theory," which, again, Iwata (2012, pp. 81–84) and Watanabe (2022, pp. 14–23) had earlier criticized. Watanabe argued that the frenzy of prices of 1974 was not the result of soaring global oil prices. According to the reflationist theory, a surge in oil prices causes energy-related prices to soar but also lowers non-energy-related prices. The assertion that indexes excluding energy prices show the momentum of inflation is a self-denial of the reflationist theory of prices. To avoid blame, the BOJ under Kuroda and Iwata revived not only the BOJ's theory of deflation but also the accounting theory (see Sect. 2.4.3).

4.4.3 Price Theory Ignores the Effects of Yen Depreciation

However, the CPI inflation rate less fresh food and energy declined from the beginning of 2016 and reached around 0% in 2017. During this period, rates of increase in the CPI less fresh food rose slightly from negative to near zero. Once again, the BOJ under Kuroda, Iwata, and Ito's outlooks were far off the mark. Outlooks based on erroneous reflationist theory were wrong again—but why?

Figure 4.3 illustrates the rate of increase in the CPI less fresh food and energy, the rate of change in the yen-dollar rate, and the rate of increase in import prices denominated in the contract currency. In 2013, import prices denominated in contract currencies declined slightly. The yen depreciated by well over 20% year-on-year, which created imported inflation. In 2015, import prices denominated in contract currencies plunged by more than 20% year-on-year because of the sharp decline in global energy prices, ending the imported inflation. Until mid-2015, however, imported inflation continued in the CPI less fresh food and energy owing to the rapid depreciation of the yen. In the second half of 2015, the yen's depreciation stopped, and the yen began to appreciate. By 2016, imported inflation in the CPI less fresh food and energy ended.

The BOJ, Iwata, and Ito's outlook were incorrect because they did not understand that the high rate of increase in the CPI less fresh food and energy was owing to

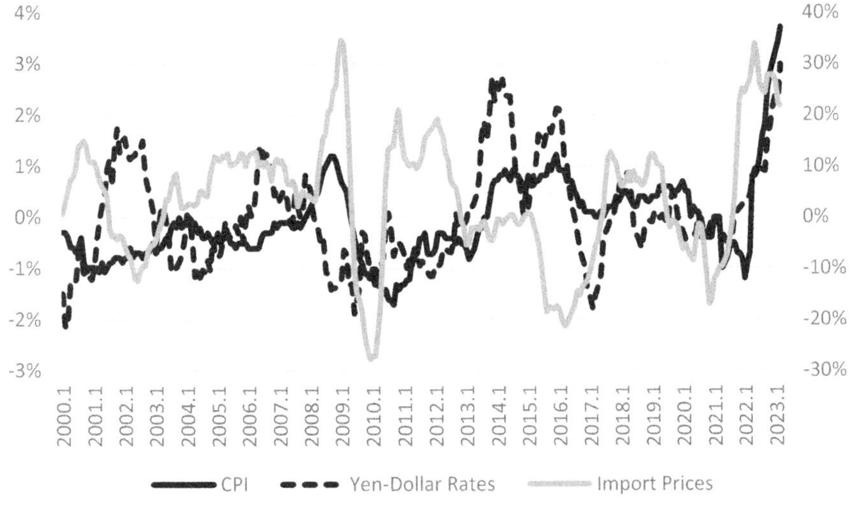

Fig. 4.3 Consumer price inflation rate, change in yen-dollar rate and import price inflation rate in contract currency (January 2000 to March 2023). *Source* Statistics Bureau, Ministry of Internal Affairs and Communications, Japan (2023) and the Bank of Japan (2023). *Note 1* "CPI" is indicated on the left-hand side axis, while others are indicated on the right-hand side. *Note 2* Year-on-year change. *Note 3* "CPI" is less food (less alcoholic beverages) and energy. "Import Prices" are in contract currencies. *Note 4* The rate of increases in "yen-dollar rate" and "import prices" were six months ago

imported inflation owing to the depreciation of the yen. In the first place, it would be a theoretical contradiction that a sharp global decline in energy prices pushes down CPI in Japan, but soaring import prices owing to the rapid depreciation of the yen does not raise CPI (see Hattori, 2017, pp. 95–105).

That the weak yen was causing CPI to rise was known. In a January 2015 report, Mizuho Research Institute (2015) presented an estimate by its econometric model that the CPI inflation rate less fresh food would be reduced by 0.1% overall, with the effects of the yen's depreciation and the effects of lower crude oil prices almost evenly matching. The BOJ (The Bank of Japan, 2016b, Appendix Chart 6–2) presents similar quantitative results. The report shows that most of the price fluctuations since 2013 have resulted from movements in the nominal effective exchange rate and real crude oil price. From 2015 to the beginning of 2016, the effects of the depreciation of the yen raising the CPI and the effects of lower crude oil price decline were almost balanced, and if the effects of both are omitted, the inflation rate has been almost zero.

While the effects of the yen's depreciation will spread to many consumption goods, the effects of lower oil prices are skewed toward energy-related products. We could assume that the sharp depreciation of the yen and the decline of oil prices were also responsible for the increase in the CPI less fresh food was negative, close to zero, and the approximately 1% increase in the CPI less fresh food and energy. Assuming this supposition is correct, once the sharp depreciation of the yen and the decline in crude oil price end, we can expect the rate of increase of both the CPI less fresh food and the CPI less fresh food and energy to be close to zero. In 2017, this outlook came true. Curiously, the BOJ's own analysis shows that most of the fluctuations in CPI in Japan are caused by fluctuations in the exchange rate and crude oil price, but leaders of the BOJ, including Kuroda and Iwata, have repeatedly made erroneous judgments and outlooks.

In 2018, Iwata (2018a) excused the inability to overcome deflation as the cause of the sharp drop in import prices. This is correct, but if it is correct, the rise in the CPI in 2013 should also have resulted from a sharp rise in import prices. However, Iwata claims that the rise in the CPI in 2013 was the result of monetary easing by the BOJ under Kuroda. This is a theoretical contradiction but a convenient argument for Iwata and the BOJ under Kuroda.

4.4.4 Blame-Shifting Theory that Denies the Reflationist Theory

The third shift of blame is that wages do not increase (much). Since the beginning of Abenomics, both the BOJ and the government have been saying, as a matter of course, that "there will be no end to deflation without wage increases." In 2016, Iwata (2016, p. 4) also showed that the rate of increase in nominal wages per hour and the inflation rate fluctuated in parallel in the long run and stated that wage increases are important. Rising import prices and consumption taxes raised the CPI through higher costs. Then, higher wages will also raise the CPI through higher costs. We and Yoshikawa (e.g., 2013, Chaps. 5 and 6, pp. 149–193; 2022, pp. 163–167) argue to this effect. Conversely, reflationists believe that the lack of wage increases is owing to continued deflation (Kuroda, 2013, p. 6; 2022, pp. 6–7). Iwata (2012, pp. 88–89) had earlier argued that wage stagnation could not be the cause of deflation. The theory of wage deflation, which reflationists had criticized, was also revived.

The fourth is adaptive inflation expectations. At a press conference in September 2016, Kuroda (The Bank of Japan, 2016a, p. 8) stated, "In practice, after the introduction of 'Quantitative and Qualitative Monetary Easing,' the inflation rate reached 1.5% in 2014. Subsequently, the actual inflation rate declined owing to the fall in oil prices and other factors, and I think it is undeniable that 'adaptive expectations formation' had a significant impact on the process". What is surprising about the theory of adaptive expectations formation is that it self-denies the core of reflationist theory. Gertler (2017) uses adaptive inflation expectations to explain why Kuroda's policies fail. Earlier, when Krugman (1998) advocated monetary policy to work on inflation expectations in 1998, Gordon and Blinder (Krugman, 1998, p. 201) argued that Krugman's policy would not work because inflation expectations are adaptable (see Sect. 3.3.1).

Inflation expectations are adaptive not only to consumers but also to ESP forecasters, who are experts in economic forecasting in Japan (see Figs. 2.1, 3.2). Inflation expectations did not affect the CPI inflation a year later. As long as inflation expectations do not work on inflation a year later, whether inflation expectations are adaptable is meaningless (see Sect. 3.2.3). In addition, if the expectations are adaptable and the BOJ under Kuroda raises prices, there would be a change in expectations regarding inflation. After all, the problem is not whether the expectations are adaptive but that soaring import prices will raise the CPI, and the BOJ under Kuroda cannot raise the CPI.

The fifth and last is the persistent deflationary mindset. Prices do not rise easily because Japanese people believe that deflation will continue as it always has. In a speech in 2017, Kuroda (2017, p. 9) stated that inflation expectations are more adaptive in Japan than in the U.S. and Europe: "The Bank of Japan aims to fundamentally dispel the deflationary mindset that has become entrenched among the public, but changing people's inflation perceptions is not easy. As Hawtrey argued, the problem is psychological." We consider this self-denial on the part of reflationists.

The fundamental problem is that the assertion that the CPI will not rise owing to a deflationary mindset is completely wrong. Kuroda himself pointed out that the inflation rate rose to 1.5% in 2014. The CPI rose within one step of the 2% inflation target. Iwata also claimed that prices had risen in 2013. Takatoshi Ito also stated that, by 2016, the economy was more than halfway out of deflation. On the one hand, it is a contradiction to say that the CPI has risen and, on the other hand, that it will not rise owing to a deflationary mindset. By 2022, the CPI inflation rate even exceeded 4%. According to the "Consumer Confidence Survey" from January to March 2023, conducted by the Economic and Social Research Institute, Cabinet Office (2023a), more than 90% of respondents said that prices would rise, and more than 60% said that prices would rise by 5% or more. However, these higher prices and higher inflation expectations are the result of higher import prices. Again, the problem is that the CPI is not rising owing to the monetary policy under the BOJ under Kuroda.

A thorough examination of excuses by Iwata and the BOJ under Kuroda reveals that costs do affect the CPI, but the BOJ's monetary policy cannot raise inflation expectations. These conclusions simultaneously support our price theory and reject the price theory of the reflationists. It was Bernanke (2017, p. 31) who stated that the excuses of the reflationists and BOJ under Kuroda were merely a restating of the fact that the BOJ under Kuroda would not end deflation through their monetary policy (see Chap. 1).

4.4.5 Iida Denies Reflationist Theory

Iida (2024, ii–iv) says that in the new neoclassical synthesis established in the 2000s, deficit financing to fight recession was to be avoided and that monetary policy should be exclusively responsible for economic stimulus. However, this common sense collapsed with the 2008 global financial crisis and many economists now believe that fiscal policy is also necessary. It was common sense to Keynesians until the 1970s that interest rates have a lower bound, at which point monetary policy could not be effective. "Monetary policy works for inflation, but not for deflation" was the favorite theory of Mitsuharu Ito,[2] a representative of Keynesian economists in Japan. Until Shirakawa, the BOJ had argued that monetary policy could not end deflation (e.g., Shirakawa, 2011, p. 5. See also Nakaso, 2022, p. 695). Conversely, the reflationists, including Iida, blindly followed the new neoclassical synthesis ideas and criticized the BOJ until Shirakawa said that deflation in Japan could be solved by monetary policy. Iida does not write about this.

Iida (2024, pp. 78–82) summarizes unconventional monetary policies such as inflation targeting and QE as policies that push down long-term interest rates by making people expect low interest rates for a long period. As the interest rate has a zero lower bound (in practice, negative close to zero), he says that monetary policy cannot overcome deflation when the neutral interest rate is negative. Therefore, Iida (2024, pp. 105–108) argues that these policies entail waiting for a chance for the neutral rate of interest to become positive owing to an economic boom that comes in cycles of 10 or 20 years.

The arguments of reflationists were quite the opposite. For example, Iwata states that, even if interest rates reached zero, monetary policy would overcome deflation by raising inflation expectations. Both the inflation target and the QE were means to that end. If inflation expectations increase, long-term interest rates will rise rather than fall as a result. When Iwata took office as the deputy governor of the BOJ, he boldly stated that the inflation target could be achieved within two years, and any failure would be his responsibility. This target was not achieved even after ten years,

[2] Mitsuharu Ito is my supervisor at my university and graduate school.

let alone two years, but neither Iwata nor anyone else took the blame. Instead, they shifted the blame for their failure onto all but monetary policy.

Iida justifies inflation targets and overshooting commitments by saying that they have the effect of raising inflation expectations. As the inflation target is a policy essential to the reflationists, it is understandable to justify it. However, we have shown that there is no basis for this claim (see Sect. 3.3.2). Besides, he does not consider the wolf-boy effect and the destruction of the BOJ's credibility when it fails to achieve its inflation target. The idea that monetary policy cannot overcome deflation when nominal interest rates reach a lower bound is a denial of the reflationist theory. Strangely, however, Iida does not admit the folly of reflationist theory.

4.4.6 Vested Theories and Vested Interests

After 2016, the BOJ under Kuroda effectively gave up on achieving its inflation target and introduced every theory and policy that the reflationists had criticized. The BOJ stopped the massive supply of monetary base and instead introduced the YCC, which was rooted in the BOJ's theory and had been criticized by the reflationists. The BOJ also stopped its commitment to the inflation target, effectively changing it to the "medo" (goal), which was criticized by the reflationists. The inflation target without a BOJ commitment and the overshooting commitment are policies of mere talk without implementation or responsibility, which Iwata and Hamada have criticized before. After only about three years, the BOJ effectively abandoned the reflationist theory.

Iwata does admit that the YCC has no effect on raising inflation expectations and that the momentum of inflation has not risen. He still defends the YCC and maintains that the reflationist theory is not wrong. Noguchi criticized the BOJ's theory but not the YCC. Harada said that an increase in the monetary base would boost nominal GDP but accepted that BOJ under Kuroda had slowed the pace of monetary base growth as the economy plunged into a recession. Even Wakatabe (2022) failed to indicate how monetary easing is possible after interest rates reach the lower bound in both the short and long term (see Sect. 3.2.1). Ignoring the fact that the BOJ under Kuroda had never achieved its inflation target, even in 2022, he claimed that the BOJ could achieve its inflation target by setting an inflation target. Iida effectively denies the reflationist theory but does not write that the reflationists were wrong.

Why do the reflationists and the BOJ under Kuroda engage in such illogical statements and behaviors? Asada (2015, 161–163) argues that many Japanese economists do not embrace reflationist economics because of their vested theories and vested interests. Asada (2015, pp. 157–158) summarizes the basic arguments of the reflationist in the following three points: First, in the medium to long term, the rate of increase in nominal money stock affects inflation rates, nominal GDP growth rates, and exchange rates. Second, fluctuations in nominal economic variables affect real economic variables such as real GDP growth and unemployment. Third, the BOJ has the greatest ability to determine the rate of increase in money stock. If it raises the rate of increase in money stock and resolves deflation, the Japanese economy will recover.

Asada (2015, p. 153) argues that these things are not a matter of personal preference or subjectivity but that of logic and data, which is superior to some extent. We agree with that. Additionally, data analysis in Chap. 2 and its Appendix shows that CPI in Japan fluctuated with import prices, not with the monetary base or money stock. Further, data analysis later in Chap. 5 shows that the massive supply of monetary base by the BOJ under Kuroda did not lead to an increase in the money stock. In Chap. 2, we also used data to show that real consumption has declined when CPI has risen in Japan since the 2000s. This indicates that prices move real variables but in the opposite direction to what Asada and reflationists believe. After analyzing the data correctly, it is clear that Asada's argument cannot be supported. However, even now that the BOJ under Kuroda has failed to end deflation, neither Asada nor the reflationists understand that the reflationists are theoretically wrong. Asada and the reflationists were obsessed with the vested theory, but those who are obsessed with the vested theory do not think they are obsessed with it.

Here, we observe a confirmation bias. The same phenomenon can yield different meanings depending on one's beliefs. Nakaso (2022, p. 695) argues that the policy by the BOJ under Kuroda confirms that monetary policy alone cannot overcome deflation. This is the traditional position of the BOJ, and it is a natural conclusion for a person directly involved with the operations of the BOJ. As shown in the "Preface," Harada (2021, p. 401) admits that the BOJ under Kuroda failed to achieve the 2% inflation target. Iwata (2018b, p. 419, p. 398) also acknowledged that the YCC could not raise inflation expectations and that deflation had not been overcome. Harada and Iwata thus argue close to Nakaso. However, neither Harada nor Iwata concludes that the BOJ under Kuroda does not have the power to overcome deflation. This is because it contradicts the reflationists' vested theory.

We believe that this is not the end of the story. At the very least, reflationists such as Iwata and Wakatabe should understand that the BOJ has abandoned the monetary policy that was first proposed by those very reflationists. At the very least, Iida probably understands that the arguments of the reflationists are no longer the common sense of the U.S. mainstream economics. To officially admit that the vested theory of reflationists is wrong and that the BOJ under Kuroda has abandoned its vested policy based on the vested theory would be a total defeat for the BOJ under Kuroda and reflationists and would damage their positions and reputations. We thus believe that they used the BOJ's theory of deflation, which they had earlier criticized, to shift the failure to overcome deflation away from monetary policy. Through sophomoric logic, they continued to make it appear that the monetary policy based on the reflationist theory is still in place and that overcoming deflation is well underway. In this sense, vested theories and vested interests are one and the same.

4.5 The BOJ Under Kuroda Has Destroyed the Reflationist Theory

Iwata and other reflationists adopted the Japanese-style inflation target and a large supply of the monetary base as policy tools to overcome deflation. These policies were in place only for the first three years at most. Unable to supply a large amount of monetary base, the BOJ under Kuroda introduced a negative interest rate policy, and then the YCC, based on the BOJ's theory, which has been criticized by reflationists, and started stealth tapering. The BOJ also stopped announcing its outlook for the period in which it would achieve its inflation target and stopped making commitments to its inflation target. It has also effectively changed the inflation target to the "medo" (goal) that reflationists had earlier criticized. The BOJ under Kuroda and the reflationists have shifted the blame for their failure to end deflation away from monetary policy and refused accountability. All their excuses use the BOJ's theory of deflation, which they once opposed. Logically, the BOJ under Kuroda and the reflationists have fully capitulated, however, admitting this would be detrimental to their positions and reputations. Therefore, they continue to insinuate that the monetary policy based on reflationist theory remains in place and that the Japanese economy is on its way out of deflation.

Appendix: Price Outlook of the BOJ

April 2013: The BOJ under Kuroda's first outlook.

Based on these factors, the outlook for prices—excluding the direct effects of the consumption tax hikes—is as follows. The year-on-year rate of change in the CPI is expected to follow a rising trend, reflecting factors such as the improvement in the aggregate supply and demand balance as well as the rise in medium- to long-term inflation expectations, and it is likely to reach around 2 percent—the price stability target—toward the latter half of the projection period. Comparing the current projection for the period through fiscal 2014 with that in the January 2013 interim assessment, the projected rates of change in the CPI are higher.

October 2014: First postponement of the date of achieving the inflation target.

Based on the above, the outlook for the year-on-year rate of increase in the CPI (excluding the direct effects of the consumption tax hikes) is as follows. It is likely to be at around the current level for the time being, and subsequently accelerate gradually and reach around 2 percent—the price stability target—around the middle of the projection period; that is, in or around fiscal 2015. Thereafter, the year-on-year rate of increase in the CPI is likely to edge up as medium- to long-term inflation expectations will converge to around 2 percent and the output gap is expected to continue expanding in positive territory. Comparing the current projections up through fiscal 2016 with those in the July 2014 interim assessment, the projected rate of increase in the CPI for fiscal 2015 is somewhat lower due mainly to the decline in international commodity prices, but that for fiscal 2016 is more or less unchanged.

October 2015: CPI inflation fell to negative owing to a sharp decline in crude oil prices.

Based on the above, the outlook for the year-on-year rate of change in the CPI (for all items less fresh food and excluding the direct effects of the consumption tax hikes, and the same hereafter) is as follows. It is likely to be about 0 percent for the time being and, as the underlying trend in inflation steadily rises and the effects of the decline in crude oil prices dissipate, accelerate toward 2 percent—the price stability target. Although the timing of reaching around 2 percent depends on developments in crude oil prices, it is projected to be around the second half of fiscal 2016, assuming that crude oil prices will rise moderately from the recent level. Thereafter, the year-on-year rate of change in the CPI is likely to be around 2 percent on average. Comparing the current projections with those in the July 2015 interim assessment, the projected rates of increase in the CPI for fiscal 2015 and 2016 are lower due mainly to the effects of the decline in crude oil prices, but the projection for fiscal 2017 is more or less unchanged.

October 2016: After the introduction of YCC. Added mention of downside risks.

The year-on-year rate of change in the consumer price index (CPI, all items less fresh food) is likely to be slightly negative or about 0 percent for the time being, and as the aggregate supply and demand balance (the output gap) improves and medium- to long-term inflation expectations rise, it is expected to increase toward 2 percent in the second half of the projection period.

With regard to the risk balance, risks to both economic activity and prices are skewed to the downside. On the price front, the momentum toward achieving the price stability target of 2 percent seems to be maintained but is somewhat weaker than the previous outlook, and thus developments in prices warrant careful attention going forward.

April 2018: Cancellation of the announcement of the outlook for when the inflation target could be achieved.

The year-on-year rate of change in the consumer price index (CPI, all items less fresh food) has continued to show relatively weak developments when excluding the effects of energy prices compared to the economic expansion and the labor market tightening, mainly against the background that firms' wage- and price-setting stance has remained cautious. Nonetheless, medium- to long-term inflation expectations are projected to rise as firms' stance gradually shifts toward raising wages and prices with an improvement in the output gap continuing. As a consequence, the year-on-year rate of change in the CPI is likely to continue on an uptrend and increase toward 2 percent.

With regard to the risk balance, upside and downside risks to economic activity are generally balanced in fiscal 2018, but risks are skewed to the downside for fiscal 2019 onward. Risks to prices are skewed to the downside. On the price front, the momentum toward achieving the price stability target of 2 percent is maintained as the output gap is expected to continue improving and medium- to long-term inflation expectations are projected to rise gradually; however, the momentum is not yet sufficiently firm, and thus developments in prices continue to warrant careful attention.

January 2020: Just before the outbreak of COVID-19 in Japan.

The year-on-year rate of change in the consumer price index (CPI, all items less fresh food) is likely to increase gradually toward 2 percent, mainly on the back of the output gap remaining positive and medium- to long-term inflation expectations rising throughout the projection period, despite such effects as of the past decline in crude oil prices for the time being.

With regard to the risk balance, risks to economic activity are skewed to the downside, particularly regarding developments in overseas economies. Risks to prices are skewed to the downside, mainly due to the downside risks to economic activity and uncertainties over developments in medium- to long-term inflation expectations. The momentum toward achieving the price stability target of 2 percent is maintained but is not yet sufficiently firm, and thus developments in prices continue to warrant careful attention.

April 2020: Amid the pandemic of the COVID-19

Japan's economy is likely to remain in a severe situation for the time being due to the impact of the spread of the Novel Coronavirus (COVID-19) at home and abroad. The year-on-year rate of change in the consumer price index (CPI, all items less fresh food) is expected to be somewhat weak for the time being, mainly affected by the spread of COVID-19 and the decline in crude oil prices.

Thereafter, as the impact of the spread of COVID-19 wanes at home and abroad, Japan's economy is likely to improve, supported by accommodative financial conditions and the government's economic measures, as well as through the expected materialization of pent-up demand (i.e., demand that has been constrained) and a projected recovery in production from the decline brought about by the spread of COVID-19. The year-on-year rate of change in the CPI is likely to increase gradually. In this Outlook Report, the impact of the spread of COVID-19 is assumed to wane on a global basis through the second half of 2020. With regard to the risk balance, risks to both economic activity and prices are skewed to the downside, mainly due to the impact of COVID-19.

Source The Bank of Japan (2013–2020).

References

In Japanese

Asada, T. (2015). Keizai Gaku no Tayō sei wo Meguru Oboegaki: Defure to Kin'yū Seisaku ni Kansuru Tokushu Nihon tekina Ronsō ni Kanren Sa sete (Notes on diversity in economics: In connection with the special Japanese-style debates on deflation and monetary policy. In K. Yagi, Y. Aruka, H. Osaka, H. Ohnishi, & M. Yoshida, (Eds.), *Keizai gaku to Keizai Kyōiku no Mirai: Nihon Gakujutsu Kaigi Sanshō Kijun wo Koete* (*Future of economics and economic education: Beyond the reference criteria of Science Council of Japan*). Sakurai Shoten, pp. 145–167.

Asahi Shimbun. (2016). Tenshin Yame, Make wo Mitome yo (Stop change of course and admit defeat): Yasunari Ueno, chief market economist, Mizuho Securities. November 18, morning.

Economic and Social Research Institute, Cabinet Office, Japan. (2023a). Consumer confidence survey. https://www.esri.cao.go.jp/jp/stat/shouhi/shouhi.html.

Fujishiro, K. (2019). Yoku Yomu to Sugoi: Ōbāshūto gata Komittomento: Ji Sedai gata no Nichigin Bungaku (That are great when read carefully: Overshooting commitment: The next generation of rhetoric of the Bank of Japan). The Daiichi Life Research Institute, Inc., *Market Flash*, September 27.

Hamada, K. (2013). *Amerika wa Nihon Keizai no Fukkatsu o Shitte iru (America knows the revival of Japanese economy)*. Kodansha.

Hamada, K. (2017). 'Abenomikusu': Watashi wa Kangae Naoshita ('Abenomics': I have reconsidered). *Bungeishunju, 95*(1), 124–131.

Harada, Y. (2021). *Defure to Tatakau: Nichigin Shingi Iin Kutō to Shikō Sakugo no Go Nenkan (Fighting deflation: Five years of struggle and trial and error for the members of the policy board of the Bank of Japan)*. Chuokoron-Shinsha.

Hattori, S. (2017). *Itsuwari no Keizai Seisaku: Kakusa to Teitai no Abenomikusu* (*Deceptive economic policy: Abenomics of inequality and stagnation*). Iwanami Shoten.

Hattori, S. (2019). Ikizumaru Ryōteki Shitsuteki Kanwa Seisaku (Quantitative and qualitative monetary easing at the dead end). *Journal of Japanese Scientists, 54*(12), 32–39.

Hattori, S. (2022). Kuroda Nichigin wa Naze Defure Dakkyaku ni Shippai Shita no ka (Why the Bank of Japan under Governor Haruhiko Kuroda failed to overcome deflation). *Doshisha Shogaku, 74*(3), 1–41.

Iida, Y. (2024). *Zaisei Kin'yū Seisaku no Tenkan Ten: Nihon Keizai no Saisei Puran* (*Turning point in fiscal and monetary policies: A plan for the revival of the Japanese economy*). Chuokoron-Shinsha.

Ito, T. (2016). Hi Dentō teki Kin'yū Seisaku ni Genkai wa Aruka? Mainasu Kinri wo Chūshin to shite (Is there a limit to unconventional monetary policy? Focusing on negative interest rates). In Japan center for economic research, (Ed.), *Gekiron*: *Mainasu Kinri Seisaku* (*Heated debates*: *Negative interest rate policy*) (pp. 199–224). Nikkei Publishing.

Iwata, Kazumasa, Samikawa, I., & Japan Center for Economic Research, (Eds.). (2016). *Maiinasu Kinri Seisaku: San Jigen Kin'yū Kanwa no Kōka to Genkai (Negative interest rate policy: Effects and limits of three-dimensional monetary easing)*. Nikkei Publishing.

Iwata, K. (1993). *Kin'yū Seisaku no Keizai gaku: Nichigin Riron no Kenshō (Economics of monetary policy: An examination of the Bank of Japan's theory)*. Nikkei.

Iwata, K. (2012) *Nippon Ginkō*: *Defure no Ban'nin* (*The Bank of Japan: Keeper of deflation*). Nikkei Publishing.

Iwata, K. (2013). *Rifure wa Tadashii*: *Abenomikusu de Fukkatsu Suru Nihon Keizai* (*Reflation is correct: The Japanese economy revived by abenomics*). PHP Institute.

Iwata, K. (2018a). Rifure Riron mo Seisaku mo Tadashii, Daga Gyakuhū de Jikan ga Kakaru: Deguchi no Meikyū: Kin'yū Seisaku wo Tou (34) (Reflationist theory and policy are correct, but it takes time due to headwinds: Maze of exits: Questioning monetary policy, 34). *Shūkan Ekonomisuto*, 96(23), 82–85.

Iwata, K. (2018b). *Nichigin Nikki: Go Nenkan no Defure to no Tatakai (Diary in the Bank of Japan: Fighting deflation for five years)*. Chikuma Shobo.

Karube, K. (2022) *Afutā Abenomikusu: Igyō no Keizai Seisaku wa Ikani Henshitsu Shita no ka? (After abenomics: How unusual economic policies have changed?)*. Iwanami Shoten.

Kodama, Y. (2018). Bukka Mokuhyō no Tassei Jiki o Sakujo (Deletion of the timing of inflation target achievement). *Meiji Yasuda Life Insurance Company, Keizai Watchi, 3*, Second week of May, 3–9.

Mizuho Research Institute. (2015). En Yasu to Gen'yu Yasu no Shōhi sha Bukka e no Eikyō: Gen'yu Yasu no Eikyō ga Masari, Bukka Osisage ni Sayō (The effects of the Yen's depreciation and lower crude oil prices on consumer prices: The effects of lower crude oil prices prevail and push prices down). *Mizuho Insight,* January 7.

Nakaso, H. (2022). *Saigo no Bōei Sen: Kiki to Nippon Ginkō (The last defense line: Crisis and the Bank of Japan).* Nikkei Business Publications and Nikkei Publishing.
Nihon Hosō Kyōkai (2023). NHK Supesharu: Shōgen Dokyumento: Nichigin Ijigen Kanwa no Jū Nen (NHK documentary: Testimonial document: Ten years of the Bank of Japan monetary easing of different dimensions). TV, April 16.
Noguchi, A. (2021). *Han Kinshuku no Keizai gaku* (*The economics of anti-austerity*). Toyo Keizai.
Okina, K. (1993). *Kin'yū Seisaku: Chūō Ginkō no Shiten to Sentaku* (*Monetary policy: Perspectives and choices of a central bank*). Toyo Keizai.
Suzuki, A. (2022) *Defure to no 20 Nen Sensō* (*The 20-year war against deflation*). Kinzai Institute for Financial Affairs.
Takashima, O. (2016). The Market: Kawase: Endaka Atsuryoku Masu (The market: Foreign exchange: Increasing pressure on the strong yen). *Shūkan Ekonomisuto, 94*(42), 90.
Tanaka, T. (2023). *Kin'yū Seisaku no Dai Tenkan: Chūō Ginkō no Mosaku to Kadai (The great transformation of monetary policy: Quests and challenges for central banks).* Keio University Press.
The Bank of Japan. (2013a). Sōsai fuku Sōsai Shūnin Kisha Kaiken Yōshi: (Summary of the press conference of the inauguration of the governor and deputy governor, March 21). March 22.
The Bank of Japan. (2013b). Sōsai Kisha Kaiken Yōshi (Summary of the governor's press conference, April 4). April 5.
The Bank of Japan. (2016a). Sōsai Kisha Kaiken Yōshi (Summary of the governor's press conference, September, 21). September 23.
The Bank of Japan. (2018a). Sōsai Kisha Kaiken Yōshi (Summary of the governor's press conference, April 27). May 1.
Watanabe, T. (2022). *Bukka to wa Nani ka?* (*What are Prices?*). Kodansha .
Yoshikawa, H. (2013). *Defrēshion: Nihon no Mansei Byō no Zembō wo Kaimei Suru (Deflation: Elucidating the whole picture of chronic diseases of Japan).* Nikkei Publishing.

In English

Bernanke, B. S. (2017). The Mayekawa lecture: Some reflections on Japanese monetary policy. *Monetary and Economic Studies, 35*, 23–37.
Bernanke, B. S. (2022). *21st century monetary policy: The Federal Reserve from the great inflation to covid-19.* W. W. Norton.
Bureau of Economic Analysis, the U.S. (2023). *Gross domestic product.* https://www.bea.gov/data/gdp/gross-domestic-product.
Economic and Social Research Institute, Cabinet Office, Japan. (2023b). National accounts for 2022. https://www.esri.cao.go.jp/en/sna/data/kakuhou/files/2022/2022annual_report_e.html.
Gertler, M. (2017). Rethinking the power of forward guidance: Lessons from Japan. *Monetary and Economic Studies, 35*, 39–57.
Iwata, K. (2015). Japan's economy and monetary policy. Speech at a meeting with business leaders in Okayama, December 2.
Iwata, K. (2016). Japan's economy and monetary policy. Speech at a meeting with business leaders in Nagasaki, December 7.
Japan Bond Trading Co., Ltd (2023) BEI rate. We are personally provided with data.
Kataoka, G. (2019). Economic activity, prices, and monetary policy in Japan. Speech at a meeting with business leaders in Kagawa, February 27.
Kiuchi T. (2015). Recent developments in economic activity, prices, and monetary policy, Speech at a Meeting with Business Leaders in Aomori, September 3.
Kohn, D., & Sack, B. (2020). Monetary policy during the financial crisis. In B. S. Bernanke, T. F. Geithner, & H. Paulson, Jr. (Eds.), *First responders: Inside the U.S. strategy for fighting the 2007–2009 global financial crisis* (pp. 421–450). Yale University Press.

Krugman, P. R. (1998). It's Baaack: Japan's slump and the return of the liquidity trap. *Brookings Papers on Economic Activity*, (2), 137–205.

Kuroda, H. (2013). Overcoming deflation and after. Speech at the meeting of Councillors of Nippon Keidanren (Japan Business Federation) in Tokyo, December 25.

Kuroda, H. (2017). The role of expectations in monetary policy: Evolution of theories and the Bank of Japan's experience. Speech at the University of Oxford, June 8.

Kuroda, H. (2022). Toward achieving the price stability target in a sustainable and stable manner: Accompanied by wage increases. Speech at the meeting of Councillors of Keidanren (Japan Business Federation) in Tokyo, December 26.

Shirakawa, M. (2011). Toward a revitalization of Japan's economy. Speech at the Foreign Correspondents, Club of Japan, February 7.

Statistics Bureau of Japan, Ministry of Internal Affairs and Communications. (2023). Consumer price index. https://www.stat.go.jp/english/data/cpi/index.htm.

The Bank of Japan. (2013–2020). Outlook for economic activity and prices. https://www.boj.or.jp/en/mopo/outlook/index.htm.

The Bank of Japan. (2015). Outlook for economic activity and prices (April 2015). May 1.

The Bank of Japan. (2016b). Comprehensive assessment: Developments in economic activity and prices as well as policy effects since the introduction of quantitative and qualitative monetary easing (QQE): The Background. September 21.

The Bank of Japan. (2018b). Strengthening the framework for continuous powerful monetary easing. July 31.

The Bank of Japan. (2020). Enhancement of monetary easing. April 27.

The Bank of Japan. (2023). BOJ time-series data search. https://www.stat-search.boj.or.jp/index_en.html.

Wakatabe, M. (2022). The future of monetary policy: Lessons from the history of monetary economics. Keynote speech at the 38th annual meeting of the Japan Association of Business Cycle Studies, December 3.

Woodford, M. (2012). Methods of policy accommodation at the interest-rate lower bound. September 16 (Revised draft of a paper presented at the Federal Reserve Bank of Kansas City symposium on 'The changing policy landscape'. Jackson Hole, Wyoming, August 31).

Yoshikawa, H. (2022). *Reconstruction of macroeconomics: Methods of statistical physics, and Keynes principle of effective demand*. Springer.

Chapter 5
Revisiting the Controversy on the Money Supply

Abstract When secular stagnation in Japan began in the early 1990s, Kikuo Iwata, who was later appointed as the Deputy Governor of the Bank of Japan (BOJ), argued that this was because the BOJ was decreasing the growth rate of the money stock. Kunio Okina countered that the BOJ was supplying the monetary base in response to demand and could not increase the money stock. Thus began the controversy on the money supply. Although the BOJ under Kuroda supplied a large monetary base, it could not raise the rate of money stock growth. Central banks in the United States and Europe also supplied large amounts of monetary base after the global financial crisis, but, eventually, they could not increase the money stock. Thus, Iwata also lost the controversy on the money supply. We will clarify not only why a massive supply of monetary base does not lead to an increase in the money stock but also the mechanism by which deficit fiscal policy increases the money stock. Based on this argument, we also clarify the fallacy of Friedman's theory of the Great Depression and reflationists' claim that Takahashi's fiscal policy in Japan in the 1930s was a monetary policy of increasing the money stock.

Keywords Abenomics · The Bank of Japan under Kuroda · Deflation in Japan · The controversy on the money supply · Theory of money multiplier · Friedman's theory of the Great Depression · Takahashi's fiscal policy · Kunio Okina · Kikuo Iwata

5.1 Introduction

In the early 1990s, the bubble in Japan burst, and secular stagnation began. At the time, Kikuo Iwata (e.g., 1993) argued that the economic stagnation was owing to the BOJ not easing monetary policy and leaving deflation unattended. In response, Okina (e.g., 1993), who worked for the BOJ at the time, argued that the BOJ could not increase its money stock. Thus, the controversy on the money supply began. Since then, the argument that an increase in the monetary base does not lead to an increase in money stock has become a standard criticism of reflationists (e.g., Suzuki, 2022,

S. Hattori, *Why the Bank of Japan Has Failed to Conquer Deflation in Japan*,
https://doi.org/10.1007/978-981-97-9408-9_5

p. 134; Ito, 2022, pp. 209–210n). Moreover, the massive supply of the monetary base by the BOJ under Kuroda once again showed that the criticism of Okina and others was correct.

This chapter clarifies why an increase in the monetary base does not lead to an increase in money stock. In exceptional cases, the money stock increases. It is also important to clarify why it increases in some cases. We will also clarify how deficit fiscal policy leads to an increase in money stock. After the global financial crisis, central banks in the United States (U.S) and Europe have also sharply increased their monetary bases, but this, too, has not led to an increase in the money stock.

Note that Friedman argued that the Great Depression of the 1930s was the result of the Federal Reserve not easing monetary policy and leaving deflation unattended. The premise of this claim is that the central bank can increase the money stock. Thus, the question of whether the central bank can increase the money stock spills over into the question of whether Friedman's theory of the Great Depression was correct.[1]

In this chapter, in Sect. 5.2, we show why the massive supply of the monetary base by the BOJ under Kuroda did not ultimately lead to an increase in the money stock. Conversely, we also show that deficit-financing policy can increase the money stock through banks' holdings of government bonds. In addition, we show that the massive supply of monetary base by the Federal Reserve after the global financial crisis did not lead to an increase in the money stock. In Sect. 5.3, we will show that the deficit-financing policy increased the money stock both in the U.S. after the Great Depression and Korekiyo Takahashi's fiscal policy in Japan in the 1930s. Section 5.4 presents conclusions.

5.2 Why Could the BOJ Under Kuroda Not Increase Its Money Stock?

5.2.1 Controversy on the Money Supply

In the early 1990s, the bubble burst, and a secular stagnation began in Japan. At the time, Iwata (e.g., 1993) was one of the first to argue that the economic stagnation was owing to the BOJ leaving deflation unattended without easing monetary policy.

[1] Hattori (2007) has already clarified that an increase in the monetary base does not lead to an increase in the money stock not only in Japan but also in the U.S. and the UK since the 1990s. We clarify that the increase in money stock while lending has been decreasing in Japan since the 1990s was the result of deficit fiscal policies. In the U.S. after the Great Depression and in Japan during Takahashi's fiscal policy, the increase in the money stock amid declining lending was the result of deficit fiscal policies. However, in the U.S., the inflow of gold after 1933 also contributed to the increase in the money stock (for more details regarding the U.S. during and after the Great Depression, see Hattori, 2022).

Iwata's rationale for the BOJ's monetary tightening was the low rate of money stock growth. He also criticized the BOJ's belief that it could not control its money stock, calling it the BOJ's theory.

Okina (e.g., 1993) refuted Iwata's claim that money stock would not increase in a situation where lending did not increase. His rebuttal has become one of the staples of the rebuttal to reflationists to this day. Iwata reiterated that banks should increase their money stock through securities purchases even if lending does not increase. Almost 20 years thereafter, Iwata (2009, pp. 178–187, p. 201) continued to hold that the money stock would increase if the monetary base surged. However, in *Nippon-Ginkō* (*The Bank of Japan*), he (Iwata, 2012, pp. 217–220) changed his opinion that an increase in money stock or lending is not necessary to raise prices. As shown in Sect. 4.4.6, Asada (2015, p 157) argues that the BOJ can increase the money stock. As discussed below, the rate of money stock growth has remained sluggish under BOJ Kuroda, but strangely, Asada has not demanded that BOJ under Kuroda increase the money stock.

The policy of the BOJ under Kuroda was also an essential historical experiment in the controversy on the money supply. Consequently, the BOJ under Kuroda surged its monetary base, however, the rate of increase in its money stock remained sluggish. After the global financial crisis, central banks in the U.S. and Europe also surged their monetary bases. However, a sharp increase in the monetary base did not lead to a sharp increase in money stock. Not only the BOJ under Kuroda but also the experiments of Western central banks proved the fallacy of Iwata's claims. As mentioned in Sects. 3.4.3 and 3.2.2, Bernanke (2022, pp. 141–144) and Woodford (Woodford, 2012, pp. 49–56) believe that an increase in the monetary base does not lead to an increase in money stock.

The source of Iwata's argument is Friedman's theory of the Great Depression. He famously claimed that the cause of the Great Depression was the Federal Reserve's tightening policy, which caused the money stock to plummet by one-third. However, if the Federal Reserve in the 1930s, like the BOJ under Kuroda and the central banks of the U.S. and Europe after the global financial crisis, could not increase its money stock, then Friedman's criticism is groundless. Thus, the problems raised by the controversy on the money supply are significant in dealing with macroeconomics and monetary policy problems.

5.2.2 Controversy Is Overwhelmingly Won by Okina

As mentioned at the beginning of Sect. 3.2.2, the monetary base and money stock are different. However, according to the money multiplier theory, the BOJ can increase its money stock by increasing its monetary base. First, suppose the BOJ purchases ¥10 billion of Japanese government bonds (JGBs) from depository institutions. At this time, the BOJ's holdings of JGBs will increase. Depository institutions will reduce their holdings of JGBs by ¥10 billion but will receive ¥10 billion in payment. Depository institutions will not make a profit by putting this money in the current account of the BOJ so that they will lend it. Borrowing companies and individuals spend most of the money and hold the rest in the form of cash and deposits. Note that spending only changes the owner of money, not the amount of it. Therefore, bank lending generates ¥10 billion in cash and deposits. Here, if the ratio of deposits to cash is 9 to 1, deposits are ¥9 billion, and cash is ¥1 billion.

Depository institutions should accumulate current accounts at the BOJ according to their deposits. If the ratio of deposits to current accounts at the BOJ is 81 to 1, the BOJ's current account will be ¥1/9 billion. If depository institutions use the remaining for lending, the above process will proceed again. Thus, the money multiplier theory states that the supply of the monetary base by the BOJ creates a multiplier times the money stock.

In the current example,

$$\text{Monetary Base} = \text{Cash} + \text{Current Account at the BOJ} = ¥10 \text{ billion},$$

$$\text{Deposits / Cash} = 9, \text{Deposits / Current Account at the BOJ} = 81$$

Therefore,

$$\text{Money Stock} = ¥90 \text{ billion, Cash} = ¥9 \text{ billion, Deposits} = ¥81 \text{ billion},$$

$$\text{Current Account at the BOJ} = ¥1 \text{ billion, Lending} = ¥90 \text{ billion}.$$

In this way, the supply of the monetary base creates a nine-fold increase in the money stock.

Table 5.1(A) shows the changes in the assets and liabilities of the BOJ and depository institutions. As Iwata says, the money stock will increase when depository institutions increase their securities holdings instead of lending. In this case, the items of depository institution assets in Table 5.1(A) replace securities such as JGBs, municipal bonds, and corporate bonds. However, while it may be changed to securities, it remains necessary to increase the assets of depository institutions.

Although omitted for simplicity in the table, the BOJ and depository institutions have liabilities other than money. For example, if a depositor withdraws a deposit from a depository institution and purchases a bond issued by a depository institution instead, the item of debt of the depository institution changes from a deposit to a corporate bond. The assets of depository institutions will remain unchanged, but the money stock will decrease. Considering this,

Increase in Money Stock
=Increase in Assets of the BOJ and Depository Institutions
– Increase in Non-Monetary Liabilities.

Figure 5.1 illustrates the changes in various assets of the BOJ and depository institutions, monetary base, and M3. The figure shows the difference from March 2013, when Kuroda became the governor of the BOJ. The figure omits claims between the BOJ and depository institutions. Claims on the central government are subtracted from liabilities since cash and deposits held by the central government do not count as money stock. The BOJ under Kuroda's massive purchase of JGBs was also a major experiment to see which of Iwata's or Okina's arguments were correct. The figure shows that the BOJ's claims on the central government have increased rapidly since Kuroda reigned over the BOJ. In tandem, the monetary base also surged, and most

Table 5.1 Relationship between the monetary base and money stock and the assets of the BOJ and depository institutions

(A) Buying operations and increase in bank lending			
Asset		Debt	
Central bank			
JGBs	10	Cash	9
		Current Account at the BOJ	1
Depository institutions			
Current Account at the BOJ	1	JGBs	10
Loans	90	Deposit	81
Consolidated tables			
Asset		Debt	
Loans	90	Cash	9
		Deposit	81
Current Account at the BOJ	1	Current Account at the BOJ	1
(B) Buy operation only			
Asset		Debt	
Central bank			
JGBs	10	Current Account at the BOJ	10
Depository institutions			
Current Account at the BOJ	10	JGBs	10
Consolidated tables			
Current Account at the BOJ	10	Current Account at the BOJ	10
(C) Direct underwriting of JGBs			
Asset		Debt	
Central bank			
JGBs	10	Cash	1
		Current Account at the BOJ	9
Depository institutions			
Current Account at the BOJ	9	Deposit	9
Consolidated tables			
JGBs	10	Cash	1
		Deposit	9
Current Account at the BOJ	9	Current Account at the BOJ	9

(continued)

Table 5.1 (continued)

(D) Issuance of JGBs and purchases of JGBs by depository institutions Central bank			
Asset		Debt	
Central bank			
Current Account at the BOJ	1	Cash	1
Depository institutions			
JGBs	10	Cash	1
		Deposit	9
Consolidated tables			
JGBs	10	Cash	1
		Deposit	9
Current Account at the BOJ	-1	Current Account at the BOJ	-1

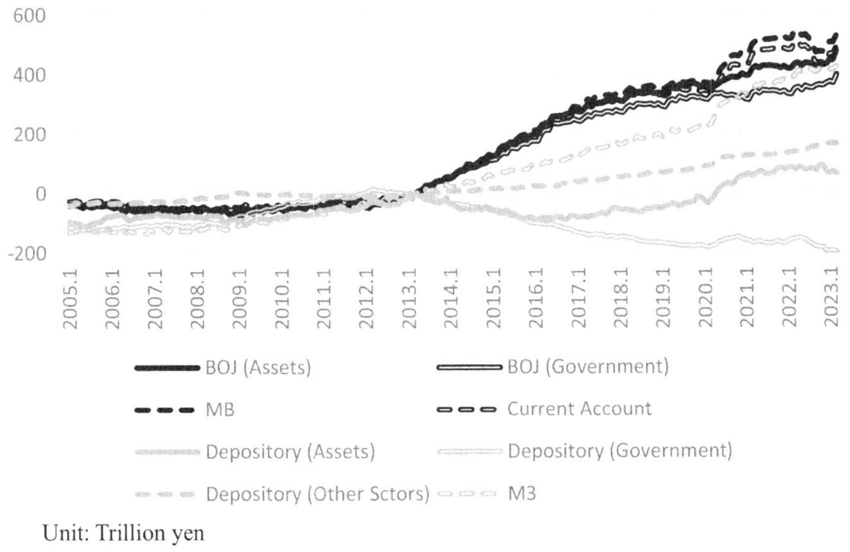

Fig. 5.1 Assets of the BOJ and depository institutions, monetary base, and M3 (January 2005 to March 2023). *Source* The Bank of Japan (2023). *Note 1* Difference from March 2013. *Note 2* "Government" is claim on the central government. "Current Account" is the current account at the BOJ. "MB" is monetary base. "Depository" is depository institutions. "Depository (Other sectors)" is depository institution's domestic credits (excluding shares), excluding those on central and local government and financial institutions. Claims between the BOJ and depository institutions are omitted from assets. Foreign assets are net claims. Claims on the central government are subtracted from liabilities to the central government

of the surging monetary base is in the current account at the BOJ. However, the pace of increase in M3 has continued to be gradual, just as it was before the BOJ under Kuroda.

From September 2014 to September 2015, the BOJ under Kuroda increased the monetary base most rapidly. Table 5.2 compares this period with the last year of the BOJ under Shirakawa (March 2012 to March 2013). From September 2014 to September 2015, the BOJ expanded its assets by ¥80 trillion. Most of this expansion was in claims on the central government (JGBs in practice). Accordingly, both the monetary base and the current account at the BOJ increased by more than ¥80 trillion. However, the combined assets of the BOJ and the depository institutions increased by only ¥48 trillion, less than the ¥56 trillion in the last year of Shirakawa. The main reason is that depository institutions sharply reduced claims on the central government. The increase in M3 in September 2015, at ¥33 trillion, is less than half the increase in the monetary base and the current account deposits at the BOJ. It is only slightly larger than the ¥28 trillion increase during the last year of the Shirakawa. The year-on-year growth rates were 2.8% and 2.5%, respectively.

Iwata argued that the BOJ's supply of the monetary base would increase the money stock through depository institutions' purchases of securities. In reality, depository institutions experienced a sharp decline in assets owing to a decrease in their holdings of JGBs, resulting in almost no change in the M3 growth rate—the opposite of what Iwata had claimed occurred. The controversy on the money supply also ended in the overwhelming victory of Okina and the critics of quantitative easing (QE). The BOJ had already implemented the QE policy from 2001 to 2006. Thereafter, the rate of increase in the monetary base was not low, except for some periods. A large portion of the massively supplied monetary base became excess reserves and, consequently, did not lead to an increase in the money stock.

The COVID-19 pandemic period in 2020 is an exception. During this period, the assets of depository institutions surged. This was owing to a surge in claims on the financial institutions other than depository institutions and the other sector. When COVID-19 spread, the number of companies struggling with cash flow, mainly in

Table 5.2 Differences in the assets of the BOJ and depository institutions, monetary base, and M3

	BOJ		Depository institutions		
	Assets	Claim on central government	Assets	Claim on central government	Claim on other sectors
March 2012 to March 2013	37.1	36.5	18.7	−14.5	7.7
September 2014 to September 2015	79.8	69.1	−32.2	−38.3	7.6

	MB	Current account at the BOJ	M3
March 2012 to March 2013	26.3	23.7	28.1
September 2014 to September 2015	85.9	80.7	33.4

Unit Trion yen
Source The Bank of Japan (2023)
Note "Other sectors" is domestic claims (excluding shares) excluding central and local government and financial institutions. Claims between the BOJ and depository institutions are omitted from assets. Claims on the central government are subtracted from liabilities to the central government

the travel industry and restaurants, increased rapidly. Owing to these special circumstances, the demand for borrowing also arose rapidly. The government and the BOJ encouraged banks to lend to companies suffering from COVID-19. As depository institutions surged lending, so did M3. However, the increase in M3 was temporary, and when firms' financial positions improved, the increase in M3 became smaller than before the pandemic. The argument that the monetary base will not increase money stock in a situation where there is no borrowing demand implies that money stock can also increase if there is a large borrowing demand. The surge in money stock during COVID-19 also proved the validity of critics of QE that money stock could also surge if there is borrowing demand.

5.2.3 Deficit Fiscal Policy Increases Money Stock

What is the error in Iwata's assertion? The premise of the money multiplier theory is that depository institutions use excess current accounts at the BOJ beyond the necessary level for lending or purchasing securities. For depository institutions to lend, companies and individuals to borrow must exist; and to purchase securities, companies and individuals selling securities must also exist. This is a necessary condition. Even if there exists a demand to borrow or securities to sell, depository institutions will not lead to lending or purchasing securities unless they judge that the benefits outweigh the risks. In the absence of attractive loans and securities from the view of the depository institutions, the BOJ's purchases of JGBs will only increase the BOJ's current account at the BOJ. This case is shown in Table 5.1(B). As Fig. 5.1 shows, when the BOJ under Kuroda purchased a large amount of JGBs, the JGB holdings of depository institutions declined sharply, reducing their asset holdings. Except for a temporary increase in borrowing demand during the COVID-19 crisis, the purchases of JGBs by the BOJ under Kuroda since the 2000s have basically created the situation shown in Table 5.1(B).

Here, there is an assumption of "*ceteris paribus*." In the real world, other things are *not* equal. If other things do change, the money stock will increase. Suppose that the BOJ purchases ¥10 billion of JGBs newly issued by the government. The government will use the money it receives for tax cuts or government spending. Those who receive money from the government hold them in the form of ¥1 billion in cash and ¥9 billion in deposits, for example. In this case, an increase in the money stock will be equal to that of an increase in the monetary base. However, the increase in current accounts at the BOJ was ¥9 billion, the same as the increase in deposits. As the money stock grows, banks will have additional excess reserves. This is the case with Table 5.1 (C).[2]

[2] Although the table assumes that government bond issuance and bank lending are determined independently, this is not always the case. When the government spends, individuals or firms earn money. They may then reduce their borrowing from banks. Thus, if the expansion of bank assets is suppressed, the increase in money will also be smaller.

Even for government bonds already issued, if the BOJ purchases them from other than depository institutions, the results in Table 5.1 (C) can be realized. Mcleary et al. (2014, pp. 21–25) explain how the Bank of England's (BOE's) QE policy increases the money stock. In their example, the central bank buys assets from the pension fund and pays for them, the payments are deposited and created money. At this time, the bank accumulates excess reserves. They further explain that the multiplier process does not proceed because this excess reserve does not go to lending. Our explanation is the same in theory as that of Mcleary et al. Additionally, in Japan, there is a broader index of money stock, broadly-defined liquidity, which includes government bonds; it has increased only when the government issues government bonds. The BOJ purchases exchange-traded funds and Japan real estate investment trusts. As the sellers would not be a depository institution, this portion would increase the money stock.

Furthermore, since the 2000s, depository institutions in Japan have had large excess reserves. In such a situation, if government bonds are issued, depository institutions will purchase them. Those who receive the payment from the government will hold it in the form of ¥1 billion in cash and ¥9 billion in deposits. In this case, the money stock will increase by ¥10 billion, but the current account at the BOJ will decrease by ¥9 billion. This is the case in Table 5.1(D).

Since the 2000s, massive issuance of JGBs has increased the money stock through depository institutions' purchases of government bonds. The BOJ, particularly under Kuroda, increased the monetary base by purchasing a large amount of government bonds from depository institutions. However, this only creates excess reserves and does not lead to an increase in the money stock (see also Hattori, 2007, Chap. 1, pp. 41–65). Since the mid-2000s, deposit institutions' lending has been on an increasing trend (it declined at some times, such as during and shortly after the global financial crisis, and the rate of increase is not so high even when it is increasing). Therefore, we do not deny that the increase in lending has also contributed to the increase in money stock to some extent.

Koo (2007, pp. 37–44, 2009, pp. 85–92) also points out that deficit fiscal policy increases money stock and that monetary policy cannot function without fiscal policy under the balance sheet recession. Reviewing Iwata's argument, we admit that, even if banks reduce lending, the money stock can increase by increasing their securities holdings (JGBs in practice). However, Iwata overlooked the fact that if the government did not issue a large amount of JGBs, banks would not be able to increase their holdings. He thus wrongly concluded that the BOJ can increase the money stock by simply supplying the monetary base through the purchase of JGBs by banks.

From the borrower's point of view, both borrowings from banks and securities such as corporate bonds are their debts, and there is no essential difference. Conversely, the difference between firms and government is significant. When the economy is stagnant, there is little need for firms to borrow. Some of the numerous firms may have significant borrowing needs. However, in a period of stagnation, lending to these firms will often be risky from the bank's perspective. Thus, lending to firms would stagnate or decline during periods of stagnation. Conversely, during periods of stagnation, government tax revenues decrease, but spending increases owing to measures against stagnation. As a result, the government's debt balloons. Moreover, in the flight to quality, government bonds are a promising investment destination for banks. During periods of stagnation, the money stock increases owing to deficit fiscal policy.

5.2.4 *Bernanke Also Failed to Increase the Money Stock*

Japan implemented the QE from 2001 to 2006. Although not as much as the BOJ under Kuroda, the monetary base surged, and even at the time, the sharp increase in the monetary base did not lead to an increase in the money stock. As noted in Sect. 3.4.3, Bernanke (2022, pp. 141–144) has stated that the QE in Japan was based on the idea of monetarism and was intended to increase the money stock but failed in doing so. He (Bernanke, 2022, p. 142) also writes that "[c]ounting on the expansion of reserve alone to stimulate the economy would be like the proverbial pushing on a string, most of us [members of the Federal Open Market Committee in 2008] believed," while Friedman supported Japan's QE policy.

Figure 5.2 illustrates the changes in the U.S. monetary base, M2, and reserves after the introduction of the QE. The figure shows the difference from September 2008, when the global financial crisis occurred. In the U.S., when three QE policies were implemented, the monetary base increased sharply. After each QE ended, the monetary base remained flat. In the U.S., tapering took the form of raising the interest rate on excess reserves before reducing the monetary base.

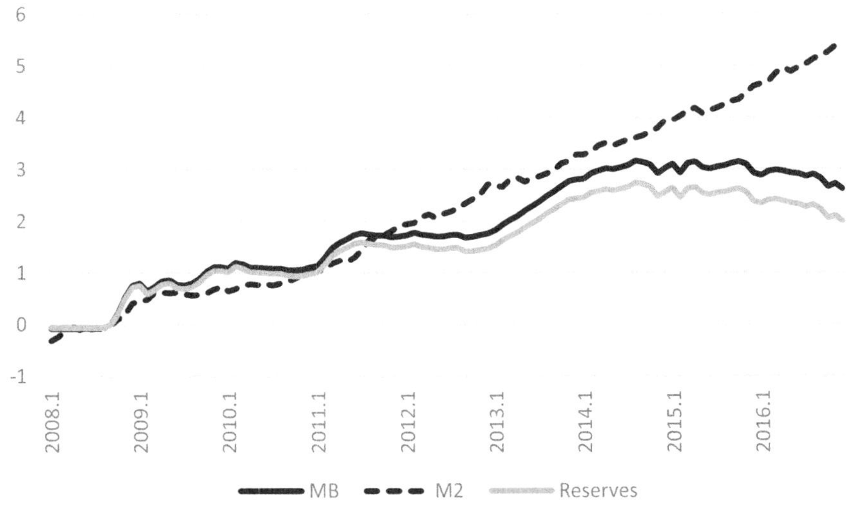

Unit: Tillion dollars

Fig. 5.2 U.S. monetary base, M2, and reserves in the U.S. after the global financial crisis (January 2008 to December 2016). *Source* Federal Reserve Bank of St. Louis (2023). *Note 1* Difference from September 2008. *Note 2* "MB" is monetary base. Seasonally adjusted except "Reserves"

In contrast, M2 continued to increase regardless of monetary base movements. Even after the end of each QE, the increase of M2 continued as before. It was reserves that were rapidly increasing in tandem with the monetary base—the same as the BOJ under Kuroda, where a sharp increase in the monetary base did not lead to an increase in the money stock but only a sharp increase in reserves.

Keister and McAndrews (2009) also explain the meaning of the Federal Reserve's provision of money to banks during the global financial crisis and hold that it does not cause inflation. Under normal circumstances, some banks have enough money, and some do not. Banks lacking funds can borrow from banks with excess funds in the interbank market. The Federal Reserve should supply the monetary base so that there is no excess or shortage of funds across the banks as a whole. However, during a financial crisis, even if a bank has a surplus of funds, it will not lend to a bank that is short but appears to be in danger. Banks that cannot borrow money from the market ultimately fail. To prevent their failure, the Federal Reserve needs to lend money to banks that cannot borrow in the market.

This way, excess reserves are supplied to the market. According to the money multiplier theory and Iwata's explanation, this excess reserve is used to lend or purchase securities, expanding the money stock. Keister and McAndrews conversely argue that if interest is charged on excess reserves, the excess reserves will not be used for lending if the rate of interest earned from lending is less than the rate of interest on the excess reserves. As bank lending is subject to the risk of default, when the lending rate is negative when adjusted for risk, banks will not lend even if the interest rate on excess reserves is zero. In such a case, a massive supply of monetary base will only lead to a sharp increase in excess reserves. Critics of the Federal Reserve's policy have criticized this excess reserve as being loaned out in the future, causing inflation. Keister and McAndrews (2009) argue that raising interest on excess reserves does not cause inflation. If economists at the Federal Reserve think that banks will use excess reserves to buy securities instead of using them for lending and increasing money stock, they will write so. Failure to write so would indicate that they do not think that banks use excess reserves to purchase securities.

After the global financial crisis of 2008, the monetary base also surged in the U. S. and Europe. As with Japan, it has not led to an increase in the money stock. In light of this, Goodhart (2010) questions the money multiplier theory, which states that the supply of the monetary base increases the money stock; however, he has long been critical of the money multiplier theory.

The experiences of the BOJ under Kuroda, or more precisely, Japan since the 2000s, as well as of the central banks of the U.S. and Europe after the global financial crisis, show that the large supply of the central bank's monetary base does not lead to an increase in money stock. As we have shown, asset purchases by a central bank may contribute to an increase in the money stock when assets are purchased from sources other than depository institutions. Even then, excess reserves do not create additional money stock through further lending or securities purchases. Our view is consistent with that of Bernanke and other U.S. and European policymakers.

5.3 The Great Depression and Fiscal Policy of Takahashi in the 1930s

5.3.1 Was the Federal Reserve Able to Increase Money Stock During the Great Depression?

Iwata's claim that the BOJ can increase its money stock is founded in Friedman's theory of the Great Depression. The Great Depression was the catalyst for the emergence of Keynesian economics and its spread worldwide. Keynes (1973[1936]) argued that monetary policy does not function in a liquidity trap with the lower bound on interest rates. Similar to mainstream American economists after the global financial crisis, he appealed to fiscal policy as an alternative to monetary policy. Just as after the global financial crisis, excess reserves were an issue in the U.S. after the Great Depression, owing to the lack of demand for funds, which meant that monetary authorities could make funds available but could not guarantee that they would be used. Thus, it is said that "monetary policy is like a string: you can pull on it, but you can't push on it." (Friedman and Schwartz, 1963, p. 348).

Friedman opposed these claims. He and Schwartz (Friedman and Schwartz, 1963, p. 348) argued that excess reserves are only excess in the legal sense. During the Great Depression, while banking crises did emerge in the U.S., the Federal Reserve did not fully perform its lender-of-last-resort function. Excess reserves were merely the result of banks, traumatized by the failure to adequately secure legal reserves and the lender of last resort, accumulating reserve deposits in excess of legal reserves.

Friedman's tool of monetary policy is money stock, and he argues against using nominal interest rates as a policy tool (Friedman, 1969, pp. 99–101). This is because when prices rise as a result of monetary easing, nominal interest rates rise. If, as Friedman says, monetary easing led to a rise in nominal interest rates after a certain period of time, it would be impossible for the zero lower bound to dry up monetary policy tools. The failure of the BOJ under Kuroda, central banks in the U.S. and Europe to increase their money stock, and the fact that interest rates are near zero in both the short term and the long term despite the BOJ under Kuroda's monetary easing of different dimensions, spills over into the larger question of whether Friedman's theories of the Great Depression and monetary policy are correct.

Friedman's theory of the Great Depression—which held that the central bank could increase its money stock by following the money multiplier process—was roundly criticized. Krugman (1998), for instance, pointed out that the movements of money stock and the monetary base during the Great Depression were not linked. Kaldor (1990[1970], pp. 517–519), arguing similarly, criticized Friedman for saying that the monetary base had increased during the Great Depression and that an increase in the monetary base had not lead to an increase in the money stock. Going back even further, in 1965, shortly after the publication of Friedman and Schwartz's (1963) *A Monetary History of the United States*, Tobin (1990[1965], pp. 211–212) noted in his review article that there had been a great deal of excess reserves after the

Great Depression, and explained it on the basis of Keynesian liquidity preferences. That is, until interest rates were close to zero, banks would hold government bonds and commercial paper, but beyond that, they would hold cash (in this case, excess reserves).

In the Federal Reserve's view in the 1930s, "excess reserves were primary unneeded surplus funds held by banks, proof of easy-money conditions and lack of private demand for credit" (Friedman and Schwartz, 1963, p. 461). Tobin's view is the same as that of the Federal Reserve in the 1930s. There is more: After the global financial crisis, Keister and McAndrews (2009), who worked for the Federal Reserve; Mcleary et al. (2014), who worked for the BOE; as well as Bernanke, Yellen, and Woodford agreed to the same effect. In Friedman's view, banks in the 1930s simply wanted to hold reserves in excess of legal reserves. Therefore, when the monetary base increases by one unit, the money stock that increases becomes smaller, but the money stock still increases. Friedman and Schwartz's view was inherited by Iwata (e.g., 2002, pp. 395–398).

5.3.2 No Link Between Monetary Base and Money Stock in the 1930s in the U.S.

Figure 5.3 illustrates the Monetary Base, M2, and Reserves before and after the Great Depression. The peak of the banking crisis during the Great Depression was in March 1933. Shortly after taking office, Franklin Roosevelt quickly ended the crisis with the bank holidays. This was the starting point for the recovery of the U.S. economy. Figure 5.3 also illustrates the difference from the peak of the banking crisis in March 1933.

The stock market crash in the U.S. occurred in October 1929. Earlier, in mid-1929, the economy had passed its peak. However, the money stock remained flat until October 1930, or at most marginally declined. As Friedman himself understands, the collapse of money began in November 1930. There were four banking crises during the Great Depression. The first banking crisis began in October 1930. Most of the money stock then was and now is bank deposits. At the time, there was no deposit insurance system, so when some banks failed, depositors withdrew their deposits from other seemingly dangerous banks. The sharp decline in the money stock resulted from the outflow of deposits triggered by the banking crisis. Cash holdings, which are not at risk of bankruptcy, rose sharply but did not affect the overall situation as cash is much smaller than deposits.

Even as the money stock declined sharply, the monetary base increased, as Kaldor and others have noted. Cash increased rapidly, and the cash-to-deposit ratio, which was less than 9% until October 1930, exceeded 20% in early 1933. Conversely, reserves did not increase, and there were several periods of decline. The reserve ratio did increase as deposits declined sharply. When the crisis subsided, the cash-to-deposit ratio dropped sharply, and reserves began to rise sharply. Thus, the claim that the cause of the surge in reserves was the banking crisis is dubious.

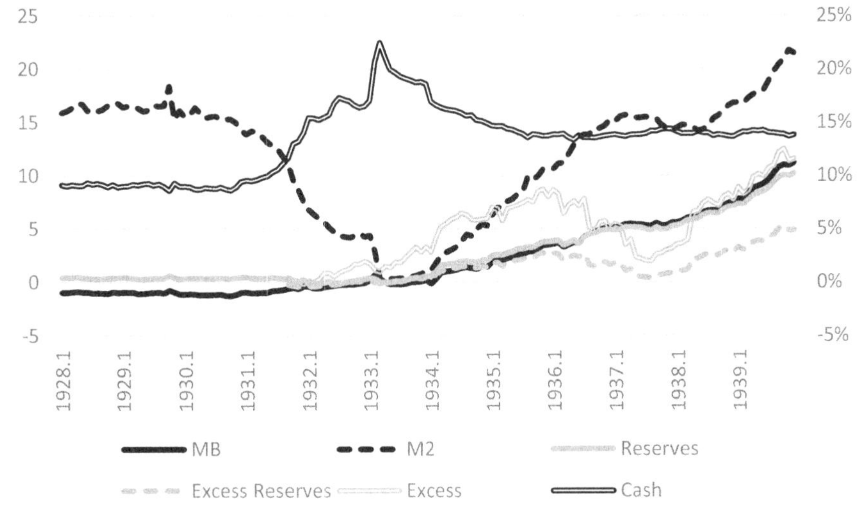

Unit: Billion Dollars

Fig. 5.3 Monetary base, M2, and reserves before and after the Great Depression in the U.S. (January 1928 to December 1939). *Source* Friedman and Schwartz (1963) and Board of Governors of the Federal Reserve System (1943). *Note 1* "Excess" and "Cash" are indicated on the right-hand side axis, while others are indicated on the left-hand side. *Note 2* Difference from March 1933 except "Excess" and "Cash." *Note 3* "MB" is monetary base. "Reserves" are banks' deposits at the Federal Reserves and banks' cash. "Excess" is the excess-reserve-to-deposits rate. "Cash" is the cash-to-deposit rate. *Note 4* Seasonally adjusted except "Excess Reserves"

After the banking crisis subsided in March 1933, the increase in the monetary base accelerated. With the establishment of Adolf Hitler's regime in Germany, the threat of war intensified, and gold flowed from Europe to the U.S. This led to a sharp increase in the monetary base. The increase in reserves was linked to this surge in the monetary base. Until July 1936, most of the increase in reserve deposits was in excess reserves. The figure shows that the monetary base, reserves, and excess reserves increased in tandem in the U.S. after the banking crisis subsided. However, the Federal Reserve raised the legal reserve requirement ratio in August 1936. As a result, excess reserves fell sharply. It also raised the ratios in March and May 1937. Consequently, from July 1936 to May 1937, excess reserves fell sharply to about one-fifth.

If, as Friedman and Iwata said, excess reserves had some economic impacts, then raising the legal reserve requirement ratio would not have significantly changed the excess-reserve-to-deposit ratio. Conversely, the ratio of reserves to deposits would have risen sharply with the raising of legal reserve ratios. In reality, the excess-reserves-to-deposit ratio plummeted to almost one-fifth, while the reserve-to-deposit ratio remained largely unchanged from the previous trend and only rose moderately. Thus, changes in excess reserves and reserves are independent of changes in deposits.

Under normal circumstances, cash accounts for the bulk of the monetary base. However, in Japan since the 2000s and in the U.S. and Europe after the global financial crisis, most of the increase in the monetary base caused an increase in reserve deposits, particularly excess reserves—just as in the U.S. after the banking crisis of the Great Depression subsided.

Keister and McAndrews (2009) state that, during a financial crisis, banks with sufficient funds will not lend to banks that are in short supply. In such a case, banks as a whole may have excess reserves, but some banks may fall short of reserves. Hence, some excess reserves may have made sense. Once the banking crisis is over, banks with insufficient reserves will be able to borrow from other banks. At the very least, stress on the interbank market should be reduced. Therefore, from April 1933 onward, the necessary excess reserves should have declined sharply, at least in terms of the ratio to deposits. In reality, excess reserves only surged after the banking crisis subsided. Therefore, most of the excess reserves can be considered simply unnecessary.

Figure 5.4 illustrates the correspondence between the assets of the Federal Reserves and banks and changes in M2 before and after the Great Depression. From 1925 to 1933, the increase or decrease in bank lending roughly matched the increase or decrease in bank assets. As the increase or decrease in assets of the Federal Reserve was small, the increase or decrease in bank lending determined the increase or decrease in the assets of the Federal Reserve and banks combined. In other words, before the Great Depression, the increase in bank lending increased the money stock. Conversely, during the Great Depression, the sharp decline in lending caused the collapse of money.

As mentioned earlier, gold has been flowing into the U.S. since 1933. The accumulation of gold did not shrink the bank's assets, thus increasing M2. This is equivalent to the conversion of the assets in Table 5.1(C) from government bonds to gold. Instead, banks increased their assets by holding a large amount of U.S. government bonds. This corresponds to Table 5.1(D). The figure shows that the increase in the Federal Reserve's assets roughly corresponded to the increase in gold, and the increase in bank assets roughly corresponded to the increase in government bond holdings.

Conversely, bank lending has remained virtually unchanged. Even in the 1930s, deficit fiscal policy was increasing the money stock (see also Hattori, 2007, Chap. 6, pp. 149–177; 2022). This is rarely pointed out, with Koo (2009, pp. 109–113) being a notable exception, who demonstrated that deficit fiscal policy increased the money stock during the post-Depression economic recovery.

5.3.3 The Beginning of All Errors

Friedman's theory of the Great Depression was not only research on history but also intended to prevent a disastrous event such as the global financial crisis. According to Friedman, the Great Depression was not caused by the bubbles that spread in the 1920s or the speculative activity that accompanied them. The Federal Reserve's

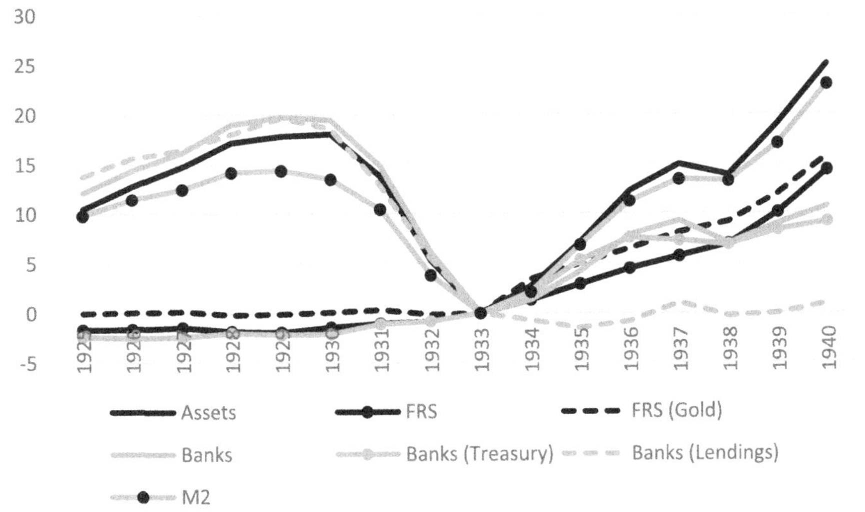

Unit: Billion Dollar

Fig. 5.4 Assets of the Federal Reserve and banks, and M2 before and after the Great Depression in the U.S. (1925 to 1939). *Source* Carter et al. eds. (2006). *Note 1* Difference from 1933. Note 2 "Assets" are the sum of the assets of the Federal Reserves and the banks. "FRS" are assets of the Federal Reserve, and "Banks" are assets of banks. Assets exclude claims on the Federal Reserve and banks. "Treasury" is U.S. Treasury securities. Assets and "Banks (Treasury)" subtract deposits of the federal government

tightening of monetary policy to crush the bubble led to the Great Depression. Moreover, the crucial mistake was to cause a sharp decline in the money stock during the Great Depression.

In 2005, Friedman (2005) compared the three post-bubble bursts in the U.S. in the 1930s, Japan in the1990s, and the U.S. in the 2000s. In all cases, stock prices plummeted after the bubble burst. During the Great Depression of the 1930s, the U.S. witnessed a sharp decline in its money stock at the same time, and concurrently, its economy fell rapidly. However, in the U.S. in the 2000s, money stock continued to increase, and the economy recovered relatively quickly. In the 1990s, Japan was between the two; although the increase in the money stock continued, it was considerably slower than before. The economy also stagnated. Friedman argued that economic stagnation can be avoided if the central bank increases the money stock even after a bubble burst.

Bernanke, chair of the Federal Reserve during the global financial crisis, agreed with Friedman's theory of the Great Depression. Bernanke (2002) argued that monetary policy should not be used to prick the bubble as it would worsen the economy. Instead, he recommended easing monetary conditions after a bubble burst to aid quick recovery. He (Bernanke, 2000) further argued that the secular stagnation of Japan in the 1990s was also caused by the BOJ not easing monetary policy and allowing deflation to continue.

If Friedman and Bernanke were correct, even if the U.S. housing bubble burst and financial institutions were saddled with non-performing loans, as long as Bernanke implemented the right monetary policy, there could be no global financial crisis that would push the U.S. and global economies to the edge of collapse. The global financial crisis was theoretically impossible for Friedman and Bernanke. Therefore, when the global financial crisis occurred, mainstream economists said that conventional macroeconomics and monetary policy theories were wrong (e.g., The Economist, 2009).

Friedman also understands that the banking crises were the cause of the monetary collapse during the Great Depression. However, Friedman (1965, p. 200) argues that banking crises brought about the economy's collapse not because they caused financial institutions to fail but because they caused a monetary collapse. He also believes that the failure of the Federal Reserve to exercise its lender-of-last-resort function and the inability of banks to redeem their deposits caused the banking crises. Applying his argument directly to the U.S. in 2008 would mean that if Bernanke had fully exercised his lender of last resort, the collapse of financial institutions would not have occurred.

Friedman (1968, pp. 74–75) appreciates the deposit insurance system created in the U.S. in 1934 more than the creation of the Federal Reserves. From the experience of the Great Depression, governments now protect deposits. There were caps on deposit insurance, but not a few countries had full protection during the global financial crisis. If deposits are protected, money should not collapse even if financial institutions fail. Protecting all deposits and money but allowing financial institutions to fail to maintain market discipline would be more in line with Friedman's doctrine of defending market freedom. In addition, both Lehman Brothers, the securities company, and American International Group, a life insurance company at the center of the global financial crisis, are not banks and do not keep deposits. According to Friedman, both companies can simply go bankrupt. However, during the global financial crisis, except for Lehman Brothers, regardless of banks and non-banks, the U.S. and European policymakers bailed out all the giant financial institutions. It was not money that mattered but financial institutions.

Most problematic are Friedman's claims about monetary policy. Friedman knows that the banking crises caused the collapse of money, but he considers the Federal Reserve's policy a failure because he believes that an increase in the monetary base would also increase the money stock. However, the experiences of the U.S. and Europe after the global financial crisis and the BOJ under Kuroda demonstrate that the monetary base and money stock are not linked. We also show this was the case in the U.S. after the Great Depression. If an increase in the monetary base does not lead to an increase in the money stock, then Friedman's criticism has no basis.

Moreover, the 1930s was a time of historically low interest rates in the U.S.; hence, officials at the Federal Reserve thought they were already easing monetary policy. However, according to Friedman, monetary easing would cause nominal interest rates to rise. Therefore, he argued that the low interest rates in the U.S. in the

1930s were not because monetary policy was eased but were caused by tightening monetary policy, which led to deflation. If this argument were correct, then the zero interest rates after the global financial crisis would be owing to the central banks in the U.S. and Europe tightening monetary policy. Particularly in Japan under BOJ under Kuroda, irrespective of the massive supply of monetary base, the growth rate of money stock was sluggish, short-term interest rates have been negative, and long-term interest rates have been almost zero or even negative in some cases. In this case, the BOJ under Kuroda is also not conducting historic monetary easing but historic monetary tightening and *creating deflation*. The BOJ under Kuroda cannot solve deflation, but this is not because it is tightening monetary policy. Instead, it cannot solve deflation despite aggressive monetary easing. Therefore, Friedman's argument is doubly wrong.

Additionally, the claim that the Great Depression could have been solved by monetary policy also means that fiscal policy is unnecessary. After the global financial crisis, critics argued that monetary policy had limits beyond which fiscal policy was needed. The reflationists in Japan have now shifted their emphasis on fiscal policy. This is also the exact opposite of Friedman's claim; however, if the increase in money after the Great Depression that Friedman pointed out was owing to fiscal policy, it is also easy to explain why fiscal policy is necessary.

The global financial crisis was supposed to be the best opportunity to make the most of the findings of Friedman's theory of the Great Depression. However, Friedman's theory of the Great Depression cannot explain why the global financial crisis occurred. The policies he proposes are completely useless or even catastrophic. But why? Friedman believed that, even if banks failed, the Federal Reserve was able to prevent what he called a money collapse if it surged its monetary base. Thus, the true cause of the collapse of money, the banking crises, was ignored. That the increase in the money stock after the Great Depression was owing to deficit fiscal policy (at least one of the major factors) was incomprehensible. For this reason, the importance of fiscal policy was also ignored. The global financial crisis revealed the fallacy of Friedman's theory of the Great Depression (see also Hattori, 2022).

5.3.4 Fiscal Policy of Takahashi

The Great Depression, which began in 1929, was also the period of the Showa Depression in Japan. Korekiyo Takahashi, who became Minister of Finance in 1932, rebuilt the Japanese economy through a deficit fiscal policy—the so-called pre-Keynes Keynesian policy. As a result, Japan became one of the fastest countries to recover from the Great Depression. While studying Takahashi's fiscal policy, Iwata ed. (2004) considered the direct underwriting of JGBs by the BOJ to be crucial and equated it with the QE policy to conclude that monetary policy overcame deflation and revived the Japanese economy.

Figure 5.5 illustrates changes in the assets of the BOJ and banks, as well as the monetary base and M2 in Japan in the 1920s and 1930s. As mentioned earlier, the effects on the money stock of the central bank's purchase of JGBs from banks and direct underwriting are completely different. Takahashi's deficit fiscal policy is unlike QE. Moreover, during the implementation of Takahashi's fiscal policy, the BOJ's asset expansion was relatively smaller. When the ban on gold exports was lifted in 1929, gold flowed out, and the BOJ's assets declined sharply. Although the BOJ's assets certainly increased during the period of Takahashi's fiscal policy, they only returned to the 1929 level in 1936.

Japan did not have a well-developed secondary market for JGBs at the time. Under such circumstances, issuing a large amount of JGBs could lead to a market collapse as nobody would be willing to underwrite the bonds. For the time being, the BOJ was asked to underwrite the bonds. Later, the BOJ sold the bonds to the market based on the situation. Despite the BOJ's underwriting, the BOJ's holdings of JGBs had not exploded. Money multiplier rose during Takahashi's fiscal policy but sharply declined in Japan after the 2000s and in the U.S. in the 1930s and after the global financial crisis. It declined even more sharply during Kuroda's reign at the BOJ. This also indicates that period of Takahashi's fiscal policy was a combination

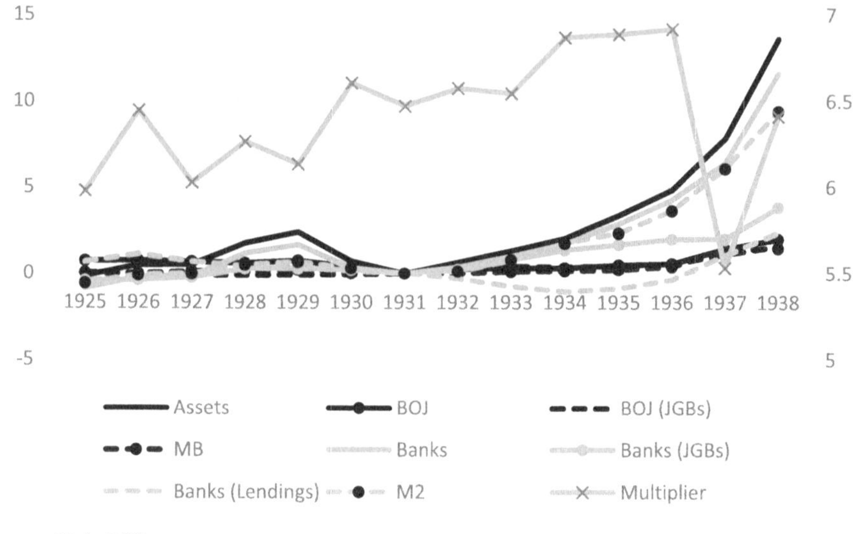

Fig. 5.5 Assets of the Bank of Japan and Bank, monetary base and M2 (1925 to 1938). *Source* Fujino (1994), Fujino and Teranishi (2000). *Note 1* "Multiplier" is indicated on the right-hand side axis, while others are indicated on the left-hand side. *Note 2* Difference from 1931 except "Multiplier.". *Note 3* "Assets" are the sum of the assets of the BOJ and banks. "BOJ" are assets of the BOJ, and "Banks" are assets of banks. "MB" is monetary base. Excluding cash from the BOJ's assets. Excluding cash, deposits, and call liabilities from the banks' assets. "Multiplier" is money multiplier

of aggressive fiscal policy and gradual monetary easing (see Hattori, 2007, pp.130–133; 2014, pp. 129–136, for the fact that Japanese banks expanded their assets by buying JGBs even in the 1930s). Iwata ed. (2004) ignores these facts.

Figure 5.5 also shows that banks were buying JGBs to a far greater extent than the BOJ. During the period of Takahashi's fiscal policy, deficit fiscal policy also increased the money stock through banks' purchases of JGBs. However, similar to Friedman, Iwata and other reflationists could not understand the mechanism by which deficit financing increased the money stock, and thus, they failed to truly understand Takahashi's fiscal policy. This is consistent with the current shift in the arguments of mainstream American economists and reflationists toward fiscal policy.

5.3.5 *Fiscal Origin of Hyperinflation*

Premised on the view that the central bank can supply an unlimited amount of the money stock, it is generally believed that hyperinflation is the result of central banks inflating the money stock. However, the massive supply of monetary base by the BOJ under Kuroda and central banks in the U.S. and Europe after the global financial crisis did not lead to an increase in money stock. The BOJ under Kuroda has been unable to find JGB sellers and has been unable to supply a large amount of monetary base. Although the BOJ under Kuroda supplied a large amount of monetary base, it was, at most, a fivefold increase. This is a tiny amount compared with the money expansion during the historic hyperinflationary period. Not only does the central bank have no control over the money stock, but it also cannot supply even an unlimited amount of the monetary base.

For the central bank to expand the monetary base without limit, financial assets must expand without limit. This was carried out through fiscal collapse. Historical hyperinflations were preceded by fiscal collapses. In such situations, no one wants to buy government bonds. Still, this situation cannot be left as is, so the central bank buys government bonds instead. Consequently, the monetary base and money stock surged. Inflation increases the amount of spending required by the government; however, since taxation is based on the economic situations earlier, the budget deficit worsens. In such a case, the central bank must buy more government bonds, which worsens inflation.

When Friedman said that inflation is a monetary phenomenon, he meant that it does not matter why money increases. Therefore, the central bank that caused the expansion of money is criticized. Conversely, he (Friedman, 1991, pp. 11–12) argued that a deficit-financing policy could not be sustained without a central bank money supply, which would result in a shortage of money to purchase government bonds. We agree that such a situation could occur. However, without a fiscal collapse, the monetary base and money stock cannot increase rapidly enough to cause hyperinflation. In this sense, contrary to Friedman's argument, the reason why money expands is also important.

5.4 Can Central Banks Control Money Stock?

Since the controversy on the money supply that broke out in the early 1990s, it has become one of the staples of criticism of the reflationists that the BOJ's provision of the monetary base does not lead to an increase in the money stock. The BOJ under Kuroda has surged the monetary base, but it has hardly led to an increase in the money stock. This chapter reiterates the reasons for this in a theoretical manner. However, this chapter also shows that, in some cases, it leads to an increase in the money stock. Even in these cases, there is no multiplier effect, as shown by the money multiplier theory. In addition, this chapter clarifies the mechanism by which deficit fiscal policy increases money stock.

These conclusions are related to Friedman's theory of the Great Depression and whether hyperinflation resulted from monetary policy failure. Friedman argued that the Great Depression in the U.S. was caused by the Federal Reserve's sharp decline in the money stock. If central banks are incapable of increasing the money stock, as the BOJ under Kuroda and other central banks in the U.S. and Europe have shown, then Friedman's argument has no basis. In addition, the BOJ under Kuroda's inability to find sellers of JGBs has resulted in the inability to supply a large amount of monetary base. For the BOJ to supply an unlimited monetary base, it would first have to issue an unlimited amount of JGBs owing to a fiscal collapse. This indicates that the ultimate origin of hyperinflation lies in fiscal policy. Thus, the controversy over the money supply in Japan is related to fundamental issues in macroeconomics and monetary theory.

References

In Japanese

Asada, T. (2015). Keizai Gaku no Tayō sei wo Meguru Oboegaki: Defure to Kin'yū Seisaku ni Kansuru Tokushu Nihon tekina Ronsō ni Kanren Sa sete (Notes on diversity in economics: In connection with the special japanese-style debates on deflation and monetary policy. In K. Yagi, Y. Aruka, H. Osaka, H. Ohnishi, & M. Yoshida, (Eds.), *Keizai gaku to Keizai Kyōiku no Mirai: Nihon Gakujutsu Kaigi Sanshō Kijun wo Koete* (*Future of economics and economic education: Beyond the reference criteria of Science Council of Japan*), (pp. 145–167). Sakurai Shoten.

Fujino, S. (1994). *Nihon no Manē Sapurai (Money supply in Japan)*. Keiso Shobo.

Fujino, S., & Teranishi, J. (2000). *Nihon Kin'yū no Sūryō Bunseki (Quantitative analysis of finance in Japan)*. Toyo Keizai.

Hattori, S. (2007). *Kahei to Ginkō: Kahei Riron no Saikentō (Money and banks: A re-examination of monetary theory)*. Nihon Keizai Hyoronsha.

Hattori, S. (2014). *Abenomikusu no Shūen (The end of Abenomics)*. Iwanami Shoten.

Ito, O. (2022). *Baburu go no Kin'yū Kiki Taiō: Zen Kiseki, 1990–2005 (Responses to financial crisis after the bubble: The complete trajectory, 1990–2005)*. Yuhikaku Publishing.

Iwata, K. (1993). *Kin'yū Seisaku no Keizai gaku: Nichigin Riron no Kenshō (Economics of monetary policy: An examination of the Bank of Japan's theory)*. Nikkei, Inc.

Iwata, K. (2002). Yoshō Keisei ni Hatarakikakeru Kin'yū Seisaku wo: Komiya Rombun Hihan (1) (Monetary policy working on the formation of the inflation expectations: A critique of Komiya (1). In R. Komiya, & Center for Japan Economic Research (Ed.), *Kin'yū Seisaku Rongi no Sōten: Nichigin Hihan to sono Hanron* (*Issues in the monetary policy debate: Criticism of the Bank of Japan and its rebuttal*), (pp. 391–418). Nikkei, Inc.
Iwata, K. (2009). *Sekai Dōji Fukyō (Simultaneous world recession).* Chikuma Shinsho.
Iwata, K. (2012). *Nippon Ginkō: Defure no Ban'nin (The Bank of Japan: Keeper of deflation).* Nikkei Publishing.
Iwata, K. (Ed). (2004). *Shōwa Kyōkō no Kenkyū (Studies on the Showa depression).* Toyo Keizai.
Koo, R. (2007). *"In" to "Yō" no Keizai gaku: Wareware wa Donoyōna Fukyō to Tatakatte Kita no ka? (The Economics of "Yin" and "Yang": What kind of recession have we been fighting?).* Toyo Keizai.
Okina, K. (1993). *Kin'yū Seisaku: Chūō Ginkō no Shiten to Sentaku (Monetary policy: Perspectives and choices of a central bank).* Toyo Keizai.
Suzuki, A. (2022) *Defure to no 20 Nen Sensō (The 20-year war against deflation).* Kinzai Institute for Financial Affairs.

In English

Bernanke, B. S. (2000). Japanese monetary policy: A case of self-induced paralysis?. In R. Mikitani, & A. S. Posen (Eds.), *Japan's financial crisis and its parallels to U.S. experience* (pp. 149–166). Institution for International Economics.
Bernanke, B. S. (2002). Asset-price bubbles and monetary policy. Before the New York chapter of the national association for business economics, New York, *October 15.*
Bernanke, B. S. (2022). *21st century monetary policy: The Federal Reserve from the great inflation to covid-19.* W. W. Norton.
Board of Governors of the Federal Reserve System. (1943). *Banking and monetary statistics 1914–1941.*
Carter, S. B. et al. (Eds). (2006). *Historical statistics of the United States: Earliest times to the present, Economic Structure and Performance,* (vol. 3) Millennial ed. Cambridge University Press.
Federal Reserve Bank of St. Louis. (2023). FRED. https://fred.stlouisfed.org/.
Friedman, M. (1965). A program for monetary stability. In M. D. Ketchum, & L. T. Kendall, *Readings in financial institutions,* (pp. 189–209). Houghton Mifflin.
Friedman, M. (1968). Why the American economy is depression-proof. In M. Friedman, *Dollars and deficits: Living with America's economic problems* (pp. 72–96). Englewood Cliffs. Prentice-Hall.
Friedman, M. (1969). The role of monetary policy. In M. Friedman, *The optimum quantity of money and other essays* (pp. 95–110). Aldine Publishing.
Friedman, M. (1991). The counter-revolution in monetary theory. In M. Friedman, *Monetarist economics* (pp. 1–20). Basil Blackwell.
Friedman, M. (2005). A natural experiment in monetary policy covering three episodes of growth and decline in the economy and the stock market. *Journal of Economic Perspectives, 19*(4), 145–150.
Friedman, M., & Schwartz, A. J. (1963). *A monetary history of the United States, 1867–1960.* Princeton University Press.
Goodhart, C. A. E. (2010). Money, credit and bank behaviour: Need for a new approach. *National Institute Economic Review, 214,* 73–82.
Hattori, S. (2022). The global financial crisis and Friedman's theory of the Great Depression. [Discussion Paper, ACDU-22-02] *The Association of Commerce, Doshisha University,* November.

Kaldor, N. (1990[1970]). The new monetarism. In J. C. Wood, & R. N. Woods (Eds.), *Milton Friedman: Critical assessments*, (vol. I, pp. 508–523). Routledge.

Keister, T., & McAndrews, J. (2009). Why are banks holding so many excess reserves? Federal Reserve Bank of New York. *Current Issues in Economics and Finance, 15*(8).

Keynes, J. M. (1973[1936]). *The general theory of employment, interest and money, The collected writings of John Maynard Keynes*, (vol. VII). Macmillan.

Koo, R. C. (2009). *The Holy Grail of macroeconomics: Lessons from Japan's great recession*. Wiley.

Krugman, P. R. (1998). It's Baaack: Japan's slump and the return of the liquidity trap. *Brookings Papers on Economic Activity*, (2), 137–205.

McLeay, M., Radia, A., & R. Thomas of the Bank's Monetary Analysis Directorate. (2014). Money creation in the modern economy. *Bank of England, Quarterly Bulletin, Q1*, 14–27.

The Bank of Japan. (2023). *BOJ time-series data search*. https://www.stat-search.boj.or.jp/index_en.html.

The Economist. (2009). What went wrong with economics: And how the discipline should change to avoid the mistakes of the past. *392*(8640), 9–10.

Tobin, J. (1990[1965]). The monetary interpretation of history—A review article. In J. C. Wood, & R. N. Woods, (Eds.), *Milton Friedman: Critical assessments*, (vol. I, pp. 203–227). Routledge.

Woodford, M. (2012) Methods of policy accommodation at the interest-rate lower bound. *September 16 (Revised draft of a paper presented at the Federal Reserve Bank of Kansas City symposium on 'The changing policy landscape.' Jackson Hole, Wyoming, August 31)*.

Chapter 6
Conclusion: Thus, the Reflationist Theory Has Collapsed

Abstract Ten years of the Bank of Japan (BOJ) under Governor Kuroda proves the fallacy of the reflationist theory. Reflationists argued that the BOJ could end deflation by raising expected inflation. However, the BOJ has failed to raise expected inflation or achieve its inflation target. Conversely, the surge in import prices since 2022 has pushed the consumer price (CPI) inflation rate up. This again showed that costs, not monetary policy, are driving up the CPI in Japan. However, imported inflation has reduced consumption in real terms. There is no basis for the strategy of reflationists that overcoming deflation will revive the Japanese economy. The reflationists' tools for raising inflation expectations were a Japanese-style inflation target and a massive supply of monetary base. The BOJ under Kuroda abandoned both of them only three years after its start, and its monetary policy ended in a historic fiasco. The BOJ then tried to save its own position and reputation by pretending to continue policies advocated by reflationists.

Keywords Abenomics · The Bank of Japan under Kuroda · Deflation in Japan · Quantitative and qualitative monetary easing · Japanese-style inflation target · Reflationists · Kikuo Iwata · Monetary policy

> If a theory justifies the false position which a certain part of society is in, then, however baseless and even obviously false the theory may be, it will get adopted and become the belief of that part of society. (Tolstoy, 1995[1898], p. 51).
>
> I know that the majority of people who are not only regarded as intelligent but are indeed intelligent, capable of understanding the more difficult scientific, mathematical and philosophical reasonings, are very rarely capable of understanding a most simple and obvious truth, if it is such as requires that they admit that a judgement they have formed about something, sometimes with great effort, a judgement they are proud of, which they have taught to others, on the basis of which they have arranged their entire life—that this judgement may be wrong. (Tolstoy, 1995[1898], p. 112).

S. Hattori, *Why the Bank of Japan Has Failed to Conquer Deflation in Japan*,
https://doi.org/10.1007/978-981-97-9408-9_6

6.1 Ten Years of Proving the Fallacy of the Reflationist Theory

Ironically, ten years of the BOJ under Kuroda can be summed up as proving the fallacy of reflationist theory. The core of reflationist theory is that deflation in Japan is a monetary phenomenon and that the BOJ can only solve deflation through monetary policy. The BOJ and reflationists argued that monetary easing would enable an end to deflation by raising inflation expectations. The BOJ under Kuroda failed to raise inflation expectations and ultimately ended up not achieving the inflation target. However, owing to the soaring import prices from 2021, the consumer price (CPI) inflation rate exceeded 4% in 2022. It was evident that CPI in Japan was driven by import prices and costs, not monetary policy or inflation expectations. The biggest theoretical problem with the reflationist theory is that it does not understand what drives the CPI in Japan.

When the BOJ under Kuroda failed to overcome deflation, the BOJ and reflationists blamed higher consumption tax, adaptive inflation expectations, persistent deflationary mindset, and so on. Imported inflation since 2022 has also proved that these excuses have no basis. The reason why CPI inflation rates did not reach the 2% target until 2022 was simply because costs did not rise sufficiently. However, as CPI rose owing to imported inflation, consumption declined in real terms. This is also contrary to the assumption of reflationists that the Japanese economy will recover if deflation can be overcome.

We also reveal that the BOJ under Kuroda implemented monetary policy based on the reflationist theory only for the first three years. It thereafter introduced theories and policies that Iwata and other reflationists had criticized in the past while making it appear as if the monetary policy advocated by reflationists was continuing. An important turning point was the YCC introduced by the BOJ in September 2016. Under the YCC, real interest rates automatically rise as deflation progresses. This is diametrically opposed to the policy ideas of the reflationists. Under the YCC, the BOJ under Kuroda passively adjusted the purchase of long-term JGBs and the supply of monetary base. This is a revival of the BOJ's theory, which Iwata and other reflationists have also criticized. That long-term interest rates are near zero is evidence that people expect the BOJ to fail to end deflation and that interest rates will remain near zero for a long time. Ergo, the fact that the yield curve is under control means that the market has judged that BOJ under Kuroda is incapable of overcoming deflation.

Iwata and the reflationists argued that the inflation target should be set as a deadline, and the commitment of the BOJ should be clarified. However, the BOJ under Kuroda stopped announcing its outlook for achieving the target to obscure its commitment to achieving its target. Concurrently, Kuroda stated that the outlook does not actually indicate the BOJ's commitment to achieving it. It must be remembered that Hamada (2013, p. 36) criticized the "medo" of the BOJ under Shirakawa as "a policy of evading criticism." However, after the introduction of the YCC, the BOJ under Kuroda conducted stealth tapering, saying that it would strengthen monetary easing.

Even after it stopped announcing its outlook for achieving the target, it continued to say that it would soon be able to achieve its inflation target. It was the BOJ under Kuroda and the reflationists who really implemented "policies of evading criticism."

Reflationists, led by Iwata, criticized the Bank of Japan, up to Governor Shirakawa, for not taking the blame for its failure to end deflation and for only making excuses. Iwata called this shifting of blame the BOJ's theory of deflation. However, the BOJ under Kuroda and Iwata shifted the blame away from monetary policy to the consumption tax hike, adaptive inflation expectations, the persistent deflationary mindset, and so on. In doing so, they revived the BOJ's theory of deflation and the accounting theory of prices. More worryingly, they now hold that CPI does not have to rise, and in turn, admitting the error of their theoretical assertion that deflation is a monetary phenomenon. This way, they have also disproved their own analysis that deflation is the cause of the current economic stagnation in Japan. The monetary policy advocated by reflationists, which pushes down real interest rates by raising prices, is impossible, but it was no problem. Gradually, the reflationists have come to reject all their theory as well as analyses of the current situation and policy.

In the past, Hamada (2013, pp. 92–96) criticized the BOJ for focusing solely on organizational defense without thinking about people's lives. He also criticized the BOJ for sophistry. However, it was the BOJ under Kuroda, the reflationists and Iwata who first defended the organization by the sophistry of defending policies that they once objected to. In the end, the BOJ under Kuroda failed to achieve its inflation target. The monetary policy advocated by reflationists was also eventually abandoned. However, criticizing the BOJ under Kuroda is criticizing Abenomics; therefore, politicians who support Abenomics cannot criticize it. Thus, severe criticism of the BOJ, up to Governor Shirakawa, has ceased. Although the BOJ has made a historic fiasco in its economic policy to end deflation, it has achieved a significant political outcome in terms of protecting the BOJ as an organization from political criticism.

When Krugman (1998) published his paper in 1998, interest rates had already fallen to virtually zero in Japan, leaving little room for interest rate cuts. Based on this premise, Krugman proposed a monetary policy to raise inflation expectations. However, Krugman was clueless regarding raising inflation expectations. This task was to be taken over by the reflationists, who also failed. Even if this problem is resolved, the problem remains that even if inflation expectations rise, actual CPI will not necessarily rise. Thus, the reflationists have self-destructed.

6.2 Why Simple Truths Cannot Be Understood

The first quote in this chapter is from Tolstoy's (1995[1898]) *What is Art?* That is, wrong theories are strongly held by people if they help justify such people's wrong acts. Even smart people, he said, cannot understand simple truths when they are fixated on erroneous theories. It was imported inflation from 2022 that once again made it clear that both the theories and strategies of the reflationists were wrong.

Soaring import prices had caused CPI to rise in Japan, and at one time, the rate of increase exceeded 4%. Both the BOJ under Kuroda and reflationists understand that this was cost-push inflation owing to soaring import prices. However, reflationists cannot generalize this fact to believe that what is driving the CPI in Japan are costs, not the BOJ under Kuroda's monetary policy or inflation expectations.

Furthermore, both the BOJ under Kuroda and the government knew that cost-push inflation since 2022 has reduced real wages and real incomes, putting pressure on people's lives. That is why the government has adopted policies that keep prices down. They, however, do not generalize this fact either, as if rising prices are not necessarily good for the Japanese economy. Both the BOJ under Kuroda and the government understood that wage increases were necessary to alleviate the plight of households. The BOJ under Kuroda also continued to ease monetary policy, claiming that imported inflation since 2022 was not accompanied by wage increases. However, the important question of why wages would rise if the BOJ under Kuroda were easing monetary policy is not explained at all. We believe that this is because the BOJ under Kuroda knows that wages will not rise with monetary easing, but publicly stating this would expose its own powerlessness. Reflationists will understand that what is happening is the opposite of what they thought would happen in theory. However, they cling to reflationist theory or assumptions. They regard inconvenient facts as simple exceptional events.

Economists are ultimately fallible human beings, which is well explained by psychology and behavioral economics. The first is confirmation bias. If soaring import prices have the power to raise the CPI and if a surge in import prices and a sharp increase in the monetary base occur simultaneously, a sharp increase in the monetary base and a rise in the CPI will occur together. Reflationists, who believe that a sharp increase in the monetary base will raise the CPI, then believe that their theory has been proven. Conversely, CPI will decline if an increase in monetary base and a sharp decline in import prices occur simultaneously. In this case, they do not consider their theory to have been disproved. Instead, they concoct something that does not exist, such as a persistent deflationary mindset, to convince themselves.

The second is the bandwagon effect. Humans are animals that live together with their fellows. When one person alone believes in a wrong theory and is criticized by everyone around him or her, he or she becomes anxious. The reflationists are a group, meaning that the individual's wrongness is protected by the group's wrongness. Conversely, a person who accepts criticism from outside the group and admits that the reflationist theory is wrong is a traitor. Thus, when a group makes a mistake, the mistake cannot be corrected. The third is the sunk cost. Similar to us, every academic person or policymaker struggles to build his or her career. To admit a mistake is to deny the hard work he or she has involved. Therefore, he or she cannot admit mistakes.

The last and the worst is negative incentives. It would be reasonable to correct mistakes upon sound realization. However, admitting a mistake lowers your valuations. Therefore, even if you understand or have a vague sense that you might make a mistake, you cannot admit it. Conversely, making excuses and shifting the blame to one thing or another will not damage your reputation. In Japan, there are sometimes reports of false charges. However, even when a retrial is conducted on a false charge, it is not uncommon for the prosecution to refuse to admit the accused's innocence. Even when a retrial results in not guilty, the parties involved often refuse to admit that they were wrong. Section 4.4 clarified how the BOJ under Kuroda and its reflationists used the theories and policies they once criticized to justify reflationists' theories and policies.

Humans make mistakes every day. Private companies will also make mistakes. However, if private companies make a big mistake and do not correct their failure thereafter, they risk bankruptcy—a type of market mechanism. However, even if it is the government or the BOJ that fails, in the end, it is the people who will suffer. The top officials of the government and the BOJ may also suffer a tiny part of the damage as part of the people. However, such damage is not a concern for them, given the pain of admitting failure and being held accountable.

6.3 Lack of Wisdom, Courage, and Luck

Not all policies will succeed. Depending on what you count as a failure, there may be more failed policies than successful ones in history. However, not all policies fail in the same way. When Abenomics began, the real growth rate of 2% and the nominal growth rate of 3% were also targets. The New Abenomics of September 2014 set a target of achieving a nominal GDP of ¥600 trillion in 2020 (if the initial nominal growth rate of 3% target could be achieved, this target could also be achieved). However, regardless of COVID-19, the target failed to be achieved. In 2016, nominal GDP increased significantly owing to the revision of the GDP standard, but still, the target of ¥600 trillion was a fantasy. However, today, the fact that such targets exist has been forgotten. This is a policy failure being faded out of existence.

One of the targets of New Abenomics was to raise the total fertility rate to 1.8. However, the fertility rate, which had been rising, began to decline after 2016. Long before Abenomics, policies to raise the fertility rate were implemented in Japan. The current Kishida Cabinet has also launched different-dimensional measures to address the declining fertility rate. However, no measure to address the declining fertility rate has ever succeeded. This is a policy failure stuck in an endless loop: policy → failure → policy → ….

In contrast, after the failure of the BOJ under Kuroda, it effectively abandoned policies advocated by reflationists. The newly introduced YCC is a policy based on the once-criticized BOJ's theory. Nonetheless, the BOJ makes it appear as though the policies advocated by reflationists are continuing. This can be said to be a policy failure of "tenshin" (changing of course)—a peculiarity of the failure of the BOJ under Kuroda and the reflationists.

In the end, the reflationists do not have the wisdom to understand that wrong policies are wrong, nor do they have the courage to admit and correct wrong policies. However, the BOJ's policies are not the only ones that drive the Japanese economy. Even if the BOJ under Kuroda continues its error, as Gertler (2017, p. 55) states, luck might have been able to overcome deflation and revive the Japanese economy. But the reflationists had no luck either. Ultimately, it is the Japanese people who are really unfortunate.

References

In Japanese

Hamada, K. (2013). *Amerika wa Nihon Keizai no Fukkatsu o Shitte iru (America knows the revival of Japanese economy)*. Kodansha.

In English

Gertler, M. (2017). Rethinking the power of forward guidance: Lessons from Japan. *Monetary and Economic Studies, 35*, 39–57.

Krugman, P. R. (1998). It's Baaack: Japan's slump and the return of the liquidity trap. *Brookings Papers on Economic Activity, (2)*, 137–205.

Tolstoy, L. S. (1995[1898]). *What is art?* (Trans. by R. Pevear & L. Volokhonsky). Penguin Press.

Author Index

S. Hattori, *Why the Bank of Japan Has Failed to Conquer Deflation in Japan*,
https://doi.org/10.1007/978-981-97-9408-9

Subject Index

S. Hattori, *Why the Bank of Japan Has Failed to Conquer Deflation in Japan*,
https://doi.org/10.1007/978-981-97-9408-9

The manufacturer's authorised representative in the EU is Springer Nature Customer Service Centre GmbH, Europaplatz 3, 69115 Heidelberg, Germany. If you have any concerns regarding our products, please contact ProductSafety@springernature.com

Printed and bound by CPI Group (UK) Ltd, Croydon, CR0 4YY
01/10/2026
02225876-0019